100 THINGS
OREGON FANS
SHOULD KNOW & DO
BEFORE THEY DIE

Chris Hansen and Rob Moseley

TRIUMPH
B O O K S

Library of Congress Cataloging-in-Publication Data

Moseley, Rob.
  100 things Oregon fans should know & do before they die / Rob Moseley, Chris Hansen.
      pages cm. — (100 things...fans should know)
    ISBN 978-1-60078-858-1 (pbk.)
  1. University of Oregon—Football--History. 2. University of Oregon—Football—Anecdotes. 3. Oregon Ducks (Football team)—History.
  4. Oregon Ducks (Football team)—Anecdotes. I. Hansen, Chris. II. Title. III. Title: One hundred things Oregon fans should know and do before they die.
  GV958.O7M67 2013
  796.332'630979531—dc23
                              2013019935

This book is available in quantity at special discounts for your group or organization. For further information, contact:
    Triumph Books LLC
    814 North Franklin Street
    Chicago, Illinois 60610
    (312) 337-0747
    www.triumphbooks.com

Printed in U.S.A.
ISBN: 978-1-60078-858-1
Design by Patricia Frey
Photos courtesy of Getty unless otherwise indicated

To all Oregon fans

Contents

1 The Pick

"Huard, going to go back and throw the ball...sets up, looks, throws toward the corner of the end zone and...it's intercepted! Intercepted! The Ducks have the ball! Down to the 35, the 40...Kenny Wheaton's gonna score! Kenny Wheaton's gonna score! Twenty, the 10...touchdown...Kenny Wheaton! On an interception!"

—Jerry Allen, Oregon radio broadcaster

Kenny Wheaton's gonna score!

Goosebumps.

Where were you on October 22, 1994? You'd know the answer if you're a Ducks fan over the age of 30.

It was the day a legend was created and the fortunes of the Oregon football team changed forever.

It was the day a redshirt freshman cornerback from Phoenix joined the likes of immortal Ducks runner Steve Prefontaine as an Oregon icon.

It was the day of "the Pick," the most famous play in the history of Oregon football: a 97-yard interception return for a touchdown in the final minute of the Ducks' 31–20 win over ninth-ranked Washington at Autzen Stadium.

It was a play that propelled the Ducks to the 1995 Rose Bowl— the Rose Bowl!—in the days before the Bowl Championship Series, when playing on New Year's Day in Pasadena, in the Granddaddy of Them All, was still the single-greatest prize for a Pac-10 team.

It's a play credited with turning a middle-of-the-road program with nine bowl appearances in its previous 95 years into one with a run of 17 bowl games and 18 winning seasons in the following 19 years, including appearances in three Rose Bowls, two Fiesta Bowls, and the 2011 BCS Championship Game.

It's a play shown on the Autzen Stadium scoreboard before the start of every home game, to thunderous applause.

Kenny Wheaton's gonna score!

But not before the Ducks almost gave the game away, allowing the Huskies to drive all the way to the Oregon 8-yard line with 1:05 left and the Ducks leading 24–20.

A touchdown seemed inevitable for Washington, and with it, another devastating loss to the Huskies that would've dropped Oregon to 4–4.

Instead, Washington quarterback Damon Huard dropped back and threw a deep out to 5'9" wide receiver Dave Janoski near the front-left corner of the end zone.

Wheaton knew from film study that the Huskies liked to throw that deep out when they got close to the goal line. He told himself that if he saw that play coming, he was going to try and jump the pass; if he missed, he knew it would be a touchdown.

He didn't miss.

"It was just a bad decision," Huard recalled on the 15th anniversary of the play in an interview with a Eugene television station. "It was a ball that I threw out late to the flat, and you know, good things don't happen when you throw out into the flat late. And the kid jumped it, read it, and ran it back."

Kenny Wheaton's gonna score!

But not if Damon Huard could make a tackle first.

Replays show the Husky quarterback had a good shot to at least slow Wheaton down when he cut back toward the field from the sideline to dodge a Washington offensive lineman around the Oregon 40-yard line. But Huard pulled up and never even got a hand on Wheaton, who then had nothing but 60 yards of open field ahead of him.

"He was a quarterback. Quarterbacks don't tackle," Wheaton said. "I was expecting him to hit me. I really was. When I made the cut I was thinking, *Okay I'll take this hit.* I just didn't want the big guy to hit me... When I didn't get touched it was like, *Well there's no way they're gonna catch me now.*"

When Wheaton made it to the end zone he was mobbed by teammates—including many who rushed in from the bench, and even some Oregon cheerleaders—as Autzen Stadium erupted into pandemonium.

Huard has since admitted he should've made the tackle but was too shell-shocked at the time.

"I think I was so *Oh my gosh! That just happened. That ball was intercepted* that I didn't go make the tackle," Huard said. "And had I made the tackle we probably wouldn't be talking about it today."

If Wheaton hadn't made that interception, many things would be different today.

2 The Natty

It took 115 seasons until Oregon played for a national championship, but that was finally the Ducks' reality on January 10, 2011, when they took on Auburn in Glendale, Arizona, in the BCS Championship Game, famously nicknamed "the Natty" by Oregon cornerback Cliff Harris.

The game was a matchup between two undefeated teams—the top-ranked, 12–0 Tigers, and the second-ranked, 13–0 Ducks—and the season's top-two scoring offenses in the nation.

It was also a matchup between Oregon's pace—blinding speed and a running attack led by Doak Walker Award winner LaMichael

James—and Auburn's SEC-style power, led by Heisman Trophy–winning quarterback Cam Newton and bruising defensive tackle Nick Fairley.

But in the end, it was a fluke run by Auburn freshman Michael Dyer and a chip-shot field goal by Wes Byrum kicked as time expired that left the Ducks on the losing end of a 22–19 game at the University of Phoenix Stadium.

Oregon had 449 yards of total offense and sophomore quarterback Darron Thomas threw for 363 yards and two touchdowns, but the Ducks struggled all game to convert their offensive production into points.

Oregon scored just 11 points in the first three quarters and was stuffed on four straight running plays inside the Tigers' 6-yard line, including a fourth-and-goal from the 1.

That series summed up an abysmal game for the Ducks' ground attack, which gained just 75 yards on 32 attempts in the game after averaging 303.8 per game during the regular season.

James, who had 1,682 yards coming into the game, was held to 49 yards on 13 carries.

"There were times when we had it rolling pretty good," coach Chip Kelly said. "And other times it wasn't going as fast as we should have been."

But what a final five minutes.

Trailing 19–11 late in the fourth quarter, Oregon got the ball back when linebacker Casey Matthews punched the ball out of Newton's hands on a scramble and the fumble was recovered by Harris at the Oregon 40-yard line with 4:54 to play.

The Ducks followed with an eight-play, 40-yard drive that ended with James scoring on a two-yard pass from Thomas. Needing a two-point conversion to tie the score, Thomas connected with receiver Jeff Maehl in the back of the end zone to knot the game at 19 with 2:33 left.

On the Tigers' ensuing drive, Dyer made what would become the defining play of the game. Two plays after the change of possession, Dyer made a short run to midfield, was tied up, and fell over Oregon linebacker Eddie Pleasant. Several Ducks gave up on the play because Dyer appeared to be down. Instead, he regained his footing and sprinted to Oregon's 23-yard line with 1:39 to play.

"That run play killed us," Matthews said. "We had the momentum, and that play killed us."

Replay officials reviewed the play and determined that Dyer didn't contact the ground with anything other than his hands or feet. The gain stood.

"It was kind of a freak play, really, when you think about it," Oregon defensive coordinator Nick Aliotti said. "To be such a critical play in the game, it even makes it tougher, you know?"

Four plays later, Byrum's field goal split the uprights to give Auburn the win.

The loss left Oregon lamenting missed opportunities to take control of the game. There was a third-down stop by Oregon that was negated when a defensive lineman jumped offside. A promising drive was undone when Fairley flew by lineman Carson York for a sack, then Mark Asper was called for holding on the next play. And there was that drive that ended at the goal line when the Ducks couldn't score from the 1 on fourth down.

Still, Aliotti said the Ducks wouldn't hang their heads.

"I think that we showed the world that Oregon football is pretty darn good," Aliotti said. "And I know that losing sucks, but I've told myself I'm not going to hang my head when I get a chance to coach in the national championship game on this stage and had a chance to win it in the end."

3 The Chip Kelly Era

The story goes that Chip Kelly, fresh out of college in 1990 and working as an assistant at Columbia University in New York, was sharing an apartment with other members of the staff in the city, and commented on a loud banging noise he took to be fireworks. No, those aren't fireworks, a buddy scoffed. They were gunshots.

Thus were the small-town roots of the man who, in six fleeting seasons, would redefine offensive football at Oregon, lead the program to new heights as its head coach, and then move on to the National Football League. A longtime assistant at his alma mater, the University of New Hampshire, Kelly tirelessly worked on improving the spread option. He revved up the pace during two years as offensive coordinator with the Ducks and then blew the doors off the college football world as Oregon's head coach from 2009 to 2012.

In the process, Oregon played for its first-ever national title in 2010 and won a Rose Bowl the next season, the first time in 95 years. The Ducks also set or tied myriad school records for offense, regularly produced Heisman Trophy contenders on that side of the ball, and saw their national profile explode. "The man's a genius," said Kenjon Barner, a running back during Kelly's time in Eugene.

It was easy to forget later that, at the time of his hiring, Kelly was an unknown commodity on the West Coast. After brief stops elsewhere, he'd spent more then a decade back at New Hampshire, coaching running backs, the offensive line, and quarterbacks. He immersed himself in the various techniques of offensive football and spent his off-seasons traveling throughout the country, learning the spread option from Rich Rodriguez and other early visionaries.

If Kelly was relatively unknown when he got to Eugene, he wasn't for long. He introduced himself to the college football nation with the Ducks' historic win at Michigan on September 8, 2007—most notably by calling for quarterback Dennis Dixon to keep the ball for a touchdown on a fake Statue of Liberty play. Later that year, the Ducks ran for a since-broken school record of 465 yards at Washington, with Dixon and running back Jonathan Stewart demonstrating a level of wizardry in the option that confounded the crowd, television cameras, and the Husky defense, none of which could figure out whether Dixon or Stewart had the ball most of the night.

Within a year, Oregon administrators and key boosters had identified Kelly as their preferred successor to head coach Mike Bellotti. In late 2008, after the Ducks set school records for average points (41.9) and yards per game (484.8) under Kelly, a formal succession plan was put into writing. Within a few months, Bellotti announced he was stepping into the athletic director's chair, and Kelly was promoted.

Kelly's head coaching career began with a debacle at Boise State, a horrible offensive performance capped off by LeGarrette Blount's postgame punch. The embarrassment immediately tested Kelly's leadership. But of all of Kelly's qualities, his focus might be the best. He brought the Ducks together, convinced them their season was far from over, and led them all the way to the Rose Bowl in 2009.

The Ducks reached Pasadena with Jeremiah Masoli at quarterback. Whether it was the bullish, strong-armed Masoli; the lanky, lightning-fast Dixon; or even Justin Roper in the 2007 Sun Bowl, Kelly repeatedly found ways to score points regardless of who was under center. That knack would be tested again in 2010 after Masoli was dismissed from the team, the most notable development in an off-season marred by repeated criminal acts by the Ducks.

With Masoli gone, Kelly and the Ducks turned to Darron Thomas at quarterback. Thomas wasn't the fastest quarterback Kelly coached at Oregon, or the most accurate, but he had toughness in spades. He led the Ducks to the first undefeated regular season in modern school history and a spot in the Bowl Championship Series title game, where they lost to Auburn. A year later, Oregon went back to the Rose Bowl—and this time won. In 2012, Kelly again had to adjust at quarterback after Thomas declared for the NFL Draft a year early. Unflappable redshirt freshman Marcus Mariota stepped in and led them to another BCS victory, this time in the Fiesta Bowl.

Throughout Kelly's time as head coach, he maintained play-calling duties for the sake of operating the offense at the fastest tempo possible. He also kept his entire staff of assistants together throughout his four years, something no other program in the country could boast during that span.

The Kelly era was not without controversy. The 2010 off-season was a trying time in Eugene, though ultimately off-the-field transgressions were diminished over the course of Kelly's tenure. His aloof manner with boosters alienated some longtime fans, and he kept media at a distance. His dealings with scouting service operator Will Lyles prompted an NCAA investigation that was unresolved when Kelly decided to leave for the Philadelphia Eagles in early 2013.

Those developments off the field soured Kelly's tenure in the minds of some. But there was no arguing with the success the Ducks enjoyed on the field with Kelly as head coach—it was simply unprecedented.

2012: Bringing Home Roses

Nick Aliotti could hardly contain himself.

"I'm extremely excited and happy to be finally winning the Rose Bowl," the longtime UO assistant coach said as his voice rose excitedly to a shout in the Ducks' locker room. "We—the University of Oregon—Rose Bowl champs!"

What a scene it was at the Rose Bowl in 2012, as confetti rained down on the Ducks following their 45–38 victory against Wisconsin to give Oregon its first Rose Bowl victory in 95 years.

On a glorious afternoon in Pasadena, California, with the temperature 82 degrees at kickoff, Wisconsin and Oregon embarked on a wildly entertaining game that wasn't over until a disputed spike by Badgers quarterback Russell Wilson came a split second after the clock expired, ending their last-chance drive at the Ducks' 25-yard line.

In the end, the Ducks outlasted the Badgers thanks to an explosive, record-setting offensive performance and a defensive effort that included two huge turnovers in the second half.

In their last game for the Ducks, LaMichael James rushed for 159 yards and a touchdown, quarterback Darron Thomas threw for 268 and three TDs, and receiver Lavasier Tuinei had the best performance of his Oregon career with eight catches for 158 yards and two scores to earn offensive MVP honors.

And then there was running back De'Anthony Thomas, who had just two carries in the game but turned them into touchdown runs of 91 and 64 yards. The freshman finished the game with 314 all-purpose yards.

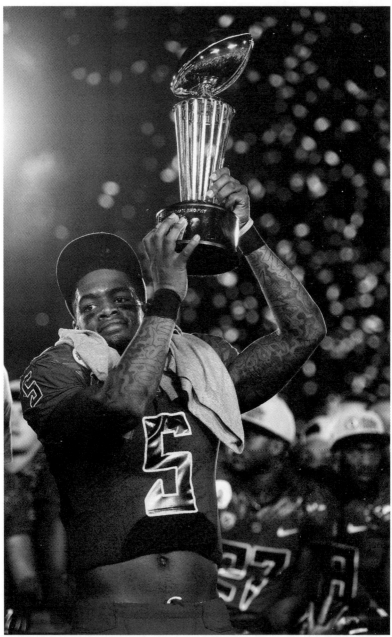

Quarterback Darron Thomas celebrates with teammates after the Ducks defeat Wisconsin 45–38 in the 2012 Rose Bowl.

His 91-yard run, which came on the final play of the first quarter, when he went untouched between the tackles, set the Rose Bowl record for longest run and longest scoring play.

The win was the Ducks' first in the Rose Bowl since 1917, ending a streak of four straight losses. It also put to rest the tired storyline that Oregon couldn't win the big one under Chip Kelly, who in three years as head coach had lost his two previous BCS bowl games, the 2010 Rose Bowl to Ohio State and the 2011 BCS Championship Game to Auburn.

Along the way the Ducks faced skepticism about their inability to crank up their high-scoring, blur offense after the long layoff between the regular season and bowl games. Oregon had scored just 17 against the Buckeyes and 19 against the Tigers.

"I was sick and tired of the missed opportunities," Oregon senior guard Mark Asper said. "But what everybody was saying, they were factual things. We didn't score as many points as usual in those games. We didn't put up as much offense as usual. That was the frustration and anxiety, wanting to perform well and take advantage of our opportunities."

Offense wasn't a problem in 2012, as the game quickly evolved into a shootout. Oregon had 621 yards of offense, Wisconsin had 508 and they came within one yard of the Rose Bowl record of 1,130 yards of combined offense set by Texas and USC in 2006.

Still, Oregon was playing catch-up for the entire first half, matching the Badgers score for score. Tuinei's three-yard TD catch with 30 seconds left in the second quarter made it 28–28 at halftime.

De'Anthony Thomas gave the Ducks their first lead of the game 49 seconds into the third quarter when he raced around the edge and went 64 yards into the end zone to put Oregon up 35–28.

The Badgers scored the next 10 points to take a 38–35 advantage late in the third quarter and were driving again when Oregon linebacker Kiko Alonso, the soon-to-be defensive MVP, made a diving interception of a Wilson pass, leading to the Ducks' go-ahead score in the opening minute of the fourth quarter.

After the Badgers went three-and-out on their ensuing drive, Oregon slowed down its offense and took 12 plays and 5:54 to march 76 yards for a 30-yard field goal, making it 45–38 with 6:50 play.

Oregon got the ball back with 4:06 to play when cornerback Terrance Mitchell forced a fumble by Jared Abbrederis after a 29-yard reception. Linebacker Michael Clay pounced on the ball as it sat motionless along the Oregon sideline for what seemed like an eternity.

The Ducks were able to run all but 16 seconds off the clock on their ensuing drive before a punt gave the ball back to the Badgers at their own 13.

That was almost too much time, as Wilson drove his team 62 yards on two pass plays. However, he couldn't get off a snap-spike to stop the clock before time expired.

After a brief review, officials declared the game over.

"We needed to win for our peace of mind," Aliotti said. "Those kids deserved to win the Rose Bowl, and we just talked about perseverance. They were really fearless on the big stage. They had unbelievable belief and faith."

5 Uncle Phil

There were many key moments in Oregon's transformation from regional also-ran to national powerhouse over the period of about 15 years that led up to the 2011 Ducks' BCS Championship Game appearance.

Of course, there was Kenny Wheaton's interception against Washington that finally clinched another Rose Bowl berth, and the addition of Chip Kelly to the coaching staff. There was also the team's ascension under Joey Harrington,. The most important, however, might have taken place in January 1996, shortly after Oregon's blowout loss to Colorado in the Cotton Bowl. It was then that Phil Knight approached head coach Mike Bellotti about becoming a more prominent benefactor to the program. The Ducks haven't been the same since.

"Before him there were [boosters] who were amazingly solid all the time," said receiver Bob Newland (1968–70). "But now with what Phil gives, it just changes the landscape of everything."

Knight, who received his undergraduate degree at Oregon, also ran track for the Ducks. He founded the company that became Nike with his UO coach, Bill Bowerman. Nike made Knight a billionaire—and he's donated hundreds of millions to the athletic department, while also making the Ducks the company's guinea pig for new equipment.

The combination of opulent, Knight-funded facilities and flashy, Nike-supplied uniforms turned Oregon into a premier destination for football recruits. The Ducks suddenly became a national player on the recruiting scene, and in turn a national powerhouse on the field—the only team in the country to make four straight Bowl Championship Series appearances from 2009 to 2012.

"Knight's influence on Oregon is so great," wrote Michael Rosenberg of *Sports Illustrated*, "that calling him a booster is like calling the Chairman of the Joint Chiefs of Staff a concerned citizen."

Knight's donations to Oregon athletics over the years have been estimated at $300 million. He was a significant contributor to the Moshofsky Center, Oregon's indoor practice facility and the most immediate result of his 1996 talk with Bellotti; the expansion of Autzen Stadium in 2002; a renovated athletic-treatment facility

Bill Bowerman

Phil Knight's co-founder at Nike, Bill Bowerman, also had twin interests in football and track at Oregon.

Bowerman, who took over the UO track program in 1948 and coached the Ducks for 24 years, was a blocking back on the football team in 1931 and 1932. He coached football in Portland and then Medford after graduating before returning to his alma mater as the head coach for track and field.

Bowerman was also hired as an assistant football coach, and served in that role from 1948 to 1952, under head coaches Jim Aiken and Len Casanova.

There was only a brief gap between the tenures of Bowerman and Bill Hayward, the former of whom was track and field coach from 1904 to 1947. And like Bowerman, Hayward also had ties to the football team, serving as an athletic trainer.

Oregon's historic track-and-field facility, Hayward Field, was in fact originally built to house a football field. A track was added two years later.

in the Casanova Center administration building; the Jaqua Center for academic support; Matthew Knight Arena, the UO basketball facility named for Knight's late son, to which he contributed $100 million as a backstop to the loans used to finance construction; and a gleaming new football operations building opened in the fall of 2013.

Knight has also given tens of millions to academics at Oregon, providing funding for construction of the university's library and law school. He has also made massive donations to Stanford, where he earned his graduate degree, and to Oregon Health & Science University. But it's his contributions to Oregon athletics that get the most notoriety—and cause the most controversy.

To some, Knight is suspected of being a meddler. He reportedly has access to a headset through which he can monitor coaches' chatter during football games and is graced with tutorials from Oregon's coaches. When Bellotti stepped into the athletic director chair to make way for Kelly to become head coach in 2009, it was thought Bellotti might have received a firm nudge from Knight.

The same was suspected when former athletic director Bill Moos had his contract bought out and was replaced in 2007 by Knight's friend and fellow booster, Pat Kilkenny. The attempts to replace McArthur Court with a new basketball arena were stalled, and some pointed fingers at Moos.

Knight denied involvement in Moos' ouster. "Bill Moos was athletic director for 12 years, and I think he did a good job," Knight said a year after the change. "He's got to look on those 12 years with pride, and the university should look on that as a good period for athletics. In those 12 years we probably had a dozen different projects that we worked on, and probably nine of them went really well, and three of them didn't go so well, and they got more publicity than the nine that went well. But on balance it was a really good 12 years and I like to think of Bill Moos as a friend. I don't think I'm the reason he isn't there."

Knight is a significant reason, however, for Oregon football's explosion onto the national scene in the years following the Cotton Bowl. He's known in Eugene as "Uncle Phil," a title earned through hundreds of millions of dollars in support of the Ducks.

Joey Harrington: Captain Comeback

In some respects, Oregon's rise to perennial elite status seemed meteoric. The Ducks under Chip Kelly were suddenly an annual BCS participant and had the most explosive offense in the country, year in and year out.

Anyone who has followed the program closely knows a different story—one in which Oregon scratched and clawed its way to prominence, winning a series of close games in progressively more successful seasons in order to ultimately enter the national title picture through force of will. And it happened largely during the era of Joey Harrington.

From the point at which Harrington was named Oregon's starting quarterback, at midseason in 1999, through the Fiesta Bowl in early 2002, the Portland native started 28 games; the Ducks won 25 of them, including 11 of the 13 in which they were tied or trailed in the fourth quarter.

By the time he graduated, Harrington was known as "Captain Comeback." There was no situation too dire for the Ducks in those days, no deficit they couldn't overcome under the leadership of their cool, charismatic quarterback.

"The difference between us and everyone else those years: We believed we were going to win the game no matter what happened," Harrington said.

In Harrington's first full season as the starter, in 2000, the Ducks won 10 games for the first time in the program's history. A year later, they won 11. He was 3–0 in bowl games, leading a fourth-quarter comeback over Minnesota in the 1999 Sun Bowl, scoring touchdowns in three different ways against Texas in the 2000 Holiday Bowl, and responding to a BCS snub by demolishing Colorado in the Fiesta Bowl as a senior in 2001.

Other Oregon quarterbacks have thrown for more touchdowns and run for more yards and led the Ducks to even bigger heights, but none so completely defined Ducks football as Harrington.

He was literally a Duck from birth. His father played at Oregon and received a letter from legendary UO coach Len Casanova upon Joey's birth, offering the family's new addition a scholarship then and there. Since the junior Harrington's graduation, Oregon has come to be defined by Phil Knight's generosity, its flashy uniforms,

Oregon's Career Passing Leaders

Name	Years	Cmp-Att-Int	TD	Yards
Bill Musgrave	1987–90	634-1,104-40	60	8,343
Danny O'Neil	1991–94	636-1,132-37	62	8,301
Kellen Clemens	2002–05	613-1,005-24	61	7,555
Joey Harrington	1998–2001	512-928-23	59	6,911
Chris Miller	1983–86	560-1,015-39	42	6,681
Dan Fouts	1970–72	482-956-54	37	5,995
Darron Thomas	2008–11	449-733-17	66	5,910
Akili Smith	1997–98	323-571-15	45	5,148
Dennis Dixon	2004–07	444-695-21	38	5,129
Tony Graziani	1993–96	362-670-18	25	4,498

Cmp-Att-Int: Completions-Attempts-Interceptions; TD: touchdowns

and the spread-option offense. Harrington played at the end of an era, when the Ducks weren't a national recruiting power but instead put together great teams by combining overlooked gems from California with gritty in-state talent.

It took an injury to junior A.J. Feeley for Harrington to get his first shot at glory, in 1999. He came off the bench to lead dramatic wins over Arizona and Arizona State. "From then on," he said, "we believed we could win every game we played, no matter the circumstances."

Harrington spent the next two seasons demonstrating just that. He quarterbacked some of the most memorable moments in UO history, including a double-overtime win at Arizona State in 2000, that season's Holiday Bowl, in which he ran, passed and rushed for touchdowns, and the 2001 Civil War in rainy, windy conditions, when playing for the national championship still seemed like a possibility.

There were memorable disappointments, too—the five-interception day in the 2000 Civil War that denied Harrington his dream of playing in the Rose Bowl and the 2001 loss to Stanford that cost Oregon a perfect regular season. There was also the BCS snub that relegated the Ducks to the Fiesta Bowl in Harrington's senior season. The Rose Bowl hosted the title game that year, and so in two straight seasons Harrington came up a game short of playing in Pasadena.

"All I ever dreamt about was getting that Rose Bowl ring," he said. "So getting snubbed by the BCS for a spot in the national title game that year has always been a tough thing for me to get over."

But the win over Colorado in the Fiesta Bowl gave Oregon a No. 2 ranking in the final polls of the 2001 season, heights to which the program had never before ascended. Harrington was a Heisman finalist as well that year, the first in Ducks' history.

Joey Harrington didn't have the strongest throwing arm of all the quarterbacks to play at Oregon. He wasn't the fastest, by a long shot. But he might have been the smartest, and he was certainly the most respected by the teammates he willed to victory and the fans who feasted on his accomplishments, when the Ducks rose from plucky underdog status to a conference powerhouse and national-championship contender.

Game Changer: Dethroning the Dawgs in 1994

Yes, Kenny Wheaton's interception in the final minute against ninth-ranked Washington at Autzen Stadium in 1994 is the seminal play in the modern era of Oregon football. But in that 31–20 victory for the Ducks, there were other significant moments as well.

Most notably, there was the defining drive of quarterback Danny O'Neil's career, and another staunch effort by the Oregon defense to hold the Huskies' powerful offense to just 20 points.

Whether or not Wheaton scored (which he did) or didn't score on his interception near the goal line with under one minute remaining in the game, that pick sealed the Ducks' upset and at 5–3 overall and 3–1 in the Pac-10, put them in the race for the conference title.

But what put Oregon in position for such a monumental victory was a 98-yard drive late in the fourth quarter to give Oregon a 24–20 lead.

It was an improbable drive led by an equally improbable hero. In his previous 33 career games, the senior O'Neil was 0–16 when the Ducks trailed in the second half. As a team, Oregon hadn't had a second-half comeback victory since 1990.

Both defied history playing against the Huskies.

Washington, which had trailed since early in the second quarter, took a 20–17 advantage with 7:44 to play on a drive that began at the Oregon 29 following O'Neil's ninth career interception against the Huskies.

A personal foul against Oregon on the Huskies' point-after attempt pushed the kickoff to the 50-yard line, and the short kick allowed Washington to pin the Ducks at their own 2-yard line.

Backed up against their own goal line and needing to drive nearly the length of the field, the Ducks put it on their embattled quarterback, who had to that point completed just 6-of-16 passes for 55 yards in the game.

On the first play of the drive, one Washington coach Jim Lambright would later call a "huge swing of momentum," O'Neil connected with receiver Dameron Ricketts for a 36-yard completion and the Ducks were off and running.

Three plays later, O'Neil completed a 10-yard pass to receiver Pat Johnson on third-and-8 from the Oregon 40, and then quickly followed on the next play with a 21-yard pass to Ricketts.

Facing another third-and-8 from the Washington 27, O'Neil scrambled for the first down at the 19. After two plays moved the ball to the 12, seldom-used running back Dwayne Jones rumbled in for the touchdown with 2:40 left to play. The Ducks needed 11 plays and 5:04 to score the game-winner, and O'Neil finished the drive 4-for-4 for 68 yards.

"I finally got it done," O'Neil said. "Not coming from behind is more than something the media has heaped on me. It was also a personal thing with me, something I needed to overcome."

Oregon was outgained 387–202 in the game and had just 11 first downs to the Huskies' 18. Nearly half the Ducks' yards (98) and first downs (five) came on that final drive.

"Danny brought this team back from what looked like a heart-breaking loss to an exhilarating win," UO coach Rich Brooks said. "Danny has taken a lot of flak, but this win is as much his as anyone else's."

The Oregon defense and special teams had put the Ducks on top early when the offense was struggling.

The Ducks initially took a 7–3 lead on an 8-yard run by Dino Philyaw at the 13:50 mark of the second quarter, a score set up by an 86-yard kick return by Ricky Whittle.

On the Huskies' ensuing possession, cornerback Alex Molden intercepted Huard on the second play of the drive to give the Ducks the ball at Washington's 19. Two plays later, Whittle scored on a two-yard run and the Ducks went up 14–3 despite just 53 yards of offense and one first down to that point.

The Ducks' defense also did a stellar job slowing Washington running back Napoleon Kaufman, the Heisman Trophy candidate who was averaging 167.3 yards per game. Oregon held him to 101 yards on 23 carries. More important, he was also kept out of the end zone.

Of course, the finest defensive play of the day was the one at the end, when Wheaton stepped in front of Huard's pass as the Huskies were driving for the lead and, well, you know the rest.

8 LaMichael James

The title of "best player in Oregon football history" can be debated endlessly. Joey Harrington led the Ducks to unprecedented heights. Mel Renfro was a dominant two-way player in a bygone era. Haloti Ngata and Gary Zimmerman became dominant NFL linemen.

However, in terms of the player who enjoyed the most decorated career in Ducks' history, it's beyond dispute. That's running back LaMichael James, the tough, speedy Texan who destroyed school rushing records and piled up honor after honor during a three-year stretch from 2009 to 2011.

James continued what had already been a strong tradition at Oregon for running backs under position coach Gary Campbell, following in the footsteps of Reuben Droughns, Maurice Morris, and Jonathan Stewart, all of whom went on to successful professional careers. But none of them matched James' production in college.

"He's certainly one of the best ever, and one of the most explosive," said Mike Bellotti, the head coach when James was recruited to Oregon.

By the time James declared himself ready to enter the NFL draft as a junior, he had run for Oregon records of 5,082 yards and 53 touchdowns. As a junior he set a single-season school record of 1,805 yards—breaking the record he'd set a year before (1,731)—and his freshman year total of 1,546 yards stands as fifth in school history.

James' phenomenal junior year included a 288-yard performance at Arizona that broke Onterrio Smith's single-game school record of 285, which was in turn surpassed just a year later by

The best running back in Ducks history, LaMichael James shows off his signature speed against the Auburn Tigers in the 2011 BCS National Championship Game.

James' best friend, Kenjon Barner. James owns four of UO's top-10 single-game rushing marks.

His dramatic cutback touchdown run of 72 yards at Tennessee as a sophomore in 2010 remains one of the most memorable plays in recent Oregon history. With LaMichael James running in Chip Kelly's spread-option, there was no stopping the Ducks.

"This offense was perfect for him," Bellotti said. "And he was a perfect fit for the offense."

James' stardom was anticipated by Oregon fans who knew of his exploits on the scout team in 2008. Even then, while he red-shirted, James was one of the best players on the field in practices, though the Ducks could afford to delay his debut because the tandem of Jeremiah Johnson and LeGarrette Blount was already on hand.

Johnson departed in 2009, when James became Blount's understudy, a quick change of pace to the burly Blount. That all changed at Boise State in Oregon's opener, when Blount was bottled up, James ran twice for 22 yards to lead the Ducks in rushing, and Blount was suspended for most of the year after punching an opposing player. The LaMichael James era at Oregon had begun.

Along with records, James piled up accolades throughout his career. He was a freshman All-American in 2009, the Pac-10's Offensive Freshman of the Year, and a second-team All-Conference pick. Then came James' remarkable sophomore campaign, when he helped lead the Ducks to the BCS Championship Game, while setting the school rushing record for the first time.

For his exploits, James finished third in Heisman Trophy balloting for the 2010 season, the best finish ever by a Duck. He received the Doak Walker Award as the nation's best running back, the most prestigious individual honor ever bestowed upon a Duck. And he was named a unanimous All-American, the first Duck so honored, earning first-team distinction from no less than eight publications nationally.

It was a tough act to follow, but James made a run at it, again setting Oregon's single-season rushing record and leading the Ducks to the Rose Bowl title in 2011. He was a finalist again for the Doak Walker Award, and also the Paul Hornung Award as the nation's most versatile player. He earned consensus All-American status, and is the only player in UO history to do so twice.

What's more, James compiled a remarkable career despite playing through several injuries that might have devastated other players. He had a finger injury throughout his sophomore year that required attention, including during a key goal-line stand by Auburn in the BCS Championship Game while James was on the

Oregon's Career Rushing Leaders

Name	Years	Att	Yards	TDs
LaMichael James	2009–11	771	5,082	53
Kenjon Barner	2009–12	582	3,623	41
Derek Loville	1986–89	811	3,296	41
Jonathan Stewart	2005–07	516	2,891	27
Terrence Whitehead	2002–05	612	2,832	18
Sean Burwell	1990–93	668	2,758	21
Ricky Whittle	1992–95	590	2,545	22
Jeremiah Johnson	2005–08	349	2,336	30
Bobby Moore	1969–71	474	2,306	22
Maurice Morris	2000–01	466	2,237	17

sideline. Earlier that year, on a memorable clock-killing drive to clinch a 15–13 win at Cal, James suffered a lower leg injury that would hamper him the rest of the season, but he didn't miss a game. And as a junior he suffered a grotesque elbow injury that sidelined him for two games, yet still set the school rushing record that season.

James' career was not without controversy. He missed the 2010 opener while suspended following an arrest stemming from an altercation with an ex-girlfriend. He also staunchly supported his mentor, Willie Lyles, the scouting service operator whose dealings with Oregon embroiled the Ducks in an NCAA investigation.

But James' story is one of overcoming remarkable odds. He never met his father, who died when James was young, and was raised by his grandmother. When she passed away, while James was in high school, he lived alone in her house in Texarkana, Texas, keeping himself on a path to Oregon, and eventually the NFL—with several stops in the Oregon record book along the way.

Double OT in the Desert

It's not often the drama of a big game matches its hype. But those who watched Oregon play at Arizona in 2009 were lucky enough to see just such a game.

As of that fall, the Ducks had gone 15 years since their last Rose Bowl appearance, and eight since they last won the Pac-10. They went to the desert in November 2009 with a chance to clinch a share of the conference title, looking to solidify their status as favorite in the Rose Bowl race.

The rub? Arizona also controlled its destiny in the race to reach Pasadena. It was a showdown of conference powers, with ESPN's *College GameDay* on hand to mark the occasion. It was Chip Kelly's first year as Oregon's head coach, and while he famously avoided putting extra importance on any single game, the Ducks were well aware of the gravity of the situation. "We know what's at stake," Oregon safety T.J. Ward said. "We've got two more games. We win them, we go to the Rose Bowl."

Arizona Stadium had been unkind to the Ducks in previous trips. In 2005, UO starting quarterback Kellen Clemens saw his career end against the Wildcats due to a broken ankle. Two years later, another Oregon quarterback suffered a career-ending injury when Dennis Dixon's knee buckled, and with it went the Ducks' national championship dreams.

So it was that Oregon went to Arizona in 2009, looking to exorcise recent history, and make some new history in the process.

The Ducks began that quest in rousing fashion, jumping out to a 14–0 lead. It looked like a blowout was in the making. But the Wildcats stormed back and held a 24–14 lead early in the fourth quarter. Thus began one of the more dramatic comebacks in Oregon football history.

It began with a rushing touchdown from tough dual-threat quarterback Jeremiah Masoli, who earlier had fumbled twice and thrown an interception. "He's just incredible," said LaMichael James, who ran for 117 yards in the game to set a Pac-10 freshman record with 1,310 in the season. "He never got down out there, even after a couple fumbles."

Three minutes later, the Ducks were in position to tie it, as kicker Morgan Flint set up for a 43-yard field goal. Flint was an incredibly accurate kicker, but his diminutive build didn't offer much leg strength. His attempt to tie the game at 24–24 looked to be short, but the kick hit the crossbar and carried through the uprights. "How far was that?" Kelly asked reporters after the game. When told the kick was 43 yards, Kelly said, "Well, that's his limit."

The Wildcats weren't about to go quietly, and answered quickly with a 71-yard touchdown from Nick Foles to Juron Criner—his second of three touchdown receptions. The Ducks ultimately got the ball back with 2:58 to play, down a touchdown and needing to go 80 yards.

As erratic as Masoli could sometimes be, he was uncommonly cool under pressure, and this game was no different. He marched the Ducks downfield 80 yards in 15 plays to tie the game. He had four completions to receiver Jeff Maehl, including an eight-yard gain on a fourth-and-5 play, before hitting Ed Dickson with a touchdown pass to force overtime. "That was one of the best drives that I've ever been a part of," Maehl said after his career day of 12 receptions for 114 yards and two touchdowns.

Overtime wasn't assured until Flint hit the extra point. The snap was low, into the turf, and holder Nate Costa had to dig it out before Flint could convert. "That was a clutch kick by Morgan," said Costa, who was named Pac-10 Special Teams Player of the Week for that recovery. "It was one of those things where, if we don't make that play, we're all going to look like a bunch of jackasses. But Morgan made a great kick and we salvaged it."

As the Ducks drove down the field, Arizona fans were pouring onto the sideline, surrounding the field in anticipation of a raucous postgame celebration. With overtime on the way, they couldn't be herded back into the stands, and so remained on the sidelines behind the team benches. "They were really loud, and we never could get rid of them," James said. "The crowd was in it the whole game."

Overtime began with Maehl's second touchdown, and then Criner's third. But in the second overtime, Arizona had to settle for a field goal, and the Ducks had an opening. They got in position to score thanks to another pass to Dickson, on a play the Ducks hadn't run since it had worked for two touchdowns against Boise State the year before.

With the game hanging in the balance, Masoli ran for the winning touchdown, his third rushing score of the game and sixth touchdown overall. The Ducks needed only to win the Civil War, and they would be off to the Rose Bowl. "This is incredible," James said afterward. "I have no words for that right now. Just incredible."

10 War for the Roses

The stage had never been bigger for a Civil War game than it was on the night of December 3, 2009.

For the first time in the 113-game history of this fierce in-state rivalry, the winner would go to the Rose Bowl.

The game was played on a Thursday night before 59,597 at Autzen Stadium and a national television audience on ESPN. It was a bitterly cold, clear night, with temperatures dropping below freezing, but the action on the field couldn't have been hotter. The No. 7 Ducks won 37–33 to earn their first trip to Pasadena since the 1994 season and their first outright Pac-10 championship since 2001.

The Ducks had to rally from deficits four times. Redshirt freshman running back LaMichael James rushed for 166 yards and three touchdowns and Oregon sealed the win with a drive that lasted the final 6:09 of the game and included two fourth-down conversions.

As former *Eugene Register-Guard* sports editor Ron Bellamy wrote afterward, "An epic stage produced an epic football game."

Oregon State came into the game with redemption on its mind. A year earlier, the Beavers had been a Civil War win away from playing in the Rose Bowl, but the underdog Ducks blasted those dreams with a 65–38 victory in Corvallis that left roses strewn on the sidelines and stands at Reser Stadium.

Oregon went on to a Holiday Bowl victory against Oklahoma State and Oregon State dropped to the Sun Bowl, the Pac-10's third-place bowl game.

"I will play Oregon anywhere on this planet," OSU cornerback Tim Clark said in the days leading up to the 2009 game.

That emotion played well for the Beavers early on. Oregon State struck first with running back Quizz Rodgers scoring on a one-yard run, capping a possession set up by an interception thrown by Oregon quarterback Jeremiah Masoli on the Ducks' opening drive of the game.

But a short touchdown run by James and a 73-yard TD strike from Masoli to receiver Jeff Maehl gave the Ducks a 14–10 lead with 3:46 to play in the first quarter.

Justin Kahut's third field goal of the game put the Beavers back up 16–14 late in the second quarter and both teams added touchdowns in the final 1:19 of the first half—first by Oregon and then Oregon State—to keep the Beavers ahead 23–21 at halftime.

The game took a distressing turn for the Ducks when quarterback Sean Canfield led Oregon State on a nine-play, 75-yard scoring drive on the opening possession of the second half to extend the Beavers' lead to 30–21. It would be the largest advantage of the game for either team.

Then the Ducks came to life. Running back LeGarrette Blount, suspended since punching a Boise State player in the opening game of the season, returned in the third quarter and scored on a 12-yard run to cut the deficit to 30–28. After Kahut's fourth field goal made it 33–28, James broke off on a 52-yard TD run to put the Ducks back on top 34–33 with 1:20 to play in the third quarter.

Kicker Morgan Flint booted a 34-yard field goal with 10:13 to play as Oregon's lead grew to 37–33.

The Beavers drove deep into Oregon territory on their ensuing possession, but on fourth-and-15 from the 27, Canfield missed receiver James Rodgers with a pass near the sideline and the Ducks took over with 6:09 to play.

Masoli kept the Ducks' 12-play final drive alive with a six-yard run on fourth down. Then, with 1:43 remaining in the game, running back Kenjon Barner took an option pitch five yards for a first down on another fourth-down play, and the Ducks were able to run out the clock.

Fans and players stormed the field once the final second had ticked away, and the on-field celebration lasted long after the Beavers had retreated to their locker room. Eventually, out of the sea of people popped the Oregon Duck, riding a wave of arms and clutching roses in its hand.

11 Mike Bellotti

Under Rich Brooks, Oregon's ascension as a football program was gradual. Under Mike Bellotti, it was dramatic.

In 1989, Northern California native Bellotti was hired as offensive coordinator, and the Ducks immediately set school records for points and yards per game. By the time Bellotti departed, Oregon had one of the top offensive traditions in the country.

In 1995, Bellotti replaced Brooks as head coach, and the Ducks tied the school record for wins in a season in his first year. By the time he was gone, Oregon was recognized as one of the nation's true powerhouses, a threat to contend for the national title in most years.

Bellotti's finale was the 2008 Holiday Bowl, after which he handed the reins of the Oregon football program to Chip Kelly. The Ducks beat Oklahoma State 42–31 that night in San Diego, making Bellotti's 14-season record 116–55, with 12 bowl appearances. "If you're only as good as your last game, okay, we're pretty good," said Bellotti, who briefly served as Oregon's athletic director before moving on to a career in television. "That part is enjoyable for me."

Before making a name as one of the most successful head coaches in Pac-10 history, Bellotti was already recognized as an offensive guru. Using a pro-style offense first implemented by predecessor Bob Toledo which aired out the football more than Oregon's teams of the past, Bellotti coached five first-team All-Conference quarterbacks, beginning with Bill Musgrave in 1990. The year before, Bellotti's first at Oregon, Musgrave and the Ducks averaged 421.5 yards and 31.6 points per game, both school records by a wide margin.

Oregon's Most Successful Coaches (min. 20 games)

Name	Years	W–L	WP
Chip Kelly	2009–12	46-7	.868
Hugo Bezdek	1906, 1913–17	30–10–4	.727
Mike Bellotti	1995–2008	116–55	.678
Shy Huntington	1918–23	26–12–6	.659
John McEwan	1926–29	20–13–2	.600
Prink Callison	1932–37	33–23–2	.586
Len Casanova	1951–66	82–73–8	.528
Jim Aiken	1947–50	21–20	.512
Rich Brooks	1977–94	91–109–4	.456
Tex Oliver	1938–41, 1945–46	23–28–3	.454

Legend: W-L: won-lost; WP: winning percentage

The 1996 team broke both records, and the Ducks did it once more in 1998, with Akili Smith at quarterback, and again in 2008, with Kelly in his second season as offensive coordinator. In all, Oregon averaged at least 400 yards of offense in 10 of Bellotti's 14 seasons as head coach, having previously only hit that mark twice, in 1970 and again in his 1989 debut as offensive coordinator. In 1994, Bellotti's final year before being promoted to head coach, he helped undersized senior Danny O'Neil develop into an All-Pac-10 quarterback. "Bellotti always believed in me, and that I was going to be the guy," O'Neil said. "I don't know if that was true for the other coaches."

When Brooks left to try his hand in the NFL after the 1994 Rose Bowl season, Bellotti was promoted to replace him. The Ducks went 9–3 in 1995 and played in the Cotton Bowl; it was the best season ever for a first-year Oregon coach. The 1996 season was one of just two in Bellotti's tenure that didn't end with a bowl, but the Ducks rallied from a 3–5 record to win three straight and finish 6–5. "I still think the very best coaching job ever, by me and my staff, was 1996," Bellotti would say after stepping aside as head coach.

The 1997 season kicked off one of the great runs in school history. The Ducks won seven games in '97, eight in '98, nine in '99, and a school-record 10 in 2000. They won 11 in 2001, won the Fiesta Bowl and finished No. 2 in the polls—the best year ever for Oregon at that point. Bellotti also established a record of being clutch when it mattered—the Ducks under Bellotti were 30–17 in regular-season games played after Halloween, and 47–12 in games decided by a touchdown or less.

In 2004, Oregon suffered its only losing season under Bellotti, going 5–6 and losing the Civil War 50–21. That off-season, he executed a daring switch in offensive philosophy, moving away from his pro-style roots and hiring Gary Crowton to implement a spread offense. Two years later, Crowton departed and Chip Kelly was hired, ushering in a new era of offensive firepower and national success for the Ducks.

Kelly's hiring was also preceded by an off-season of soul-searching for the coaching staff. The Ducks went 7–6 in 2006 and were embarrassed by BYU in the Las Vegas Bowl. "I was just disgusted with our program," Bellotti said of the time. How did the Ducks respond? In 2007 they were in the thick of the national-title hunt, until Dennis Dixon's knee injury.

The Bellotti era ended in 2008, in fitting fashion—with one more 10-win season and one more bowl win. But to Bellotti, his time at Oregon was defined just as much by his impact off the field. "I got the great opportunity to have some discussions with Len Casanova while he was still alive," Bellotti said. "He'd come into my office and talk to me about the team. He would always ask, 'How are the boys?' I would tell him. And then later on I would have people talk to me about how important Cas was in their life. And these were older men that are 50, 60, 70 years old, about what an influence Cas had on them. My goal and desire was to hopefully be as important in people's lives as Cas was. The nice thing is, there have been people over the years that said [of] Oregon football, we played hard. That's something I'm proud of."

12 Bill Musgrave

In the 2012 season, Chip Kelly and the Oregon Ducks won 12 games for the third straight season, a total of 36 victories that matched the program's win total in the 1970s—the *entire decade* of the '70s.

Somewhere in the interim, the Ducks pivoted from annual also-ran to perennial title contender—conference titles, yes, but national titles, too. Certainly, the ascension Oregon enjoyed during the Joey Harrington era, capped by the 2001 Fiesta Bowl season, completed the realization of that turnaround. But by then the Ducks were already a yearly bowl participant, and a solid competitor in the Pac-10.

No, Oregon's true pivot from nobody to somebody happened a few years earlier. It happened during the four years when Bill Musgrave was on campus playing quarterback. Ron Bellamy, the longtime sports columnist for the *Register-Guard* in Eugene, called Musgrave "the reason—more than any other single player—that the Ducks went from losing records to bowl berths."

When Musgrave arrived in Eugene from his home state of Colorado, there were signs that the Ducks were emerging under head coach Rich Brooks. They were fleeting signs, but signs nonetheless: Oregon enjoyed a winning season in 1984 and had a chance at another in 1985 before losing the final game of the year. "I felt confident in the direction of the program when I signed on," Musgrave said years later. "They seemed ready to turn that perpetual corner."

Musgrave would go on to enjoy just one fully healthy season at Oregon: his junior year of 1989. But that season he led the Ducks to their first bowl since 1963, and then to another the next year, graduating as the school record-holder in both passing yardage and total offense, records that still stand. And he helped usher in a new era of Oregon football, contributing to a success that helped the athletic department raise funds for the skyboxes that now mark the north side of Autzen Stadium and to begin fund-raising for the Casanova Center administration building, the opening salvos in what became the West Coast's most impressive facilities expansion.

After redshirting in 1986, Musgrave took the starting job as 1987 dawned. His first game was in his home state of Colorado, and the Ducks prevailed 10–7. A loss at Ohio State followed, but Oregon then reeled off wins against San Diego State, Washington, and USC. It had been more than 20 years since the Ducks started better than 4–1, and fans were climbing the goal posts after each successive win. "To start 4–1 against some pretty quality opponents felt significant," Musgrave said. A leg injury sidelined the freshman quarterback, and sent the Ducks into a tailspin, but he returned six games later to lead a 44–0 rout in the Civil War that made Oregon 6–5, a winning record.

Things looked even more promising in 1988. The Ducks started 6–1, with wins over Washington State, Stanford, and Washington. Then another injury to Musgrave, in this case a broken collarbone, stalled the season. Oregon wouldn't win another game, finishing 6–6.

Musgrave's will was being tested, but he had faith in himself and teammates such as running back Derek Loville, safety Rory Dairy, and lineman Todd Kaanapu. "None of us were necessarily

Musgrave's Debut

Bill Musgrave's storybook career at Oregon included a first chapter that couldn't have been scripted any better by Hollywood.

Musgrave, a native of Grand Junction, Colorado, made his debut with the Ducks on September 12, 1987, in his home state against the Colorado Buffaloes. Defying the odds, the young redshirt freshman who lacked experience and superior arm strength led Oregon to a 10–7 victory.

On Oregon's first possession, Musgrave completed a touchdown pass to Terry Obee. He finished the day 16-of-24 for 175 yards. While not overwhelming statistically, it was more about what he didn't do—commit a killer mistake that put the dominating UO defense in a tough spot.

"I have great confidence in Bill Musgrave," UO coach Rich Brooks said after the game. "He's mature beyond his years. I knew if we helped him, he'd have a good game."

As the 1987 season opened, there were questions about how Oregon would replace outgoing quarterback Chris Miller, a first-round NFL draft pick earlier that year. Musgrave put those to rest at Colorado, kicking off a career that ended with two bowl appearances.

"The protection was great," Musgrave said after his debut. "I could stand in there until things shuffled out and my vision wasn't blocked. We ran things I can do. Colorado played a lot of zone, and the receivers did a good job of finding the holes. It was just toss-and-catch out there."

blue chip recruits, but I think we all knew that the essence of playing football and succeeding is toughness and being resilient," Musgrave said. "And it happened that a lot of us had those traits."

It showed in 1989, Musgrave's junior year. The Ducks were 3–1, then lost to regional rivals Washington State and Washington. They were 3–3, another .500 record, when they visited Arizona State. It was a crossroads moment. "We talked about how the program was going to break the bowl drought, and we would be more proud of ourselves if we were the ones that did it, rather than [being] proud of future generations who accomplished that," he said. "So that was our mind-set." The team responded by winning four of its five remaining games and earning a berth in the Independence Bowl. It was Oregon's first postseason trip since the 1963 Sun Bowl, and the Ducks beat Tulsa 27–24 to finish 8–4.

For sheer drama, nothing could match Musgrave's senior season. He was stopped short of the goal line late in the game for a 22–17 loss at Arizona. He outplayed eventual Heisman Trophy winner Ty Detmer in an upset of fourth-ranked BYU. And he led the Ducks back from an 11-point deficit in the final 10 minutes to upset UCLA in his final home game.

Musgrave was injured yet again that day, and missed the final two regular-season games. But he returned for Oregon's second postseason game in as many years and threw for 392 yards and three touchdowns in the Ducks' Freedom Bowl loss to Colorado State. His career was over, but the Oregon football program would never be the same.

13 Civil War

During his four years as Oregon's head coach, beginning in 2009, Chip Kelly tried his best to instill the attitude in his team that no single game was more important than any other. "Every week is the Super Bowl," he often said. Longtime Ducks fans appreciated the sentiment—and the victories it produced. Still, to the Oregon faithful, there's nothing quite like beating the Beavers.

By the time Kelly left Eugene in 2012, the Ducks were riding a five-game win streak against their in-state rivals, and hadn't lost in regulation since 2006. The 2006 game was the last of nine straight in which the home team won the Civil War, a stretch more indicative of the back-and-forth nature the series has had over the years.

"There's no better feeling than pummeling those guys up there, especially at that old, crappy stadium," said Josh Wilcox, a former Oregon tight end who grew up in Junction City, between Eugene and Corvallis. "They don't like coming down here to play, we don't like going up there. I respect those guys, I like those guys—good people—but it's the backyard, man."

The Civil War has a colorful history dating back to the first year it was staged, in 1894. The 1911 game was canceled after fans of what was then Oregon Agricultural College chased the Ducks back to the train station following their 1910 win in Corvallis. The two teams brawled on the field in 1934, and in 1937 the Beavers won, prompting their fans to drive to Eugene the following Monday to celebrate on Oregon's campus—which was not well received.

The Ducks took their share of lumps from Oregon State during the middle part of the 20th century. Legendary all-purpose back Bobby Moore, who later changed his name to Ahmad Rashad, never did beat the Beavers. "That was the toughest thing for me," Rashad said. "But man, those guys. I've never been so keyed on any more in my life, I'm telling you. They used to just beat me up something terrible. Whatever our differences were, Oregon and Oregon State, they took it out on me. They were a pretty conservative bunch, and I was the most liberal guy at a liberal school, I guess."

Former place-kicker and defensive back Ken Woody (1968– 70) recalled his experience in 1966 with the freshman team, then coached by former Ducks lineman Norm Chapman. The Oregon freshmen were down 3–0 at halftime, and Chapman was stalking the sideline, ripping into his players. "Then he takes a drag of his cigarette, jumps onto the taping table, and screams, 'I hate these guys!'" Woody recalled. "I was so fired up. We had to punt right after that, and I was on the punt team. The Oregon State guy called a fair catch, and I just went in and leveled him. Like four penalty flags hit me. I remember getting off the field and Norm said, 'Great hit. Great hit.' Obviously getting late hits against Oregon State was okay in his book."

But for all the success Oregon State had through the '50s and '60s, Rich Brooks turned the tables. The former Oregon State player went 14–3–1 against his alma mater while coaching at Oregon from 1977 to 1994. Even when the Ducks were muddling through two-win seasons in 1977, 1978, and 1981, they managed to win the Civil War. "We always tried to circle the Beavers game in those days," former Oregon defensive lineman and assistant coach Michael Gray said, "because that was one game where we always had a good chance of winning.… The games were always close, and it seemed like every play mattered. The Civil Wars were the defining games for us, because we didn't have a chance to go to any bowl games."

Nobody won in 1983, the infamous "Toilet Bowl": a scoreless tie played in awful weather that resulted in an ugly parade of turnovers. Oregon quarterback Chris Miller had the ignominy of playing in that game, but he went on to beat the Beavers the next three years, closing out his career with a 49–28 win in 1986. "Afterward we were all smoking cigars, hanging out in the locker room with some of the alumni and coaches," Miller said. "That was a pretty good way to end it. It was special."

Oregon mostly controlled the series until 1998, when the Ducks came into the game 8–2 and ranked No. 15 in the nation; the Beavers posted a 44–41 win in double overtime. "More than anything I remember us not being able to stop Ken Simonton," quarterback Akili Smith said. "He scorched us that game." Back and forth the rivalry then went, including a 2000 victory for Oregon State with a bid to the Bowl Championship Series on the line. Joey Harrington endured the worst game of his college career, with six turnovers. "Oregon State didn't beat us; we beat ourselves," cornerback Rashad Bauman said.

But the Ducks got revenge the next year, winning 17–14 despite miserable conditions to finally break through for a BCS berth. The key play was a punt return for a touchdown by Keenan Howry, one of the most memorable moments in school history. "The punter had been struggling with the bad weather all day," Howry recalled. "He kicked a low line drive right to me, so when I caught it I had time to look and see where everybody was. I set up a block for Ty Tomlin. I kind of hesitated and hopped to the right so he could get his block, and right when I hopped to the right it was like nobody was there. Everybody had made perfect blocks. All I had to do was run straight, and that's pretty much all I did."

The stakes were again high in 2009, the "War for the Roses," when the Pac-10 title was on the line. Oregon prevailed, winning 37–33 in Eugene. The Ducks won again in 2010 to clinch a spot in the BCS Championship Game, proving that the Civil War can be memorable even when the results are lopsided.

14 Dreams Shattered: Dixon Goes Down

The lasting image of the 2007 regular season should've been quarterback Dennis Dixon laughing as he strolled untouched into the end zone against Michigan in September on a fake Statue of Liberty play, the signature moment in a significant win for the Ducks.

Instead, it will forever be the picture of Dixon on the Oregon sideline, tears streaming down his face after his knee gave out against Arizona in mid-November.

It was in that moment that the Ducks' magical season—its first with Chip Kelly as offensive coordinator—crash-landed in Tucson and a team that seemed destined for the BCS championship, and its senior quarterback a sure thing to be in New York City in early December, went down with it.

"Where were you when it ended?" asked George Schroeder, the *Register-Guard* sports columnist. "When a national title shot, and a Heisman campaign, too, crumpled with Dennis Dixon to the turf?"

For most Ducks fans, it was staring in disbelief at their TV screens as Dixon's knee buckled in the first quarter against the Wildcats on a noncontact play in the backfield as he attempted to avoid a sack.

A torn ACL was the diagnosis. Dixon's Oregon career was done, and the second-ranked Ducks, leaders of the Pac-10, never recovered.

As it turned out, Dixon actually damaged his knee during the previous game, in a 35–23 victory against No. 6 Arizona State on November 3. With 13 minutes left in that game, Dixon, who had thrown four touchdown passes in the game, fell to the turf when he tried to make a cut on a running play.

There was a collective gasp among the then-record-setting crowd of 59,379, then silence, as he was tended to by trainers. He didn't return against the Sun Devils and the injury was eventually called a sprain. With 10 days to get ready for Arizona, it was generally assumed Dixon would be ready to go against the Wildcats.

And he certainly appeared to be when he took off on a 39-yard, straight-ahead touchdown run just 2:36 into the game which gave the Ducks an 8–0 lead.

But seven minutes later, Dixon went down and the shell-shocked Ducks went on to lose 34–24.

Dixon's stats when his season ended were 2,136 yards passing and 583 yards rushing in 10 games. He threw for 20 touchdowns and only four interceptions, and rushed for nine other TDs.

"I feel bad for Dennis, obviously, because this year was one of those magical years, and it looks like it might be at an end," coach

Mike Bellotti said after the Arizona game. "I think overall, though, I'm more concerned about my team. We have two more games that are very, very important to play for the conference championship. We need to rally a little bit and find some ways to move the football a little bit better."

The Ducks would lose 16–0 to UCLA the following week and then end the regular season with a 38–31 loss to Oregon State in overtime.

Oregon's other three quarterbacks—Brady Leaf, Cody Kempt, and Justin Roper—all played in Dixon's absence in the final 2½ games but combined to throw for just 472 yards with two TDs and six interceptions as the Ducks finished the regular season 8–4 and 5–4 in the Pac-12.

But they also qualified for the Sun Bowl and a game against South Florida. With almost a month off to collect itself, Oregon destroyed the Bulls 56–21 in El Paso, with redshirt freshman Roper getting the start and throwing for 180 yards and four TDs.

Almost two months between victories, the Sun Bowl win was a pleasant ending to a season that once offered so much more.

15 Dressed for Success

The mid-1990s were an important time in Oregon football history because the team was in the early stages of becoming nationally relevant following back-to-back appearances in the Rose Bowl and Cotton Bowl.

But with very little history or tradition to speak of, and no true identity, the Ducks were mostly known as the team with the Disney character as a mascot.

Two months after losing to Colorado in the Cotton Bowl on New Year's Day 1996, Nike cofounder and Oregon booster Phil Knight put together a design team that included Tinker Hatfield, Nike's renowned shoe and uniform designer, who was also a former Oregon pole vaulter.

"How can we help the University of Oregon attract better students and better student athletes?" Knight asked the group.

"He didn't say 'rebrand,' he just asked the question," Hatfield told the *SportsBusiness Journal* in 2011.

But the message was clear: Oregon was going to re-create its own identity, and it would happen through aggressive reinvention and marketing.

The Ducks couldn't sell their tradition to prospective recruits like Michigan, Penn State, or Alabama. They needed to be new, hip, cool, unconventional and innovative, and the main target was Oregon's uniforms.

Thus began the effort to move the Ducks' design away from the standard green and yellow with the interlocking UO on the helmet. In 1999, the Ducks underwent their first radical uniform change, most significantly going to a redesigned *O* logo on a solid green helmet.

No more than every three years since then, and with increasing frequency, the Ducks have undergone a major uniform makeover.

There was a clear drive to "turn up the dial on being unexpected and edgy," Hatfield said. "We wanted to be out there, to be purposely controversial. That's a part of what we do that's not very well understood.

"A lot of the sportswriters at first hated it and that's actually what we wanted. If you're purposely trying to stir up the nest and increase visibility, you want them saying something. And what's a more visible way to turn up the heat and create a personality than through the football uniforms? So many millions see them on TV that uniforms become your biggest branding tool."

What the Ducks struggled to build on the field—an identity—they manufactured through design. Through their willingness to wear just about any color combination, they built one of the most unmistakable brands in college sports—one built on innovation and fun, the *SportsBusiness Journal* wrote.

And it's worked, said Hatfield, who used to visit sports camps across the country to talk with young athletes. He would always ask them about Oregon.

"They'd say, 'Is that close to California?'" Hatfield said. "Now you can go from the sticks of Utah to the swamps of Louisiana and people know how to form the *O* with their hands. That's marketing. That's a successful program."

The frequent uniform redesigns have rarely come without heaps of criticism and ridicule from national media and college football fans. When the 2006 version was unveiled, with its nearly 400 potential combinations and diamond plating patterns on the shoulders and knees, the website Deadspin.com panned Oregon's "next step in uniform development" as only being true if "that step involves playing football during an Elton John concert."

In 2007 the Ducks unveiled an all-white look against Washington, and in 2008 against Arizona the Ducks went all-black and debuted wings on the shoulder pads, a pattern that would be the standard look through the 2011 season.

In the 2012 Rose Bowl, Oregon wore its "liquid metal" helmet with wings on the sides for the first time.

Along the way, as the Ducks became a national power because of their performance on the field, they slowly turned from being jokers to innovators in regards to their uniform style. Soon, other college programs started taking an "Oregon approach" by redesigning their own looks.

Oregon's ascent has created an "industry-wide acknowledgment of the importance of brand development," Brad Bishop, cofounder of Dallas-based Torch Creative, told the *SportsBusiness*

"Uncle Phil" Knight, Nike cofounder and one of the University of Oregon's biggest donors, was the architect behind the team's rebranding, underwriting the team's uniform overhaul, among many other efforts.

Journal. "You didn't hear athletic directors five, six years ago talking about their brand like you do now. There's definitely much more of an evolving concern."

Meanwhile, another change at Oregon is no doubt in the works, another debut in store in the coming seasons.

"It's who we are," Oregon athletic director Rob Mullens said.

16 Len Casanova: Architect of a Program

Football coach, athletic director, fund-raiser, and more, Len Casanova is truly one of the bedrocks on which Oregon athletics was built.

Upon retiring as football coach after a 16-year run that included three bowl appearances, Casanova became athletic director for four years, helping oversee the completion of Autzen Stadium. He stayed active in the UO athletics community for decades afterward, and when the Ducks opened an athletic administration building 20 years after Casanova's retirement, it was named in his honor.

"Everything that Oregon athletics is today, it owes to Len Casanova," former Oregon athletic director Bill Moos said after Casanova's death in 2002.

Under Casanova's guidance, the football team enjoyed its first golden era. Before the Ducks lured him away from the University of Pittsburgh in 1951, they had played in three bowl games in the program's history. By the time Casanova was finished, he doubled that number, in an age when bowl games weren't nearly as numerous as they are today. The Ducks were 82–73–8 in 16 seasons, making Casanova the team's winningest coach until Rich Brooks came along. The 1957 team played in the Rose Bowl, and the 1958 team might have featured Oregon's best defense ever, allowing only five points per game.

But it was the men who Casanova nurtured, players and assistant coaches, who became his legacy. He coached the likes of Mel Renfro and Dave Wilcox, and hired assistants such as John McKay, John Robinson, and George Seifert, who went on to illustrious coaching careers of their own. "Len Casanova was just a one-of-a-kind person and human being," said Willie West, a halfback from 1957 to 1959. "He was just a renaissance man, a multifaceted guy—not only a father figure but a counselor. He was much more than a coach."

Casanova was a man who rarely let his emotions boil over. But he wasn't a man to be crossed. "If you got in trouble, whoever else you got in trouble with was the least of your worries because you had to talk to Cas," said Dave Wilcox, an end from 1962 to 1963. "So a lot of people decided that getting in trouble wasn't the way to go."

Rather, Casanova commanded respect through decency and a firm hand. He would ask the most of his stars—"Come on, Shanley, a good back would run through those arm tackles," he would bark to halfback Jim Shanley during film sessions—but never overlooked anyone. "He didn't care if you were a first-string guy or a fourth-string guy," quarterback Bob Berry recalled. "He was building young men."

"The thing about Cas was, he was tough," Mel Renfro said. "He had great coaches and he let them do a lot of the coaching, but he was the guy in charge, and if he needed to tell you something specifically, he would bypass the position coach and come and tell you directly." Casanova's office door was always open, too. "You could always talk to him about your issues and how you were doing, and he kept track of how you were doing academically," Renfro said. "If there were situations or areas where you needed help, he would always recommend somebody who could help you."

West said Casanova would call a player in for a one-on-one meeting "and you'd think, *Oh, what did I do?* and he would just want to talk." The coach forged relationships that endured years later. "I couldn't believe how close in touch he stayed with me over all those years," said Jim Shanley, who played from 1955 to 1957. "Wherever I went, whatever I was doing—coaching, selling insurance—Cas would always call me and keep up with me."

After Casanova left coaching, his opportunities seemed endless. "I believe he could have run for governor," Berry said. But the California native stuck to the new roots he had laid down in Oregon. Casanova was selected to the National Football Foundation's Hall of Fame in 1977, and was honored with the Amos Alonzo Stagg Award for contributions to the sport by the American Football Coaches Association in 1990.

To his players, though, Casanova's legacy wasn't about the schemes he coached or the games he won. They remember a tough father figure who knew when to employ a gentle touch or a firm hand. Years later, they found themselves emulating the great man, who taught hard lessons that made them into men. "I'm not saying it was all fun and games for us," said Norm Chapman, a lineman from 1955 to 1957. "But after we were gone, we appreciated it more."

17 Ducks and Dawgs

For the recently converted among the Oregon fan base, the idea that Washington should be considered one of the Ducks' most hated rivals might seem strange.

After all, in 2012 the Ducks beat the Huskies 52–21, Oregon's ninth straight win over Washington, all of them by at least 17 points. What kind of rivalry is that? And why does everybody make such a big deal about that Kenny Wheaton interception in 1994, anyway?

Consider this: Prior to Oregon's upset of the Huskies in 1994, which was clinched by Wheaton's dramatic interception return for a touchdown, Washington had gone 37–13–1 against Oregon in the years dating back to World War II. Back then, it was Husky fans who didn't put much stock in the idea of a rivalry with the Ducks. "Washington is good today, but back then they were '*Washington*,'" said quarterback Danny O'Neil, who directed the touchdown drive that put the Ducks in the lead prior to Wheaton's interception in the 1994 game. "It was a bigger deal than today."

In the early years of the programs, freshmen weren't eligible to play with the varsity. There were freshman teams, instead, which played only a handful of games against regional opponents. In Oregon's case that meant Oregon State, Washington State and Washington. So the hatred was implanted in player early on. "Even though Oregon State was a big rivalry, the Huskies were the big one for me," said halfback Larry Hill (1961–63).

The Oregon-Washington rivalry really took off in 1948. That year, the Ducks and California finished tied atop the conference standings. A vote of conference teams was held to pick their representative to the Rose Bowl—in which Cal had played just 10 years earlier and Oregon hadn't been since 1920. The Bears were picked. How could that be, since the Pacific Coast Conference then had six Northwest teams among its 10 members? Legend holds that not only did Washington officials pick Cal, they also convinced Montana to vote the same way. And with that, a rivalry was stoked.

Bob Berry, who quarterbacked the Ducks from 1962 to 1964, recalled playing in Seattle in 1961 with the freshman team, which was coached by future NFL head coach John Robinson. "We were up I think 21–0 on them at halftime, and he came in and was ranting and raving like we were losing the game, because he just hated them so bad," Berry said. "He had us line up and do live tackling practice at halftime of the game.... I think we ended up winning 51–0. But Robbie was so fired up, he had tackling practice at halftime. It was crazy, but that's how intense he was about beating the Huskies."

In 1951, Len Casanova's first year with the Ducks, before freshmen had been declared ineligible, he was forced to play 13 of them against the Huskies. Washington put a 63–6 whooping on the Ducks. The 1974 game was worse—a 66–0 Washington win.

Oregon had actually pounded the Pups in 1973, 58–0. But more common in those days were narrow Ducks victories over the Huskies, such as the 3–0 win in Seattle in 1968, when Ken Woody was carried off the field after his field goal provided the game's only points. "The week that we played the Huskies, I could never sleep," Woody said. "I would just tremble in bed. I hated them so much."

The most crushing UO defeat in the series, the one future Oregon assistant Steve Greatwood said "I will take to my grave," came in 1979. Mark Lee returned a punt 59 yards to give the Huskies a 21–17 win just when the Ducks had seem poised to win for the first time in five years. "We had controlled the game from the outset, but they found a way to win, and we found a way to lose," Greatwood said. "That one still hurts."

Defensive lineman Vince Goldsmith at least managed to find a small silver lining in the defeat. "We had Washington beat for three quarters and 14 minutes, and lost," said Goldsmith, who grew up in Washington. "That hurt.... My father and I actually grew closer because of that game. Afterward he came in the locker room, and we looked at each other and both started crying. I guess that's the power of sports—man, it hurt, and it helped to share it with someone who you knew understood."

Everything changed, however, with O'Neil's touchdown drive and Wheaton's interception in 1994. Washington has won just four times in the series since then, while Oregon has celebrated Pat Johnson's game-winning touchdown catch in Seattle in 1997, the wizardry of Dennis Dixon and Jonathan Stewart running the option in 2007, and the dominating recent wins of 53–16 in 2010 and 52–21 in 2012, both at Autzen Stadium.

Yes, the Oregon-Washington rivalry has a rich history—even if it might be hard to tell in the last few years.

18 Mel Renfro

For all that Oregon has accomplished in recent years, one might have to go back five decades to find the greatest player ever to suit up for the Ducks.

Mel Renfro was a two-way star who left Oregon in 1963 as an All-American and the school's all-time leading rusher. He went on to a 14-year pro career with the Dallas Cowboys that included four Super Bowls and 10 Pro Bowls, and was eventually inducted in both the college and NFL halls of fame.

With the Ducks, Renfro was a member of the famed "Firehouse Four" along with quarterback Bob Berry, halfback Larry Hill, and fullback Lu Bain. Hill had played against Renfro in high school, and was only too glad to team up with him again in college. "No doubt about it, Renfro was the best football player I've ever been around," Hill said. "He was fantastic." Berry got to Oregon in 1962, and Renfro's presence was part of assistant coach John Robinson's recruiting pitch. Berry had been a little skeptical of the hype—until he got to Eugene. "I was just flabbergasted," he said. "Mel was a world-class athlete."

Mel Renfro, seen here in a Dallas Cowboys uniform in 1974, followed up an All-American collegiate career at Oregon with 14 seasons in the NFL and a Pro Football Hall of Fame induction.

Indeed, Renfro burned up Hayward Field—the home of Oregon football in those years—on the track as well. He helped Oregon's 4x440 quartet set a world record in 1961, and finished second in the NCAA 120-yard high hurdles the next year. But it was in football that he truly made his athletic mark.

Renfro's Oregon football debut came in 1961, and it was a memorable one. "I thought it would be a big jump," he said. "But on my second play of the first game, against Idaho, I ran 80 yards for a touchdown." He ended up leading the Ducks in rushing and earning All-Coast honors (Oregon didn't have a conference affiliation at the time) as he would do for all three years of his career.

His best season offensively was in 1962, as a junior. Renfro ran 126 times for 783 yards—at the time a school record—and 10 touchdowns, while also throwing five passes for 114 yards and two touchdowns and catching 16 passes for 298 yards. His crowning moment that season was a win at Rice, which made an exception to its segregation policy and allowed several of Renfro's family members, including his grandfather, into the game. After Oregon won 31–12, one local headline read: RENFRO RUNS RICE RAGGED. "That was probably the highlight of my whole college football career," Renfro recalled.

The 1963 Ducks won eight games, and Renfro again was the team's leading rusher. That season, all-time Oregon great Dave Wilcox was moved from end to guard on offense. If he was not entirely comfortable on the interior of the line, he picked up at least one element of the offense quickly. "The one thing I made sure to do was stay out of Mel Renfro's way," Wilcox said. "He didn't need me in his way."

The biggest disappointment of Renfro's career was his lack of a Civil War win. The Ducks lost in 1961 and 1962, with Renfro's former high school teammate from Portland, Terry Baker, leading

Oregon State to victories. Oregon won to cap Renfro's senior year in 1963, but he was unable to play after cutting his hand in an accident, having punched a mirror in frustration after learning of John F. Kennedy's assassination.

His college career over, Renfro left Oregon as the leading rusher in school history, with 1,540 career yards. "I probably would have set a lot more records and done a lot more offensively as far as yardage and touchdowns had I stuck with offense," Renfro said. "I was on the field all the time—offense, defense, special teams—and I played hard every play." Little did Renfro know at the time, all that effort would pay surprising dividends in the NFL. The Cowboys drafted him in the second round in 1964 with the intention of using him on offense. But a series of injuries prompted a shift to defense, and Renfro went on to become one of the league's all-time greatest defensive backs, as well as the Cowboys' career leader in average kickoff return yards.

As amazing as Renfro's career was, it almost went a vastly different direction. He grew up in Portland and played high school football with Baker, who went on to win the Heisman Trophy at Oregon State. Renfro was intent on joining his former teammate in college, with the Beavers, until his father stepped in and convinced him otherwise. Oregon football coach Len Casanova and track coach Bill Bowerman had developed a good relationship with Renfro's father, and thus Mel became a Duck. "I was the type of guy who was going to do what my parents told me to do," Renfro said. "I just obeyed their wishes. And the rest is history."

19 A Return to the Rose Bowl

It had been 37 years since the Ducks enjoyed the sweet smell of roses, but there they were, on January 2, 1995, in Pasadena, as one of the most unexpected participants in the history of the Rose Bowl.

Oregon started the season 1–2, was booed off its own field by a half-full stadium after a loss to Utah in September, then miraculously recovered to end the season with six straight wins and claim its first outright conference championship in school history.

"What a long, strange trip it's been, what a magical mystery tour, from there to here, from then to today," columnist Ron Bellamy wrote in the *Register-Guard* the day of the game. "What an utterly special experience. Cherish it. And never forget the defiant improbability of it all."

Having already shocked those who follow the conference, could the Ducks also shock the world? Oddsmakers didn't think so; they gave No. 2 Penn State a 17-point edge.

The Nittany Lions did those odds one better, winning 38–20. However, the game was more competitive than the final score would indicate, leaving the Ducks to lament how it let what they deemed a "winnable" game get away from them so quickly in the second half.

"We're very disappointed," coach Rich Brooks said. "We didn't come down here to pick grapes. We played hard, we took our best shot, but we weren't able to take advantage of the opportunities we had, and consequently we fell short."

As beat reporter John Conrad wrote in the *Register-Guard*, it simply came down to Oregon making plenty of little plays, but not enough big plays, despite a record-setting afternoon by quarterback

Danny O'Neil, the game's co-MVP, who completed 41-of-61 passes for a Rose Bowl-record 456 yards.

Freshman kicker Matt Belden, so steady throughout the season, also missed all three of his field-goal attempts, and the offense failed to score on a drive at the end of the first half when time ran out and the Ducks at the 5-yard line.

Defensively, Oregon couldn't stop Penn State All-American Ki-Jana Carter, who rushed for 156 yards and three touchdowns, including one on an 83-yarder on the Nittany Lions' first offensive play of the game.

In the end, the teams combined to tie the Rose Bowl record for total offense with 931 yards (501 Oregon, 430 Penn State) and total offensive plays with 162.

"We were moving the ball. That wasn't the problem," Brooks said. "The problem was not scoring when we got into scoring territory."

Oregon followed Carter's long TD run with a four-play, 80-yard drive that ended with a 1-yard pass from O'Neil to tight end Josh Wilcox to tie the score, 7–7.

The Ducks had their first chance to go on top later in the first quarter on a drive that stalled at the Penn State 6-yard line. Belden's subsequent 23-yard field-goal attempt was no good.

The Ducks again had a chance to take the lead midway through the second quarter when defensive lineman Troy Bailey recovered a fumble by Carter at the Penn State 33. But after three plays, Oregon was stuck at the 27 and Belden came in for a 44-yard attempt with just under four minutes to play in the half. This time he was wide right.

The Nittany Lions followed with a 73-yard drive that resulted in a touchdown for a 14–7 advantage.

With 1:26 left in the half, Oregon nearly drove 82 yards to tie the game. With 11 seconds left and no timeouts, O'Neil completed a pass to Cristin McLemore, but the receiver was stopped at the 5-yard line as time expired. Penn State led 14–7 at the break.

The Ducks didn't waste their next chance to even the score. After linebacker Reggie Jordan picked off Penn State quarterback Kerry Collins and returned the interception 38 yards to the 17, Oregon needed just two plays for O'Neil and McLemore to hook up on a score. Suddenly it was 14–14 with 4:54 left in the third quarter.

The Oregon sideline was energized; the Ducks fans among the 102,247 in the stands were rocking. It looked like all the momentum was with Oregon.

Then, just like that, it changed.

Penn State scored on its next two possessions to take a 28–14 lead into the fourth quarter. Then they scored the next 10 points to go up 38–14 with only a few minutes left in the game.

The Nittany Lions' powerful offense finally got on track and the Ducks couldn't slow it or keep up. Oregon scored one last time, with 2:44 to play—not that it mattered with the game all but decided.

Still, the loss did little to dampen what had otherwise been a magical ride to an unlikely destination.

20 Hail to the Victors

Tradition met innovation when Oregon and Michigan played a home-and-home series in 2003 and 2007, and both times the new-wave Ducks came out on top.

Both wins were the highlight of their respective seasons, for obvious reasons.

The game in 2003 proved the Ducks, just two years removed from an 11–1 season and Fiesta Bowl victory, could still be players on the national stage, even against the winningest program in college football history.

Oregon manhandled Michigan before the Wolverines staged a late comeback attempt. The Ducks held on for a 31–27 victory, and Autzen Stadium was never louder or more intimidating.

The game in 2007 proved to be a changing of the guard when the Ducks, with their spread offense and fancy uniforms, took tradition behind the woodshed in a nationally televised romp at the Big House.

The 39–7 victory in Ann Arbor was Chip Kelly's second game as Oregon's offensive coordinator and proved to be a harbinger of things to come, as the Ducks went 65–14 in the six years when Kelly was either an assistant or head coach.

Oregon went into Michigan Stadium as underdogs for sure, but buoyed by the fact the Wolverines had lost a shocker the weekend before to Appalachian State, another spread-offense team with speed. The loss dropped the Wolverines from No. 5 all the way out of the Associated Press Top 25.

Still, no one could have predicted what happened in the first three quarters.

Oregon flashed the exciting brand of offense it would become known for under Kelly, full of speed and demoralizing quick-strike potency.

Quarterback Dennis Dixon had touchdown passes of 85, 61, and 46 yards, and he also scored on a fake Statue of Liberty run that left the CBS announcers laughing in the booth and the crowd of 109,733—the largest ever to witness an Oregon game—stunned in their seats.

The loss was the most lopsided in 39 years for Michigan, who actually held an early lead before Oregon exploded for 36 unanswered points. The Ducks' 624 yards of total offense was the second most by a Michigan opponent in its previous 128 years of football.

"We didn't take advantage of everything, in all honesty," UO coach Mike Bellotti said. "I think we could have got on them worse."

The Ducks led 32–7 at halftime, and Michigan Stadium's aisles began to fill with fans who had seen enough after Dixon connected with Jaison Williams for a long TD to make it 39–7 in the fourth quarter. The Big House was so quiet that a small pocket of Oregon supporters could be heard chanting: "Let's Go Ducks! Let's Go Ducks!"

It was a similar situation on September 20, 2003, when No. 3 Michigan came to Eugene for what remains the most high-profile nonconference opponent to ever play at Autzen Stadium with maybe the exception of Notre Dame's visit in 1982. But that Irish team brought more "tradition than trepidation" wrote the *Register-Guard*, and the end result was Notre Dame needing a late score to force a 13–13 tie against a winless Oregon team.

But Michigan in 2003 was different. The Wolverines were built to win a national championship. They had the country's top rusher in Chris Perry and a defense that had allowed just one touchdown in three games and no points in the first half all season.

That quickly changed against the Ducks.

After falling behind 6–0, Oregon scored three touchdowns in the second quarter on a 19-yard run by running back Terrence Whitehead, a 15-yard run by quarterback Jason Fife, and a 61-yard punt return by Steven Moore to lead 21–6 at halftime.

The Ducks went up 24–6 early in the third quarter, and then 31–21 midway through the fourth on a blocked punt recovered by Jordan Carey in the end zone.

Quarterback John Navarre tried his best to rally the Wolverines, throwing for three TD passes in the second half and 273 yards in the fourth quarter alone, but it wasn't enough. Perry—who would go on to be the Big Ten MVP and finish fourth in Heisman Trophy voting—finished with just 26 yards on 11 carries and Michigan rushed for –3 yards total in the game.

When it was over, the crowd of 59,023—then the largest ever at Autzen Stadium —stormed the field for an all-out celebration, with university president Dave Frohnmayer right in the middle of it.

"Awesome!" Frohnmayer exalted. "Greatest game I ever saw here!"

The following week, the Ducks made the cover of *Sports Illustrated* with the headline: DAZZLING DUCKS—RICH, COOL AND 4–0 (QUACK, QUACK).

"These kids believed," Bellotti said. "Michigan is a great program, very storied in its history, but I told my players, 'history is what you make it.'"

And they made it, all right. Twice.

21 Oregon Football's First Family

The Winns and Harringtons left quite a legacy, but the first family of Oregon football is probably the one located just a few miles to the northwest of Eugene, on the Wilcox family farm in Junction City.

When future NFL Hall of Famer Dave Wilcox joined the Ducks in 1962 out of Boise Junior College—now Boise State—he was following in the footsteps of his brother, John. Years later, Dave's sons, Josh and Justin, would enjoy standout careers of their own with the Oregon football team.

While he was being recruited out of Junction City High School, Josh Wilcox was also pursued by Oregon State. But given the family history, there was little question where he'd end up. As a kid, he worked as a ball boy at Autzen Stadium. Apparently Wilcox men were just born to be Ducks. "That never wore off on me," Josh Wilcox said. "Getting to play for the Ducks was the most important thing in the world for me."

The family was originally from Oklahoma, and moved to Vale in eastern Oregon. It was there that John and Dave grew up; the only time they left the city limits was for high school football games. And on a team that lost just twice during Dave's career, that meant a lot of traveling.

John first enrolled at Oregon in 1956, but decided he needed a more gradual adjustment to college and so went to Boise Junior College. He rejoined the Ducks for the 1958 and 1959 seasons. Dave took note of his brother's path and went straight to Boise after getting his high school diploma, eventually arriving in Eugene in 1962. The adjustment wasn't easy. "We were farm guys coming to the city," Dave Wilcox said.

Dave Wilcox was a backup tight end in his first season, when everybody played both ways. His toughness quickly stood out to his new teammates. "Dave was just a big old country boy, and you just didn't mess with him," star halfback Mel Renfro said. "He was like a bull rider, big and tough."

As a senior, Dave Wilcox moved to guard on offense, clearing the way for Renfro on an Oregon team that went 8–3 with wins over West Virginia, Indiana, Oregon State, and, in the Sun Bowl, Southern Methodist. Playing on the interior of the line was foreign at first. "I had no idea what to do, but they told me they would work with me," he said. "So I ended up moving. On defense I got to rush the quarterback, so that was better." Indeed, Wilcox was a third-team All-Coast pick in 1963, when the Ducks lacked a conference affiliation, and went on to play 11 seasons in the NFL, making seven Pro Bowls and ultimately being elected to the Pro Football Hall of Fame for his exploits on defense.

Thirty years later, the Oregon football team was graced with the presence of another Wilcox, Dave's son Josh. A tight end by trade, Josh Wilcox finished his career with 103 receptions, the most ever by a tight end when he graduated in 1996. No catch was bigger than his touchdown in a 10–9 win over Arizona in 1994, a monumental victory in the Ducks' drive to the Rose Bowl. "That was a play that we had game-planned all week, and Mike Bellotti, the offensive coordinator then, made the right call," Josh Wilcox said. "Danny O'Neil threw it perfectly, and I guess that's when practice paid off."

Throughout his career, Josh Wilcox stood out for this willingness to try anything, on and off the field. As a senior, he joined the kickoff team, looking to spark a struggling Ducks team through his unselfish actions. "I wasn't worried about my stats or anything like that," he said. "I just wanted to win. I was there to win." Wilcox's unique spirit shined off the field too; he later pursued interests in professional wrestling and sports talk radio—no surprise to those who recall his charisma while at Oregon. "I had fun with it," Josh Wilcox said. "I wore it on my sleeve. Sometimes good, sometimes bad, but why fake people out with who I am? I'm a Duck, and that's important to me."

Josh Wilcox left in 1996 and played two years in the NFL, but by then his brother, Justin, was on campus. A much more buttoned-down personality than his brother, Justin Wilcox proved to be just as unselfish on the field. The star high school quarterback moved to defense in college, and played cornerback even though his skills were probably better suited to safety.

He got by with his acumen and preparation, and thus it was no surprise Justin Wilcox went on to a distinguished coaching career, with stops in Boise State, California, Tennessee, and Washington. For the first family of Ducks football, that last stop took some getting used to.

22 The Dutchman

Trace the quarterback lineage back through Oregon's history, past names like Mariota and Dixon, Harrington and Musgrave, Miller and Fouts, all the way back to the 1940s, and you'll find one of the original stars of professional football: "the Dutchman," Norm Van Brocklin.

A 12-year veteran player of the NFL, Van Brocklin led the Los Angeles Rams and the Philadelphia Eagles to championships, and he was named the league's MVP. He set a single-game record of 554 passing yards in 1951, a record that still stood six decades later. But before all of that, Van Brocklin was a Duck.

A South Dakota native, Van Brocklin took a circuitous route to Oregon. His family moved to the San Francisco Bay Area, and he graduated from Acalanes High School in Lafayette, California. In 1943, Van Brocklin entered the United States Navy, serving in World War II until 1945.

It was only afterward that Van Brocklin began his Oregon career. And what a career it was. He took over as the starter in 1947 and led the Ducks to a 7–3 record. As a sophomore that year, Van Brocklin completed 76-of-168 passes for 939 yards and nine touchdowns, with 11 interceptions. The Ducks lost three straight after winning their opener, but finished the year on a six-game winning streak which included the Civil War.

That set the stage for the next year, one of the finest seasons in school history. The Ducks lost just once in the regular season, at Michigan, and posted wins over northwest rivals Washington, Washington State, and Oregon State. Van Brocklin completed 68-of-139 passes for 1,010 yards, a school record at the time and most in the Pacific Coast Conference. He threw seven touchdowns and seven interceptions for a passer rating of 116.5. In both seasons, Van Brocklin also led the conference in punting.

By leading the Ducks to a 9–1 regular-season record and a clean sweep of their seven Pacific Coast Conference games in 1948, Van Brocklin helped Oregon win a share of the conference title. The Ducks were tied with California, and since the two didn't play, the PCC's Rose Bowl representative was selected by a vote of member schools; a majority of the others, including hated Washington, voted for Cal, and the Ducks headed off to the Cotton Bowl instead (and loathed the Huskies even more than they did before).

There, Van Brocklin and the Ducks went head-to-head with famed SMU running back Doak Walker, the Heisman Trophy winner that season (Van Brocklin finished sixth). The quarterback got the better of the individual matchup, throwing for 145 yards and a touchdown while Walker was held to 79 rushing yards. But Oregon lost 21–13, in just its third bowl appearance ever and first since the 1920 Rose Bowl.

Van Brocklin was named an All-American for his efforts that year, his last at Oregon. Because he had served in the navy, and thus had been out of high school more than four years, Van Brocklin was eligible for the NFL despite not playing as a college senior. He was a fourth-round draft pick of the Rams, and was inducted into the Pro Football Hall of Fame for his achievements as a player and, later, a coach.

23 Building an Empire

The legendary tale goes something like this: Following the Ducks' loss to Colorado in the 1996 Cotton Bowl, Oregon's second-straight major bowl loss following the 1995 Rose Bowl defeat by Penn State, uber-donor Phil Knight met with UO brass to discuss strategy.

"He asked me, 'What do we need to do to get to the next level?'" said Mike Bellotti, then Oregon's coach. "I said an indoor practice facility. He said, 'How soon can we get it done?' I said, 'Well, we've got to do some fund-raising and we've got to do some—' He said, 'No, no, no. How soon can we get it done?'"

Two years later, the Moshofsky Center opened, and what followed was more than a decade of unprecedented expansion at Oregon that put the athletic department front and center in the NCAA football "arms race" and helped turn the Ducks into a national power.

Also included in the building boom was the addition of new outdoor practice fields, the expansion of Autzen Stadium, a state-of-the-art locker room, the Athletic Medicine Center, and finally, the construction of a football-only building opened in the 2013 season.

But it all started with the "Mo" Center, a 117,000-square foot indoor facility that houses a full-size artificial-turf field. It cost $15 million to build and was at the time the first indoor facility on the West Coast.

At the same time, Oregon built natural grass outdoor practice fields in front of the Casanova Center. The team no longer had to cross four lanes of traffic on busy Martin Luther King Boulevard to get to their practice field.

During the off-season in 2002, Autzen Stadium underwent a $90 million expansion that, among other enhancements, increased its seating capacity by 12,000 and added 32 luxury boxes.

In 2003, Oregon built a two-story football locker room inside the Cas Center that cost $3.2 million. It included ventilated lockers that reportedly cost an estimated $26,000 apiece and a lighting system that adjusts to the light outside so eyes don't have to adjust.

In 2007, the Athletic Medicine Center was built for $10 million in donations. It's another state-of-the-art facility.

In 2010, Oregon opened the opulent Jaqua Center, a three-story, 37,000-square-foot student-athlete academic center that sits on the edge of campus. The $41.7 million building was a direct gift from Knight. As is Oregon's latest project: A six-story, 130,000-square-foot expansion of the Casanova Center.

The new building will essentially be a "centralized football operations center that will include nine dedicated football position meeting rooms, two team video theaters, offense and defense strategy rooms as well as a larger conference suite for the entire coaching staff. The centralized area will be flanked by office and locker facilities for coaches, staff and student-athletes. Additional amenities will include a players' lounge, a recruiting center to host prospective student-athletes, dedicated areas to accommodate professional scouts, a media interview room as well as an advanced video editing and distribution center," according to Oregon's own website, GoDucks.com.

The expansion will also include a 25,000-square-foot weight room, one natural grass practice field, two artificial turf fields, and a full-service dining facility.

In addition, the ground floor of the new facility will feature a lobby and reception area that will celebrate the history of the football program.

"This project epitomizes a long line of world-class facilities that has enhanced the university, and will add to the support we offer all our student-athletes," athletic director Rob Mullens said.

Seventeen years later, it's fair to say Knight got it done, indeed.

24 Rich Brooks

When Rich Brooks took over the Oregon football program in 1977, the Ducks had enjoyed just one winning season in their previous dozen. By the time he left, 18 years later, the athletic department felt it appropriate to name the field in Autzen Stadium in his honor.

If Mike Bellotti was the man who made Oregon nationally relevant and Chip Kelly was the one who made the Ducks a perennial title contender, Rick Brooks dug the program out from a decade of a mediocrity to set the stage for his successors' success. Granted a level of loyalty from the athletic department that is rare these days, Brooks took a downtrodden program and made it a regular bowl participant before he moved on to the NFL.

Brooks was hired to replace Don Read, who had won only nine games in three seasons. At the time there was a nationally syndicated sports column ranking the 10 worst teams in the country. "A big achievement for us back then was to not get yourselves mentioned in that," said offensive lineman Steve Greatwood, a player when Brooks was hired and later a long-tenured assistant with the Ducks.

Brooks' primary motivational tactic? "Fear," Greatwood said. "It ended up being the greatest experience of my life to have him and his staff coach me. But a tough tone was definitely set right from the start." Indeed, Brooks installed an off-season conditioning program in early 1977 that pushed his players to their limits. "I don't think I've worked that hard in my life," said defensive lineman Neil Elshire (1978–79). "He wanted to find out who was willing to make the sacrifices to make a winning program."

That hard work continued in fall camp. NCAA regulations have now limited such policies, but Brooks would hold two-a-day practices daily for two weeks straight—except for skill position players, who sometimes had to endure a third workout. "The afternoons weren't too bad, because you were awake by that point," defensive lineman Vince Goldsmith (1977–80) said. "But the morning, they're beating on the door with hammers to shock you out of bed, and then it was right to work."

The Ducks' improvements under Brooks came in stages. During his first seven years, Oregon had two winning seasons and an overall record of 24–49–4. "You start to question yourself after losses, but Rich was good at being stern and telling us to stay the course," said defensive lineman (1981–82) and future Oregon assistant Michael Gray.

At the time, simply being a .500 team was a reasonable goal, and Brooks stabilized the Ducks around that level from 1984 to 1988. Relying on local talent like quarterback Chris Miller and defensive back Anthony Newman, Brooks led the Ducks to a 28–28 mark over those five seasons, never winning—or losing—more than six games. The success didn't change his tough demeanor with players, particularly underclassmen. "I love playing for Rich Brooks," said Newman (1984–87), "but I was scared to death of that man."

Despite the middling overall success early in his Oregon tenure, Brooks was dominant in at least one regard: the Civil War. He was 14–3–1 against the Beavers while coaching the Ducks, a mark that includes victories in all four of the two-win seasons Brooks coached. A former Oregon State defensive back, he had been spurned for a coaching job with his alma mater—and he never missed a chance to get revenge. "I don't know if it's ever burned hotter in anybody," Greatwood said. "It was something. He basically willed teams to win."

After a decade of gradual improvement, the Ducks experienced their first major breakthrough under Brooks in 1989. With Bill Musgrave quarterbacking his offense, Brooks led the Ducks to eight wins and a bowl appearance—the first in 26 years. In 1990, Oregon won another eight games and played in the postseason, making back-to-back bowl appearances for the first time in school history. In his final six seasons, Brooks led Oregon to a 39–32 record, with four bowl appearances.

His final season in Eugene was 1994, and early on few predicted it would be one for the local history books. The Ducks, with senior Danny O'Neil at quarterback and a talented defense, beat Portland State but lost to Hawaii and Utah. Some fans were calling for Brooks' job, yet again. "That next week was a tough week of practice," said tight end Josh Wilcox (1993–96). "Rich Brooks realized he had a young team, and if he put us through Hell Week there were enough guys who would step up."

The coach was right. The Ducks rebounded to beat Iowa, then won at USC. After a loss to Washington State, Oregon won six straight—including, of course, against the Beavers. Brooks had led Oregon from conference doormat status all the way to the Pac-10 title and a Rose Bowl appearance.

He did it, too, while serving the dual role of football coach and athletic director from 1992 to 1994. Small wonder, then, that the surface in Autzen Stadium was christened Rich Brooks Field in 1995, when Brooks finally departed Eugene to take over the St. Louis Rams of the NFL.

Through the years, he rarely shed his tough exterior with players. "Since then I've golfed with him and hung out with him, and he's super fun and nice, a great guy to hang out with," said linebacker Rich Ruhl (1992–95). "But he had this thing about him where he was stone cold with his players. I think he wanted that intimidation factor." If Brooks was a stoic figure atop the Oregon football program for nearly two decades, then the Ducks' results under his leadership spoke loudly.

25 Autzen Stadium

Autzen Stadium has built its reputation nationally as providing one of the greatest home-field advantages in college football.

It's loud, it's intimidating, it's always full, and seldom does Oregon lose at home.

Then again, those are not unusual home-stadium features for elite football programs. What *does* make Autzen so unique is its size—just 54,000 in capacity—and its construction. Built into an earth-filled bowl with only a concourse on the upper rim, and little space between the stands and the playing field, there isn't anywhere for the noise to escape.

"That's the loudest stadium per person that I've ever been in," ESPN *College GameDay* analyst Lee Corso famously said during a 2007 broadcast from Eugene.

Through the 2012 season, the Ducks had an 89-game sellout streak in progress, including numerous games for which attendance far exceeded capacity.

CBSSports.com college football columnist Bruce Feldman, when he worked at ESPN, listed Autzen No. 1 on his most "intimidating stadiums for one game and one game only."

Matt Hayes of the *Sporting News* also called Autzen the most intimidating stadium in college football in a 2006 column.

Due in part to its unique dug-in architecture, Autzen Stadium, seen here in 1998, has a reputation as one of the loudest venues in college football.

"Trust me on Autzen," Hayes wrote. "Just go to the place and soak it all in. Before they throw dirt on you, take a trip to Eugene one fall Saturday…Autzen Stadium is a zoo; there's no other way to say it. Get inside your own 20 in a tight game and you can forget about A.) hearing B.) avoiding false starts and ·C.) success."

Then there was this gem from J. Brady McCullough of the *Michigan Daily* after the Wolverines lost to the Ducks in 2003.

"Sitting in the foothills of the Cascade Mountains, Oregon's Autzen Stadium is one of college football's hidden jewels. Before kickoff, Autzen is as peaceful as the Willamette River, which runs through Eugene just a few minutes from the stadium. After kickoff,

The First Touchdown

The first touchdown scored at Autzen Stadium was by Ducks receiver Denny Schuler on a 26-yard sliding catch in the end zone made just before he went out of bounds.

The Ducks lost 17–13 to Colorado that day, but Schuler had his moment.

"I like to say I caught 15 passes that day, and 14 were in pregame warm-ups," Schuler said years later. (He actually finished with four catches for 59 yards.) "I was lucky, very fortunate."

Schuler went on to a long career as an assistant coach, including a six-year stint as defensive coordinator at Oregon (1986–92).

He learned years later that the Colorado defender he beat on the touchdown play was Hale Irwin, a two-time all-Big Eight defensive back who became more famous for his 87 wins as a professional golfer.

the fans—even the alumni—forget who they are, where they come from, and what their degree is in. The audience adopts a new collective identity for the next three-and-a-half hours: the 12th, 13th, and 14th man. Autzen's 59,000 strong make the Big House collectively sound like a pathetic whimper. It's louder than any place I've ever been, and that includes "the Swamp" at Florida, "the Shoe" in Columbus, and "Death Valley" at Louisiana State. Autzen Stadium is where great teams go to die."

Autzen was completed in 1967 for $2.5 million and named after Portland lumberman, sportsman, and philanthropist Thomas J. Autzen.

The stadium is situated on a 90-acre site adjacent to Eugene's Alton Baker Park, north of the Willamette River and is approximately one-quarter mile north of the main campus.

Views from the concourse include the Coburg Hills to the north and, on a clear day, the snow-capped Three Sisters mountains can be seen to the east. It's as picturesque a stadium setting as there is in college football.

In the first game played at Autzen Stadium, nationally ranked Colorado defeated Oregon 17–13, on September 23, 1967. The Ducks recorded their first win in the stadium almost a month later, when they beat Idaho 31–6 on October 21.

The stadium underwent a massive renovation prior to the 2002 season that added 12,000 seats and 32 luxury boxes to the stadium's south-side skyline. The $90 million facelift was completed during the off-season.

Other changes have taken place through the years as well. In 1969, after just two years playing on natural grass, Oregon installed its first artificial turf. That surface was replaced in 1976 and a new covering of OmniTurf was installed before the 1984 campaign. In 2001, the Ducks played on NexTurf before quickly upgrading its surface again in 2002 to FieldTurf, which remains today.

In 2010, under the direction of then-head-coach Chip Kelly, Oregon flattened the field's infamous crown. The decision was somewhat controversial at the time since many considered the crown to be part of Autzen's advantage. As it turned out, not so much. In the three following seasons, Oregon went 19–2 at home.

2001: The First Fiesta Bowl

It was, without a doubt, a statement.

Snubbed by the BCS after finishing No. 2 in the national polls at the end of the 2001 regular season, the Ducks capped their greatest season to date with their most significant bowl victory: a 38–16 thumping of Colorado in the Fiesta Bowl.

The message was clear. The Ducks thought they should've been playing Miami for the national championship in the Rose Bowl instead of Nebraska, and they let their play against the Buffaloes remind everyone why.

Heisman Trophy finalist Joey Harrington threw for 350 yards and four touchdowns, and the defense shut down one of the nation's best running games and dominated a Colorado offense that had defeated the Cornhuskers 62–36 in November.

"Make your move," coach Mike Bellotti told his team the night before the game. "I've told this group, all you can do is all you can do…what they did tonight to Colorado was a significant victory and a significant statement about Oregon football."

That statement, wrote *Register-Guard* columnist Ron Bellamy, "was loud and eloquent, and it spoke volumes about an Oregon team with talent and heart of a champion, and a program that has come to regard a national championship not as a dream, but as a goal."

Oregon fell behind 7–0 when Colorado scored first on a one-yard touchdown run by Brandon Drumm midway through the first quarter.

But Harrington brought the Ducks right back, hitting wide receiver Keenan Howry with a 28-yard touchdown pass on third-and-13 to tie the game.

Harrington later connected with receiver Samie Parker on a 79-yard scoring play and then tossed a shovel pass to running back Onterrio Smith for a six-yard score that gave Oregon a 21–7 lead at halftime.

Running back Maurice Morris provided the backbreaker on the first series of the third quarter when he broke for a 49-yard touchdown run. Morris appeared to be tackled at the Colorado 21, but instead he landed on top of Buffaloes linebacker Joey Johnson, got up, and raced into the end zone to give Oregon a 28–7 lead.

A 47-yard field goal in the third quarter by Jared Siegel made it 31–7, and then Harrington connected with tight end Justin Peelle on a short scoring pass to go up 38–7 with 9:38 to play.

During that span of 38 straight points, the Oregon defense was relentless. It held Colorado to 49 yards rushing, and cornerback Steve Smith had three interceptions that led to 17 points.

"No question, our defense was the story of the night," Bellotti said. "Everybody felt Colorado would run all over us, but our kids would not allow that to happen. I'm pleasantly surprised because I thought it would be closer, but our kids made it one-sided."

Colorado's usually powerful ground game, which had gained 380 yards in the Nebraska victory, failed to convert on third-and-1 situations on consecutive possessions in the second quarter.

"We came out with an extreme amount of emotion," linebacker Dave Moretti said. "We wanted to make a statement. We didn't feel we've gotten any respect as a defense, and all we heard was how Colorado was going to run all over us. We stuffed them, twice on third-and-1, and we knew if they couldn't convert those, they weren't going to do anything."

Miami would go on to rip Nebraska in the Rose Bowl and the Ducks would finish No. 2 in the Associated Press poll—but they wanted more.

"It's the biggest win on the biggest stage, and we did it in an emphatic manner," Harrington said. "We scored 38 unanswered points on Colorado and shot down the hottest team in the country. We showed that we deserve to be playing for a share of the national championship."

27 Disney's Duck

It began with a random meeting in 1947 and ended amicably and officially in 2010.

But for those 63 years in between, Oregon's mascot was tied to the Walt Disney Co. and its famous cartoon character Donald Duck. The association dated back to a handshake deal between then-UO athletic director Leo Harris and Walt Disney himself.

"That same year, the Duck made its first appearance at Hayward Field," wrote the *Oregon Quarterly* magazine in 2012. "Time may have robbed its feathers of their original sheen, but even so this ugly duckling had a frumpy, non-Donald look, with spindly legs, straggly yellow yarn hair, a pale beak, and limp faux feathers. In contrast, the image appearing on pennants and T-shirts was far more sprightly—a ticked-off Donald emerging from a stylized *O*, waving his arms in a show of Duck pique."

Though no contract was signed, there is a photo dating to 1947 that shows Harris with Disney, who is wearing an Oregon jacket bearing the Donald Duck logo, crouching alongside a live duck.

That photo, in fact, was used as proof of Oregon's informal agreement after Disney's death in 1966 when the Walt Disney Co. couldn't locate a formal contract granting Oregon permission to use Donald Duck's image.

With threats of legal action looming, UO archivist Keith Richard produced the old photo.

"Disney accepted it," Richard said in the *Oregon Quarterly* story, and in 1973 the two parties signed a written contract.

"On the surface, the relationship between Duck and Disney seemed smooth," wrote *Oregon Quarterly*. "In 1984, for Donald's 50th anniversary, Disney flew its own Donald—the one with the smaller head and trademark blue sailor suit—to the Eugene Airport, where he was met by thousands of fans, declared an honorary alumnus of the University, and presented with a scroll signed by hundreds of locals. But beneath the surface, the waters churned. A 1988 letter from Disney said the University's use of the Duck logo infringed on Disney's copyright and again demanded immediate sale of all items using the logo.

Forget RoboDuck. Oregon's Disney-fied mascot is one of the most beloved in all of sports.

"In March 1989, athletic director Bill Byrne stuck a deal with a Disney executive that allowed the university to sell items with the Duck logo from its own suppliers, but stipulated the vendors pay Disney royalties.

"Then in 2010, the Duck was set free when Disney acknowledged that the 'current incarnation of a costumed character featured at the University of Oregon's athletic and promotional events (the "Oregon Duck") is not substantially similar' to Disney's Donald Duck character."

Wrote the Eugene *Register-Guard* when the deal was announced:

"In an amicable split, the folks at The Walt Disney Co. have agreed that the University of Oregon's feathered mascot, which appears at sporting events, is not Donald Duck and that the mascot is no longer subject to Disney's trademark. That leaves the Duck Who Is Not Donald free to go on its cheerleading way, subject only to UO rules.

"…Under its formal licensing agreements with Disney, the UO had to get Disney's permission to use the Duck in any setting outside those described in the agreements, which set out strict rules for how the UO can use Disney trademarks. And when the Duck strayed—and yes, the Duck has strayed—the university had to scramble to smooth any ruffled feathers in the Magic Kingdom.

"No more, as far as the Duck mascot is concerned. The UO/ Disney licensing agreement remains in effect for the printed logos on sweatshirts and the like. But the costumed Duck mascot now answers only to the university."

"What a wonderful thing for Disney to do," Matt Dyste, the UO's director of marketing and brand management told the *Register-Guard*. "It's marvelous. It's incredibly gracious on their part."

28 2009 Rose Bowl: I Smell Roses

Oregon returned to Pasadena for the first time since 1994 when its 2009 regular season ended with a 10–2 record and its first Pac-10 championship since 2001.

The Ducks' opponent in the Rose Bowl on New Year's Day 2010 was No. 8 Ohio State, also 10–2, and the champions of the Big Ten.

It was a matchup of Oregon's speed and skill versus the Buckeyes' brawn and power, a classic Pac-10/Big Ten confrontation played in the traditional New Year's Day setting between the champions of both conferences—under a cloudless Southern California afternoon sky with the temperature in the low 70s and a crowd of 93,963 packed into the Rose Bowl.

Oregon came into the game supremely confident after winning its final three games of the regular season, including a double-overtime win against Arizona followed by a thrilling victory in the Civil War against No. 13 Oregon State.

Redshirt freshman running back LaMichael James and junior quarterback Jeremiah Masoli led an Oregon attack that averaged 37.6 points and 424.6 yards per game during the regular season despite an eight-point performance in its season-opening loss to Boise State.

Oregon's odds were also buoyed by the fact that the Buckeyes' two regular-season losses came against Southern California (18–15) and Purdue (26–18), two teams the Ducks scored a combined 85 points against in regular-season wins.

But Ohio State came into the game with a defense that had allowed just 12.1 points per game and a 6'6", 230-pound, dual-threat quarterback, sophomore Terrelle Pryor, who had led the Buckeyes to five straight wins to end the regular season.

In the end, those two elements, along with a few critical Oregon mistakes, proved to be the difference.

Pryor accounted for 338 yards of offense and threw two touchdown passes, while the Ducks turned over the ball twice, missed a field goal, and were held scoreless in the first and fourth quarters in the 26–17 loss.

Oregon's offense had the ball for just 18:23, running just 53 plays. The Buckeyes, meanwhile, had the ball for 41:37—a Rose Bowl record for time of possession—and ran 89 plays. They also outgained the Ducks in total yards, 419 to 260.

"They kept us off the field," lamented Ed Dickson, Oregon's All-Pac-10 tight end, who was held without a catch. "That's the one way to beat us."

Oregon wasn't without its chances, however.

After falling behind 10–0 in the first quarter, the Ducks finally got rolling with 10 straight points early in the second quarter on a 24-yard field goal by Morgan Flint and a three-yard run by running back LeGarrette Blount, tying the game with 9:14 to play in the half.

But the Buckeyes followed with a clock-eating drive that lasted 8:00 and ended with a field goal that put Ohio State back up 13–10.

Oregon got the ball back with 1:05 left before halftime and Masoli completed a pair of quick passes to get the Ducks to the Ohio State 43-yard line. He then got intercepted by Ross Homan, who returned the ball back into Oregon territory, and the Buckeyes were able to tack on one more field goal before time expired to take a 16–10 lead into the break.

The Ducks looked sharp on the opening drive of the second half, with Masoli capping a 12-play drive with a one-yard TD run to put Oregon up 17–16, its first lead of the game.

That was it for the Ducks, however, as they later lost a fumble in the red zone after falling behind 19–17, and missed a field goal late in the fourth quarter trailing 26–17. Ohio State did its part by controlling possession for 11:24 of the fourth quarter, including the final 5:10, to secure the win.

In the end, James, who rushed for a Pac-10 freshman record 1,546 yards and 14 TDs, was held to just 70 yards on 15 carries. Worse, he never found the end zone. Masoli was also limited to a season-low 81 yards on 9-of-20 passing and an interception. He ran for just nine yards.

"The whole night, we were just a little off," Masoli said.

One bright spot for the Ducks was the emergence of redshirt freshman running back Kenjon Barner, who had a breakout game with 227 all-purpose yards, including 64 on seven carries and 122 more on four kick returns.

The game also marked the start of four straight BCS bowl games for the Ducks.

29 Haloti Ngata: The Most Dominant Duck?

The greatest defensive lineman in Oregon football history thought so much of his future college team that when he first started hearing from the Ducks, as a recruit, he was so intrigued by the prospect of playing for them that he took all the recruiting letters he received from them and deposited them directly into the trash.

"I didn't think I would go to Oregon," Ngata said. "I just threw away the letters. I hadn't heard about them all that much."

Four years later, Ngata would be the most dominant defensive tackle in the Pac-10, a top NFL draft pick about to embark on a career as one of the league's best interior linemen. But in late 2001, the top-rated high school defensive lineman in the country was just a Utah kid looking to play football and explore his Mormon faith at a school in his home state.

But a new addition to the Oregon staff, Mike Gillhamer, had coached Ngata's uncle and namesake, Haloti Moala, at Utah. Moala was intrigued by the prospect of his nephew playing for the former coach whom he still greatly respected. And in the Tongan culture, the opinion of a young man's elders—particularly someone for whom one was named—carries massive weight.

Ngata visited Eugene with his father, Solomone, and was convinced he wanted to become a Duck. His mother wasn't as sure, but when Olga took a trip to Oregon just before signing day, she relented. The Oregon football program had signed one of the most high-profile recruits in school history.

As a freshman, Ngata had 44 tackles in 12 appearances, and broke into the starting lineup five games into the season. He was named a freshman All-American and the team's top newcomer.

But entering Oregon's Seattle Bowl appearance, tragedy struck. In early December, Solomone Ngata was killed in an auto accident. Haloti traveled between Utah and Eugene that month to juggle practice and family obligations, but he was intent on playing. "This is what I want to do, and I think it's what he would want me to do," Ngata said.

The Seattle Bowl was the first game of Ngata's life that his dad didn't attend. Instead, 50 family members were there in his place—his teammates helped round up enough tickets for all of them. "I just confronted the team and said, 'If you can spare any tickets, Haloti's family really needs them,'" defensive lineman Igor Olshansky said. "The team came through real well, and we got the tickets in no time."

With his father gone, Ngata saw himself as the new head of the family. Providing means to support them was of more importance, and so he passed up the chance to take a church mission in order to speed up his arrival in the NFL. "I decided that I could stay here and portray the church by the way I play, and the way I do things on the field," he said years later. "It's been a good decision for me."

Then, disaster: In the first half of the first game of 2003, Ngata suffered a season-ending knee injury at Mississippi State. It would be the middle of 2004 before he felt back to full strength, good enough to earn second-team All-Conference honors, but not the level of consistency coaches hoped to see. "I came back a little slower than I thought I would," Ngata said late that season. "The first part of the season, I didn't think I did as well as I could have, but now I think I'm playing where I'm supposed to be at. I wish I could have been there earlier."

Ngata got to the level everyone expected of him as a junior. He had 61 tackles in 2005, including a remarkable 14 against California, an unheard-of total for a defensive tackle. Combining mammoth size and strength with uncanny quickness, the former youth rugby standout was named the Morris Trophy winner as the Pac-10's best defensive lineman, and a consensus All-American.

In Oregon's Holiday Bowl loss to Oklahoma, which capped the 2005 season, Ngata suffered another knee injury, this time a sprained MCL. That scare was enough to cement his decision to leave early for the NFL, if it hadn't been made already. "I've loved it," he said of his Oregon career, prior to officially announcing his intention to declare for the draft. "All the experiences that I've had, all the fun, all the friends that I have, [the] lifetime of friends that I got. It is nothing that I will ever experience in my life again. I'd never take that back or regret it. It's been a blessing for me."

Ngata's UO career didn't end before taking one more tragic turn—his mother, crippled by grief and health problems since her husband's death, passed away prior to the 2006 NFL Draft. But he was picked in the first round, 12th overall, by the Baltimore

Ravens, and went on to become a dominant force in the NFL, just as he'd been from 2002 to 2005 with the Ducks.

30 Returning to the Postseason

At kickoff for the 1989 Independence Bowl in Shreveport, Louisiana, between Oregon and Tulsa, the temperature registered 29 degrees. Late in the game, it dropped to 25; a few fans in the parking lot resorted to building bonfires for warmth.

A sub-freezing day in Louisiana? The Oregon football team couldn't be happier. For on December 16, 1989, the Ducks made their first bowl appearance since 1963.

"We were so excited to be going to a bowl game," quarterback Bill Musgrave said. "And we didn't care whether one bowl was better than another. It was the ultimate for us to go to Shreveport. I know that people in the crowd still talk to this day about how cold that was. But I don't think any of us were even aware of it."

Despite Oregon's inability to reach the postseason the previous 30 years, the Independence Bowl must have seemed like a no-win situation in some respects. The Ducks had gone 7–4 but were facing 6–5 Tulsa, and were a two-touchdown favorite. The athletic department had agreed to buy 14,000 tickets to guarantee the berth, and risked losing money on the trip.

But Oregon's fans came through, flocking to Shreveport for the game. And the team came through as well—eventually.

Midway through the third quarter, Tulsa was shocking Oregon, having taken a 24–10 lead. Musgrave had thrown two interceptions, and a blocked punt had resulted in one Tulsa touchdown.

Chris Oldham had two picks for the Ducks, but to that point it hadn't helped.

Musgrave had some magic in him, though. With 2:05 left in the third quarter, he threw a touchdown pass to Joe Reitzug. Early in the fourth, Musgrave ran for a touchdown, the first of his career.

Midway through the fourth quarter, Tulsa was driving, looking to regain the lead. Passing up the chance to pin the Ducks deep with a punt, Tulsa tried to convert a fourth-and-1 by giving the ball to fullback Brett Adams on a dive. Linebacker Mark Kearns made the stop, and the Ducks had another chance.

For a moment, it looked like Oregon would ice the game with a touchdown. But with the Ducks just shy of the goal line, Musgrave peeled back from the line, tried to pitch the ball to Derek Loville, but watched it hit the turf and get recovered by Tulsa. In a stroke of fortune, though, Musgrave was ruled down before the fumble.

"My foot got caught in the grass or something," Musgrave said. "Trying to get the ball to Derek was pretty stupid. I thought it was a fumble, but as I fell down I heard the whistle. Maybe I was down. I don't know. I was lucky on that one."

Gregg McCallum converted a 20-yard field goal instead, Tulsa couldn't score in the final three minutes, and the Ducks had not only their first bowl appearance since 1963, but a victory. "I felt all along if we lost this game it would tarnish a very good season," Brooks said. "But maybe winning this game makes it a great season."

Author Brian Libby later called the win "cathartic validation that, after years of frustration, the program had been turned around." Brooks agreed. "The Independence Bowl was a huge, huge step forward for Oregon," he said. "That game as much as anything turned Oregon's football fortunes."

Indeed, the Ducks were right back in a bowl the next year—and it was just as dramatic. Trailing Colorado State 32–25 late in the Freedom Bowl, the Ducks drove 79 yards to a short rushing touchdown by Sean Burwell, pulling Oregon to within a point. Brooks decided to go for two, with 1:01 left on the clock. "I like to win football games," Brooks said. "I've never gone for a tie in my life, and we didn't bring 20,000 Oregon fans down here to kiss our sister and go home."

Musgrave, who was 29-of-47 for 392 yards on the day, dropped back and passed to Michael McClellan, who had nine receptions for 148 yards and a touchdown. But, to cap a game that also featured three fumbles and a muffed point, the Ducks committed one more miscue, as McClellan cut off his route right at the goal line; the ball never crossed into the end zone.

Thus ended Musgrave's final appearance in an Oregon uniform. "He laid it on the field and gave everything he had, and he made a lot of really good plays," Brooks said. "We just made too many errors to win the game. We basically gave that game away."

Just two years later, the Ducks found themselves right back in Shreveport. Thanks in part to six takeaways, including an interception for a touchdown by Alex Molden and a fumble return for a score by Herman O'Berry, Oregon jumped out to a 29–10 lead against Wake Forest. But the same secondary that accounted for those turnovers was burned for big plays of 30, 35, 40, 60, and 61 yards, and Wake Forest roared back to win, 39–35.

"This loss is one of the toughest I've ever experienced," Brooks said, "because of the significance a bowl win would have had for this team and this season." After three bowl berths in four years, the program had taken a big enough step forward that just appearing in the postseason was no longer good enough.

31 Win the Day

Just weeks after his arrival at Oregon as its new offensive coordinator, New Hampshire native Chip Kelly would coin a phrase that would set the tone for his six-year stay in Eugene: "Win the Day."

It was a theme Kelly first used years earlier while at the University of New Hampshire to get a better effort from his players during the monotony of spring practices, by recognizing daily winners each practice at their respective positions.

At Oregon, however, the slogan needed to resonate a little stronger.

The 2006 Ducks ended the season with four straight losses, including a humiliating 38–8 loss to BYU in the Las Vegas Bowl. Their final record was 7–6 despite a 4–0 start, a 7–2 record through early-November, and a national ranking that peaked at No. 11 the week of October 2.

As *Register-Guard* reporter Rob Moseley wrote in a 2007 article, the Las Vegas Bowl loss left the team adrift, and it lingered through the early months of the 2007 off-season.

"A pall set in over the UO program. The players went about their off-season conditioning regimen. Coaches assembled a top-notch recruiting class. But the mood just didn't feel right. The family atmosphere was gone."

"From the Vegas Bowl to recruiting, everybody just kind of went their separate ways," UO associate head coach and offensive line coach Steve Greatwood told the *Register-Guard*. "There was just a lot of things that were…well, there was no closure. We felt like we needed that."

They found it just a few miles away from team headquarters on a rainy March night.

Coach Mike Bellotti called a mandatory team meeting during the final week of winter term. He then had the players and staff loaded onto buses and taken to Camp Harlow, an outdoor recreational facility operated by the First Baptist Church of Eugene.

Once there, everyone filed into the cafeteria, where they were instructed to write everything they didn't like about the program on easel paper. Then the group discussed everything that was written.

What followed was an hours-long, clear-the-air, cleanse-the-soul open forum for both players and coaches.

"When you allow an open forum, a gripe session, you can bring up things that can be uncomfortable for everybody," Bellotti said. "And there [were]. We talked about some things that made me uncomfortable, made other people uncomfortable. But everybody got their say."

Afterward, Bellotti told the players to make another list, this time of what could be done to change the program for the better. Those lists were posted in the UO locker room for months afterward.

The following day, during a coaches meeting to discuss moving forward from the previous night's events, Kelly mentioned the phrase he had once used to motivate his players at New Hampshire.

"It was like heaven sent: win the day," defensive backs coach John Neal said. "That encompassed everything that we do. Go to class. Do your studies. Get in the weight room. Do what you have to do…. Win the day [encapsulated] all those ideas into one idea. That's it, win the day. Don't try to win the Pac-10 championship before you win the day."

Years later, Win the Day is the Ducks' unofficial motto. It's on billboards and T-shirts and bumper stickers. It's written in giant letters on the players' entrance to Autzen Stadium, in their locker room, and has even been become a silly salutation among Oregon fans, in the same mold as "Roll Tide" at Alabama.

"To me, it means you take care of what you can control, and what we can control is today," Kelly told the *Oregonian* in 2010.

"I think people too often look way down the road—you know, 'I want to do this, I want to do that, I want to be conference champion, national champion.' If you don't take care of Tuesday, that's not going to happen."

That 2007 team reached No. 2 in the country before quarterback Dennis Dixon was injured and lost for the season. Still, the team finished 9–4 and routed South Florida 56–21 in the Sun Bowl. Since Kelly's Win the Day motto emerged, the Ducks responded with a 65–14 record in the next six seasons.

32 The Punch

The local paper, the *Register-Guard* of Eugene, called it "an unmitigated disaster." Columnist Dwight Jaynes, an institution in Oregon, said it was "waaaay beyond embarrassing." And Dennis Dodd of CBS Sports wrote that "the whole scene is best described as chicken-bleep."

There have been finer nights in the history of the Oregon football program than the one the Ducks endured September 3, 2009, in Boise. Pretty much any night in the team's history qualifies, really.

In what could have been Chip Kelly's triumphant introduction to the head coaching ranks, the new Oregon coach instead endured what would be one of the rare nights of offensive frustration in his UO tenure. His leadership was tested further when running back LeGarrette Blount caused an embarrassing scene after the final play, punching a Boise State player, slapping a teammate, and nearly mixing it up with fans before being dragged from the field. "I couldn't have envisioned anything worse than this right here,"

Blount said afterward, as the collective Oregon football fan base nodded in agreement.

Even before an incident that became known as "the Punch," things had gone horribly awry for the Ducks.

As can be the case in an opener, both teams struggled to find their rhythm early on. On its two first-quarter drives, Oregon went three-and-out twice. The Broncos were at the Ducks goal line but backed themselves up with mistakes, and settled for a 29-yard field-goal attempt—which Kyle Brotzman missed.

Oregon had scored in the first quarter of every game in 2008, so going scoreless to open the 2009 season was notable, though at that point the game was still tied. It was when the Ducks went into halftime still without so much as a first down, with Boise State leading 13–0, that something seemed truly amiss.

The Oregon offense finally got going with a touchdown and a two-point conversion in the third quarter. By then, though, Boise State already led 19–8 and the writing was on the wall. The fourth quarter was scoreless, and the Ducks had suffered their most inept performance since being shut out at UCLA following Dennis Dixon's knee injury in 2007. "We shot ourselves in the foot a couple times with penalties," quarterback Jeremiah Masoli said afterward. "If you don't get any first downs, you're three-and-out every time. We only had, what, 10 or 13 plays in the first [quarter]? Especially in our offense, it goes quick."

The most memorable part of the evening hadn't even happened yet, however. As time expired with Blount and the Oregon offense on the field, Boise State's Byron Hout ran up to Blount, slapped his shoulder pads, and reminded Blount of his pregame comment about the Ducks owing the Broncos one, to avenge Boise State's victory in Eugene the year before. Hout quickly turned away, then dropped to the turf after Blount hit him on the chin with a right cross.

"As the game went on, it just got more and more frustrating," said Blount, who ran eight times for –5 yards and was tackled for a safety in the second quarter. "Me in general, I was kind of fed up. I should have just [taken] it to the locker room. I shouldn't have said anything, I shouldn't have did anything, I should have just [come in]to the locker room. I shouldn't have taken it to that level."

Receiver Garrett Embry approached Blount on the field and was violently turned aside. The running back finally made his way toward the locker room, amid heavy taunting from fans who were watching the incident replayed continuously on the stadium scoreboard. At one point Blount thought a fan was about to throw a chair in his direction, but before he could engage in another confrontation he was dragged from the field by receivers coach Scott Frost.

The incident dominated the college football landscape for the next two days. Oregon had the misfortune of representing itself so poorly during a nationally televised Thursday night game, which provided ample fodder for Friday talk shows. Thus, lost in the noise was the stout performance by the Ducks' defense. "That's a pretty explosive offense, and if somebody had said to me that we'd only give up 17 points, or somebody even said 19 points…but it wasn't enough," UO defensive coordinator Nick Aliotti said. "It was just one of those days."

Early Friday, Oregon president Richard Lariviere released a statement calling Blount's behavior "reprehensible," and promising "appropriate action" from the Ducks. It came later that day, when Kelly announced that Blount was suspended for the season—though not dismissed from the team, despite calls for as much from some pundits. "LeGarrette Blount needs this football team; he needs structure," Kelly said. "I think he's taken this very hard, and he understands he made a mistake. He has to pay for that mistake, but we're not going to throw LeGarrette Blount out on the street."

Blount ultimately was reinstated from the suspension for the final month of the regular season—another early decision by Kelly that drew howls from columnists. Blount returned to the field for the Civil War, then scored a touchdown in the Rose Bowl; he also lost a key fumble.

Yes, the Rose Bowl—despite the humiliation in Boise, Oregon regrouped, won the conference, and earned a spot in Pasadena. "We're men. We can take a loss," Masoli had said that night in Boise. "This doesn't make or break our season. That's what we're going to get across to our guys tomorrow." Ultimately, that message was received loud and clear.

33 The Assistants

Maybe it's something in the water, since Eugene is a community based at the confluence of the Willamette and McKenzie Rivers. Whatever it is, there's something about working at Oregon that compels assistant coaches to stick around for years and years, sometimes in multiple stints, with the Ducks.

Entering the 2013 season, the Ducks had six assistant coaches on staff with at least a decade's worth of experience at Oregon. Prior to Chip Kelly's departure, his entire staff had spent four seasons together, the longest continuous tenure in the country at that point. But Oregon's tradition of long-tenured assistant coaches extends back for generations.

The tradition began in earnest under legendary coach Len Casanova. His first staff, in 1951, included Jack Roche, who remained an Oregon assistant through 1970 and returned in 1975 for another two-year stint. Over the next few years, Casanova's assistants included Jerry Frei (1955–66), Phil McHugh (1958–68), Max Coley (1959–68), and John Robinson (1960–71).

McHugh played tight end under Casanova from 1954–56, before becoming an assistant. "Coming back to Oregon and getting a chance to coach, that was very special," McHugh said. "To listen to Roche coach his defensive plans, and Johnny [McKay] and his offensive plans, as a player it was very exciting. And then to suddenly be sitting in the meetings and hearing how all these things came about? It was wonderful."

Several coaching changes during the '70s limited the chance for staff longevity. But when Joe Schaffeld returned to his alma mater as an assistant under Don Read in 1974, he kicked off the next generation of longtime Oregon assistant coaches.

Schaffeld remained on staff until 1997, and 15 years later he still dropped by practices from time to time. "To this day, he's like a grandfather," former Oregon safety Anthony Newman said recently. Like many assistants, though, Schaffeld had a different demeanor during his coaching days. "He wasn't easy to play for," said Michael Gray, a former Oregon defensive lineman who, like Schaffeld, also returned to the Ducks as an assistant. Schaffeld was "a little different, a little sterner."

That description also fit the man who was Schaffeld's counterpart on the other side of the line for many years, Neal Zoumboukos. An assistant primarily on the offensive line from 1980 to 2006, the man known as "Zoomer" commanded respect from his players. "Zoomer would hide in the bushes outside the dorms and try to catch people who were sneaking out," legendary Oregon offensive lineman Gary Zimmerman recalled. "He had some creative coaching methods back then, too. He'd use all kind of props: a hammer, a starter's pistol.... [But] looking back, Zoomer was hard on me, and that's what I needed."

Schaffeld and Zoumboukos were joined for much of their tenures by linebackers coach Bill Tarrow, another former Oregon player, who was an assistant from 1977 to 1996. And that trio worked from 1983 to 1994 with receivers and special teams coach John Ramsdell.

That generation of long-serving Ducks assistants overlapped with the present group. Running backs coach Gary Campbell was hired in 1983 and remained on staff three decades later, having mentored all but two of the 19 single-season 1,000-yard rushers in school history. He recruited and coached Derek Loville, Reuben Droughns, Jonathan Stewart, and LaMichael James, players who experienced not just college success but also made an impact in the NFL.

Steve Greatwood returned to his alma mater in 1982, left with Rich Brooks after the 1994 Rose Bowl season, and returned in 2000 for another decade-plus run. Tight ends and special teams coach Tom Osborne worked six seasons with the Ducks beginning in 1995, left in 2001, and returned in 2007. Linebackers coach Don Pellum also briefly left Eugene after having played for the Ducks but returned in 1993.

Pellum grew up in Los Angeles and recalled the recruiting trip on which he first came to love Eugene, rain and all. "A lot of people don't like that kind of weather, but I can't stand the heat," Pellum said. "I called my mom on the trip and told her I was going to go to Oregon. It was just a different place from what I was used to in Los Angeles. I was in a convenience store in Eugene, and out of the blue a guy said, 'Hi.' I looked around, thinking he was talking to somebody else.… After seeing how other people do things, I was like, 'Whoa, I'm going back to Oregon. My roots go really deep here.'"

Ditto for defensive coordinator Nick Aliotti, who was first on staff under Brooks from 1988 to 1994, left, and then returned in 1999. One of his defensive assistants, John Neal, was hired in 2003 and stuck around for a decade. And that's not to mention Oregon's legendary strength and conditioning coach Jim Radcliffe. While not officially a member of the football staff, he is considered one of the unsung heroes of the Ducks' success throughout the last 30 years.

Among the secrets of the Ducks' success, clearly, is staff continuity, considering the several assistants who had no problem spending multiple decades in Eugene.

34 Harrington Wills a Win

Oregon under quarterback Joey Harrington had a string of remarkable fourth-quarter comeback victories. None was as improbable as what happened at Sun Devil Stadium on the last Saturday of October 2000.

The final score was 56–55 Oregon, won in double-overtime after four hours and 14 minutes of game time and a combined 1,232 yards of offense. The game also boasted the most combined points scored in a single game during the modern era for Oregon football—until the Ducks and USC combined for 113 in 2012.

The seventh-ranked Ducks trailed Arizona State by 14 points, 49–35, with 3:21 to play when Harrington connected with Marshaun Tucker on a 32-yard scoring strike to cut their deficit to seven.

Oregon got the ball back with 1:22 remaining, but tight end Justin Peelle was stuffed at the 1-yard line on fourth-and-goal, giving the ball back to the Sun Devils.

It was a 58-yard catch and run by Peelle that put the Ducks in a position to tie the game late, but after he was stopped four plays later, all hope seemed lost for Oregon, which was being serenaded by chants of "Overrated" by the Arizona State crowd.

There Oregon was, 82 seconds away from losing sole possession of first place in the Pac-10 and in desperate need of a miracle.

It got one.

The Sun Devils appeared to ice the game when running back Mike Williams rushed for first-down yardage with 33 seconds left but he fumbled when tackled by linebackers Michael Callier and Matt Smith, and Oregon's Jermaine Hanspard recovered.

On the very next play, Harrington found Peelle in the corner of the end zone from 17 yards out for the game-tying touchdown with 27 seconds left.

"I lost the ball in the sun and I wasn't sure I was in bounds," Peelle said of his TD catch. "But I knew I needed to come through, and I was glad the coaches had the confidence [in me] to come back my way."

But they were far from through. With the score tied 49–49, the Ducks and Sun Devils went to overtime.

Oregon stopped Arizona State on its first possession of overtime when cornerback Steve Smith picked off Sun Devils quarterback Jeff Krohn.

The Ducks ran three straight times on their drive to set up a 42-yard field-goal attempt that kicker Josh Frankel sent wide left.

Oregon got the ball first in the second overtime and on the third play of the drive, running back Allan Amundson ran for a one-yard score. Frankel converted the extra point and the Ducks took their first lead of the game, 56–49.

The Sun Devils answered, getting their own one-yard TD run from Williams. They then lined up for what would've been the game-tying extra-point kick, but instead Krohn took the snap and rolled out for the surprise two-point attempt, and his pass glanced off the hands of tight end Todd Heap in the end zone, ending the game.

"Sometimes you get lucky," conceded Harrington, who completed 26-of-43 passes for a career-best 434 yards and a school-record-tying six touchdown passes. "But the thing about that is you can't get lucky unless you battle your butt off, and that's what we did today even when things didn't look good."

It was the second straight season in which the Ducks stole a win from the Sun Devils. In 1999, Harrington connected with Tucker with nine seconds left to beat Arizona State 20–17 at Autzen Stadium.

Tucker was a favorite target again for Harrington in this game, catching 11 passes for 138 yards and three touchdowns. Keenan Howry also had four catches for 125 yards and two TDs.

As for Peelle, the junior finished with three catches for 80 yards—all in the final minutes of regulation—and one game-tying touchdown grab.

"I've never felt so high or so low in my life," he said. "I can't even describe it."

35 Bobby Moore

Before there was Ahmad Rashad, NFL star and national sportscaster, there was Bobby Moore, one of the most versatile offensive weapons in Oregon football history.

A Portland native who went to high school in Washington, Moore chose Oregon over Notre Dame—in part because, ironically enough, he'd always liked the Ducks' uniforms, something that would become their hallmark decades later. He played wide receiver in 1969, then moved to running back in 1970, and was named All-American at the position as a senior.

Years later, the Ducks revolutionized a spread-option offense that featured running quarterbacks such as Dennis Dixon, Jeremiah Masoli, and Marcus Mariota. Those who played with Moore—and saw him throw passes in practice that traveled a rumored 70 yards—can only wonder about how he might have flourished in

Before he was Ahmad Rashad, NFL superstar, he was Bobby Moore, a dominating offensive force for the Ducks.

such a role. "If it had been 20 years later, he might have been a quarterback," said receiver Bob Newland (1968–70). "He could do everything.... He could have been a linebacker, a safety, a corner— [he] just had it all."

Moore played in some of the most prolific offenses in Oregon's early history. The 1969 Ducks set a school record with 361 yards per game; Tom Blanchard was the quarterback, and Moore and Newland were his receivers. "We rolled in thinking, 'We don't care whom we're playing, we're going to put some points on the board,'" said Rashad, who took a new name upon converting to

Islam in 1972. "That was kind of our attitude, and that's the way it was for three years."

Those were the days before freshmen were eligible, not that Moore couldn't have helped Oregon his first year on campus. He caught 10 touchdown passes and scored 15 times overall, both Pac-8 records at the time, and recalled "thinking it felt easy. I was having a good time out there."

"Every once in a while the ball would be in the air—and as a pass blocker you're supposed to say, 'Well, I guess I can run down the field 60 yards and block for him'—but there's a moment where you're just watching what happens," said offensive lineman Tom Drougas (1969–71). "You couldn't help it; you had to watch Bobby try and make a play.... We had this guy out there that was in the same league as O.J. Simpson in Bobby Moore, where at any given moment something could happen that was great."

Both Moore and Newland returned in 1970, and the offense set records for points and yards that weren't surpassed until 1989. Newland's 1,123 receiving yards mark still stands, and his 67 receptions stood until Samie Parker eclipsed them in 2003. But the Ducks also had a talented junior receiver in Leland Glass, and so coach Jerry Frei requested that Moore move to running back. "My first couple games I wasn't very good, and Jerry came to me and told me if I wanted, he'd move me back to receiver," Rashad said. "I just said, 'No, I'll stick with this.' And I got it down pretty much after that."

Did he ever. As a junior, Moore ran for 924 yards and a league-leading 11 touchdowns. The rushing yardage broke Mel Renfro's school record.

Against UCLA that fall, Rashad scored two key late touchdowns in Oregon's 41–40 win, in which the Ducks came back from 19 points down in the final five minutes. One was a screen pass on which he eluded three defenders; he later called it "one of the coolest plays I've ever been involved in."

But Moore's signature performance might have come a month later, against Army—in, of all things, a tie. The Ducks looked to Moore when they needed a late touchdown while playing for the tie, and called a blast play up the middle from about 60 yards out. "He ran through the entire Army football team," quarterback Dan Fouts remembered. "Everybody on that team had a shot at him. He either bounced off, ran away from, or stiff-armed every one of them." Legendary basketball coach Bobby Knight was at Army then, and to this day mentions it when he sees Rashad. "That might have been the greatest single play I've ever seen," Knight told him.

For all Moore's efforts, the Ducks were still down by two. They needed a two-point conversion for the tie, and Fouts threw a short pass to—who else—Moore, who caught it a couple yards shy of the goal line and then fought his way into the end zone. Fouts described Moore as "about as fantastic an athlete as you could ever imagine. But I think what I came to respect more than his athletic ability was his toughness. People don't realize the pounding and sacrifice he made for us. He was an All-American wide receiver, and we needed a tailback so he took that responsibility and became an All-American running back. In those days it was five yards and an AstroTurf burn, so a position change like that was a lot to ask. But he took it on."

Moore was even better as a senior, posting the first 1,000-yard rushing season in school history, with 1,211 yards. He was named All-American and was the fourth pick in the 1972 NFL Draft. His greatest success professionally was back at receiver, but as the Oregon faithful saw from 1969 to 1971, there was nothing Moore couldn't do.

36 Midnight Madness

Admit it. You left.

Or at least *thought* about leaving, or turning off the TV and just going to bed.

That was the reality for many Ducks fans who witnessed Oregon blow a 10-point, fourth-quarter lead against No. 16 USC in the last weekend of September 1999.

A fumbled kick return in the final minutes appeared to seal a 23–20 loss for the Ducks and sent many in the crowd of 45,660 at Autzen Stadium that night heading for the exits early.

Bad decision.

In one of the wildest victories in program history, the Ducks rallied to defeat the Trojans 33–30 in three overtimes—a four-hour, 20-minute marathon that didn't end until third-string kicker Josh Frankel converted a 27-yard field goal.

"We had a bunch of kids saying they weren't going to lose," coach Mike Bellotti said.

Frankel got his opportunity to be the hero after regular kicker Nathan Villegas was injured after tying the game at the end of regulation and then No. 2 kicker Dan Katz failed on a field-goal attempt in the first overtime.

"At first I was surprised when they called me, but I guess it was my turn to win a game," Frankel said. "It's funny how two teams can fight so hard and the whole thing comes down to a kicker, and a third-string kicker at that. That never happens. I made the most of my chance and I'll never forget it."

It was a chance he almost didn't get.

The Ducks led 20–10 going into the fourth quarter when USC reserve quarterback Mike Van Raaphorst, pressed into duty after

Carson Palmer was knocked out of the game just before halftime, engineered two touchdown drives, the last coming with 3:08 to play.

But in one of the many strange twists to the game, USC missed the extra point when the snap went over the holder's head. On the ensuing kickoff, Oregon's Jason Cooper was spun 360 degrees and fumbled. The Trojans recovered, but David Newbury missed a 30-yard field goal with 2:16 left.

The Ducks got the ball and quickly drove down the field with quarterback A.J. Feeley completing a 24-yard pass to LaCorey Collins to put the ball at the Trojans' 8. After three unsuccessful downs, Villegas connected to tie the game with 30 seconds left.

Villegas suffered a torn ACL in his kicking leg while celebrating with holder Joey Harrington, forcing Katz into action in overtime.

Newberry missed from 51 yards in the first overtime, giving Katz a chance to end the game, but the senior's attempt from 33 yards out sailed far left.

Oregon went up 30–23 in the second OT on a one-yard pass from A.J. Feeley to Todd Brooks.

Frankel, who hadn't attempted a kick since missing two extra-point attempts in the 1997 Las Vegas Bowl, got his shot and the junior delivered the point after in the second overtime, "that gave me some confidence and gave the team some confidence," Bellotti said.

"I just felt like I didn't want to put that pressure on Dan again—not that he couldn't handle the kick, but that I didn't think it was fair to him," Bellotti said. "It wasn't any kind of guarantee, but I felt good about Josh's kick on that extra point."

The Trojans responded with a touchdown drive of their own to force a third overtime.

Southern California got the ball first but Newbury missed his third field-goal attempt of the night when he came up short on a 37-yarder.

Oregon took over and moved the ball from the 25-yard line to the 11 on a pair of rushes by Derien Latimer.

Back in came Frankel, who was true from 27. The remaining fans stormed the field in delirium.

"I can't imagine sitting here, having played that hard, invested that much time and emotion, and not have won it," Bellotti said the day after the game. "It was certainly emotionally draining…but to come away with a victory hopefully replenishes a lot of that."

37 That BCS BS

From 2009 to 2012, the Oregon football program became one of just four schools in the history of the Bowl Championship Series era to play in BCS games in four straight seasons.

The first was the University of Miami, whose streak of four straight BCS games beginning in 2000 was matched by the Ducks in 2012. Southern California held the longest BCS streak, seven games beginning with the 2002 season, and Ohio State went to six straight, the last of which was the 2011 Sugar Bowl.

For its first three BCS appearances—the 2010 Rose Bowl, the 2011 BCS National Championship Game, and the 2012 Rose Bowl—Oregon secured its spot in those prestigious games on the field. The Ducks won a conference title in each case to secure an automatic BCS bid, and in the 2010 season finished second in the BCS standings to reach the title game.

In the 2012 season, however, the Ducks needed a little help. They finished fourth in the final BCS standings of the year. They played in the 2013 Fiesta Bowl, but as an at-large selection, the only one among the BCS participants that year.

Oregon's selection was notable in that it extended the Ducks' run of BCS appearances. And it was notable, too, because the BCS hadn't always been kind to the UO football program, leaving some fans skittish in 2012, even as Oregon seemed like a lock for the Fiesta Bowl.

In both 2001 and 2005, the Ducks seemed worthy of more than the BCS formula granted them. The 2001 team had the look of a national championship contender, but was denied a spot in that game. The 2005 team was shut out of the BCS entirely, despite finishing fifth in the standings.

In 2001, Oregon was 10–1 after the regular season and Pac-10 champions. The only blemish was a wild, back-and-forth, seven-point loss to Stanford. Heisman contender Joey Harrington was at quarterback, and the Ducks were enjoying the best season in school history, sitting at No. 2 in the human polls.

The problem: Nebraska, which hadn't even won the Big 12 that year—hadn't even played for the conference title, in fact—eked ahead of both Oregon and Big 12 champ Colorado in the final BCS standings.

The Buffaloes beat the Cornhuskers 62–36 to end the regular season and deny Nebraska a Big 12 championship shot. And yet when the dust settled after all the BCS number crunching, Oregon and Colorado were relegated to the Fiesta Bowl and Nebraska faced the Miami Hurricanes in the Rose Bowl, which hosted the title game that year. Thus Harrington was denied not only a BCS title shot but also his dream of playing in the Rose Bowl, even though the Ducks were Pac-10 champs.

"I liken the BCS to a bad disease, like cancer," said Oregon coach Mike Bellotti, explaining later that in each case a feeling of powerlessness exists. "Not to take anything away from Nebraska or Colorado—they're great football teams—but one has two losses and the other didn't win its conference championship. We're No. 2 in both polls, but those things don't have a lot of merit, obviously."

It got worse: The Cornhuskers were destroyed 37–14 by the Hurricanes in the title game. Oregon, meanwhile, took out its frustrations on Colorado, 38–16.

That Miami team was special, boasting 38 future NFL draft picks including safety Ed Reed, tight end Jeremy Shockey, and linebacker Jonathan Vilma. Some believe the Ducks dodged a bullet, benefitting from the chance to win a BCS game rather than suffering a fate similar to Nebraska's. And yet, "I still wonder, 'What if we'd had a shot at the title?'" Harrington said years later. "I really do."

Oregon was forced to play the "what if?" game again four years later. The 2005 team also finished the regular season 10–1, having lost badly at home to USC. The Ducks were No. 5 in the BCS standings, but unavailable for at-large consideration to the Fiesta Bowl, because Notre Dame and Ohio State took the "at-large" spots through new automatic qualifying rules that had been instituted.

"I can't complain too much," Bellotti said at that point. "I think we do deserve to be in that [game]. I won't say over anybody else because I'm not going to point any fingers.

"I think the reality is the BCS people are trying to do the very best they can to create an opportunity for one national champion. I have come full circle. I am a huge proponent of bowl games and the traditional bowl matchups, but I think they should be used in a playoff format now to determine a national champion."

38 Joey Heisman

The Ducks were coming off the program's first 10-win season in 2001 and receiving preseason mention as BCS title contenders when they took a bold step toward nationalizing their brand on the back of their star quarterback.

On a hot June day in New York, the Ducks unveiled a 10-story-tall billboard of Joey Harrington on the side of a building near Madison Square Garden in Manhattan.

The $250,000 billboard featured Harrington standing in his Oregon uniform, helmet in one hand, football in the other, with JOEY HARRINGTON HEISMAN over OREGON FOOTBALL plastered across the front.

It was supposed to run for three months but instead was up for five.

The project was the brainchild of Portland, Oregon, businessman Ken O'Neil, a longtime Oregon booster and close friend and former Oregon classmate of Nike's Phil Knight. O'Neil had been walking through Times Square in the summer of 2000 while he was in town for the U.S. Open tennis tournament, when he came up with the idea to push Joey Harrington as a candidate for Heisman by advertising on the side of a New York City building.

"You never get recognized by the East Coast," O'Neil said. "And to me, this is the East Coast, right here in New York. And we thought a lot of people would ask, 'What are these guys doing? Who is this guy? Where's Ore-gone?' It was kind of the ultimate tickler ad."

The idea was passed along to UO assistant athletic director Jim Bartko and immediately it began to gain traction. Though none of the money needed for the project came from Knight, Oregon did use Nike's advertising agency, Wieden+Kennedy, to buy the billboard space. Wieden+Kennedy also came up with the idea to put the billboard by Madison Square Garden instead of Times Square, where it would get lost among the bright lights and other billboards.

The Harrington billboard was also vigorously supported by then–UO president Dave Frohnmayer.

"I think Joey being a serious Heisman candidate says an important thing about our program," Frohnmayer said. "He makes a

Billboard or not, Joey Harrington was the face of Oregon football at the turn of the millennium.

statement about the University of Oregon…. I think Joey represents the scholar-athlete that we believe should typify what we do in intercollegiate athletics, at a time when many question whether we're doing the right thing by scholar-athletes, or whether they represent the right things about our universities."

Frohnmayer and Oregon's idea of promoting its student-athletes in this manner was hardly universally accepted.

The *New York Times* wrote an editorial panning the billboard on August 8, 2001, stating: "Though the billboard seems unlikely to win Harrington the Heisman, it does serve a useful purpose. It dramatizes the skewed priorities of high-powered college athletic programs. Athletic directors, awash in television revenues from football and basketball programs and generous alumni donations, are increasingly running their departments as independent fiefs. It is hard to believe there was no more constructive way for the University of Oregon to spend $250,000."

Even the *Register-Guard* wrote a disapproving editorial.

Whatever anyone thought on the subject, however, what couldn't be ignored is that in December 2001, Harrington found himself in New York as a finalist for the Heisman Trophy.

Of course, that probably had as much to do with what he did on the field during Oregon's 10–1 regular season.

Harrington threw for 23 touchdowns and just five interceptions, and rushed for seven more scores for the Ducks, who won the Pac-10 Conference and gained a then-all-time high ranking of No. 3 at the time of the ceremony. Oregon would finish the season by beating Colorado in the Fiesta Bowl.

"I knew there would be the risk of a backlash, maybe more directed toward Joey than anything else," Frohnmayer said. "Ultimately I was comfortable with it. I didn't then and wouldn't now walk away from it…. And if that [billboard] hadn't happened, would he have gotten the same attention?"

39 The Autzen Experience

There is nothing quite like game day at Autzen Stadium.

From the pregame party outside the stadium to the postgame celebration on the field, you haven't truly experienced life as a Ducks fan until you've attended a game and completely taken in the whole Autzen experience.

Pregame begins four hours before kickoff when the parking opens and those lucky enough to have secured a reserved parking spot (all of which go to donors) begin to set up their tailgate parties.

If you're not in the lot, fear not. There are other options for those wanting to tailgate, though they fill up fast.

Directly across Martin Luther King Boulevard on the stadium's north side are a handful of businesses that allow game-day parking and tailgating in their parking lots and surrounding grass fields, including the Masonic Lodge, the Boy Scout Center, the Serbu Youth Campus and Juvenile Justice Center, Lane County Mental Health, and the lot at the old Armory.

Across Leo Harris Parkway on the stadium's south side are the Science Factory and the BMX track lots.

What this creates is an incredibly lively and festive atmosphere surrounding the stadium. Even if you aren't tailgating yourself, just walk through the lot and enjoy the sounds and smells, and chances are you will end up joining a handful of fellow fans for some postgame beers and food.

However, if tailgating isn't your thing or the weather isn't the best for standing outside for four hours, head to the Moshofsky Center. Oregon's 117,000-square foot indoor practice facility turns into an indoor tailgate party for 5,000 on game day.

Doors to the "Mo" open three hours before kickoff and fans can enter for free and enjoy live music, live pregame radio broadcasts, watch other games on the TVs throughout the center, and shop for some new game-day gear at the Duck Store. There are also interactive games for the kids, and of course, lots of food and adult beverages.

The highlight, however, comes two hours before kickoff when the entire football team, led by the Green Garter Band, the cheerleaders, and the Duck, parade down the center of the Mo Center on their way to the locker room.

Once inside the stadium, get to your seat in time to watch the pregame highlight video on the scoreboard, and make sure to cheer loudest when Kenny Wheaton makes his interception against Washington.

When the video ends, you'll feel the rumble of the Harley, as the Duck roars out of the tunnel on the back of a motorcycle, followed by the players and coaches.

After every Oregon score, count along with the crowd as the Duck does his push-ups, and before the start of the fourth quarter, sing along to "Shout."

But most important, bring your voice and don't be afraid to use it—Autzen Stadium has a reputation for being the loudest in the nation for a reason.

When the game is over and the Ducks have won—and they usually do; they've gone 82–15 at home between 1998 and 2012—be sure to stay after and go down on the field.

Notice we didn't say "rush" the field. Five minutes after every home game, fans are allowed onto the field for pictures, to throw a ball around, or to simply have a look. Just be patient and wait for the horn to blow, signaling it's okay to head down.

And whatever you do, leave your umbrella at home. It won't be allowed inside, not that you'll need it. Remember, it never rains at Autzen Stadium.

40 The Toilet Bowl

In recent years, the Civil War rivalry between Oregon and Oregon State has featured overtime drama and championship moments and even, in 2009, a head-to-head battle for a berth in the Rose Bowl.

Still, the most famous game in the series between the two in-state rivals featured no drama. No points, either.

The Civil War was first contested in 1894, and Oregon's fifth straight victory, during the 2012 season, came in the 116th edition of the game. The other 115 were downright barn burners—regardless of their circumstances—when compared with the atrocity that was the 1983 Civil War. That season, the Ducks and Beavers played to the last scoreless tie in major college history, a 16-turnover monstrosity that to this day is remembered as the "Toilet Bowl."

"It was ugly," said Oregon quarterback Chris Miller. "Even if it had ended 3–0, it would have gone down as one of the ugly games of all time. It will live in infamy."

The stage wasn't exactly set for a titanic showdown, the sort that would become more commonplace between Oregon and OSU over the ensuing decades. The Ducks had just beaten Stanford to end a three-game losing streak, and had clinched their third straight losing season at 4–6 entering the Civil War. Oregon State was 2–8, the Beavers' 13th straight losing season (the streak would reach 28 years).

Given the Beavers' run of futility, Oregon had an eight-game Civil War win streak entering 1983. The Ducks were the superior team that season, and were playing at home. They had every reason to be considered favorites to win. But there were no winners that day.

"It was just a pitiful game," Oregon offensive lineman Gary Zimmerman said. "And the weather was awful."

Indeed, fans in attendance sat through a driving rainstorm, which only dragged down the quality of play even further. The final reckoning: 11 fumbles, five interceptions, four missed field goals, and zero points.

"We went up and down the field and just kept fumbling and missing field goals," recalled Don Pellum, an Oregon linebacker that day and later a long-serving assistant coach with the Ducks.

Twice the Ducks managed to cross the goal line. Both times, the scoring play was nullified by a penalty. The field-goal attempts were little more than chip shots. They weren't any more successful.

"It's comical to me when I think back on it," Miller said. "It was ugly. I remember throwing a flat route to Ladaria Johnson's feet—probably a 10-yard throw that would have been a touchdown had I been able to get it to him."

Over the years, all the participants could do when looking back on the Toilet Bowl was laugh. They share in a piece of history—overtime rules later adopted by the NCAA ensured that the 1983 Civil War will be the last scoreless tie in college football history.

There's no avoiding the ignominy.

"Even now, that's what most people remember about me at Oregon is that I played in the Toilet Bowl," said Zimmerman, an All-American who went on to a Hall of Fame career in the NFL that featured a Super Bowl title. "I saw a little kid one time and even he said, 'Hey, you played in the Toilet Bowl!'... It was the most memorable game from back then. I laugh at it now. It's pretty funny."

The fans who stuck it out to the end thought briefly they'd received some resolution. On the final play of the game, with the Ducks deep in their own territory, Miller completed a pass to Kwante Hampton, who lateraled to Johnson. For a second it looked as if the Ducks were about to complete a miraculous, 82-yard touchdown pass for the winning score as time expired.

Instead, Johnson was tackled at Oregon State's 14-yard line. And the officials ruled he'd stepped out of bounds near midfield, anyway.

"It was almost," Oregon coach Rich Brooks said, "like neither team wanted to win."

And thus, neither did—for the last time in major college history.

41 Sorry Sooners

At the end of the 2012 season, Bob Stoops had won 149 games in 14 seasons as the head coach at Oklahoma.

Anyone associated with the Sooners program would look you dead in the eye and say that total should be 150.

And they'd be right—and wrong.

In one of the most talked-about games of 2006, No. 18 Oregon defeated No. 15 Oklahoma 34–33 after some controversial officiating decisions in the final 72 seconds helped the Ducks overcome a late 13-point deficit.

After the Ducks pulled to within 33–27 on a 16-yard run by quarterback Dennis Dixon with 1:12 left, they needed to recover an onside kick to have one last shot.

That's when things got crazy.

On the ensuing kick, Oregon's Brian Paysinger appeared to make contact with the ball in the air before it had traveled the required 10 yards. No matter, because seconds after the ball hit the ground, Oklahoma's Allen Patrick had possession, so it was the Sooners' ball anyway.

Or was it?

Gordon Riese

Retired Pac-10 referee Gordon Riese was in the Autzen Stadium replay booth that afternoon. In an interview with *Sports Illustrated* in 2009 he talked about how, three years later, he was still torn by the blown calls and also by the game's aftermath.

Riese received death threats, vulgar phone calls, hostile letters, and harassing e-mails for months after the game, and following his one-game suspension by the conference, he chose not to return to the booth in a decision-making capacity.

Riese explained that on the controversial onside kick review, he was able to see just one replay—an end-zone shot—on a 16-inch monitor that was blurry and didn't allow him to rewind, fast-forward, or run plays in slow-motion.

Though other replays showed that an Oregon player had touched the football before it traveled 10 yards, Riese couldn't tell from his angle. And by rule at the time, he couldn't tell the referee what he *had* seen: Oklahoma's Allen Patrick had recovered the football.

He stuck to the rulebook for his decision, but later regretted it, saying, "The ultimate goal is to get it right."

Replay officials now have much greater latitude on those types of calls, and the technology in the booth has been vastly improved.

Even as Patrick stood above the pile of players with the ball in his hand, the referees ruled Oregon had recovered the kick. The Oklahoma sideline was incredulous.

Despite Oregon safety Patrick Chung's claim that he actually had possession first and only released the ball after the whistle had blown, video of the play appeared to show otherwise; the ball was knocked around on the ground until squirting through a pair of legs and right to Patrick, who scooped it up.

The play went to a booth review, but only to determine whether Paysinger had touched the ball early, and not to determine who had final possession.

The booth ruled the play inconclusive and so the official ruling on the field stood. Oregon got the ball back.

On the second play of the ensuing drive, Oklahoma was called for pass interference on a ball that Dixon later acknowledged was first tipped by a Sooners defensive lineman. But a review of that play also proved inconclusive, and on the Ducks' next down, Dixon connected with Paysinger for the 23-yard go-ahead score.

Still with time left, Oklahoma returned the kickoff 55 yards to set up a 44-yard field-goal attempt. It was blocked by Oregon linebacker Blair Phillips to end the game.

It didn't take long for the national media to chime in on the blown calls that "robbed" Oklahoma of a victory.

Stoops, too, was livid about how the final 72 seconds played out—especially the ruling that Oklahoma didn't recover the onside kick.

"We're taking a knee. Game's over," he said.

In the following days, there was more national uproar about the game. David Boren, president of the University of Oklahoma, asked the Big 12 Conference to see if it could get the game "eliminated from the record book."

By Tuesday, the Pac-10 Conference took action.

"Errors clearly were made and not corrected, and for that we apologize to the University of Oklahoma, Coach Bob Stoops, and his players," said Pac-10 commissioner Tom Hansen in a statement. "They played an outstanding football game, as did Oregon, and it's regrettable that the outcome of the contest was affected by the officiating."

With that, the Pac-10 suspended the seven-man officiating crew for one game. The same penalty was given to the two men in the replay booth.

Stoops was unmoved by the decision.

"I think it's fair to say that a one-game suspension compared to the way our season now is altered—I don't know if it fits the situation," said Stoops, who also described the performance of the officiating crew as "[a]bsolutely inexcusable and unacceptable."

Despite Boran's request, Oregon wasn't about to surrender a victory, even one as tarnished as this. And truth be told, Oklahoma still had a chance to stop Oregon from scoring in the final minute and missed its potential game-winning field goal.

"We did a lot of things right to win the football game, and if we're the beneficiary of some calls or the bounce of the ball, that happens," Oregon coach Mike Bellotti said. "We've all been on the wrong side of calls at some point in time and certainly those that affect games, but I have nothing but pride for our players and the way that they played and the heart and resolve that they showed."

42 Dan Fouts

The 1970s were not kind to Oregon football. The Ducks enjoyed just two winning seasons, and finished the decade with 36 wins—a total they'd later match in a three-year span from 2010 to 2012.

The decade got off to a good start, with a 6–4–1 mark in 1970. It would be Oregon's last winning record until 1979. But what a memorable season it was, thanks in no small part to a skinny sophomore quarterback named Dan Fouts.

Fouts came to Eugene from San Francisco, following in the footsteps of his high school teammate and future Ducks center Jim Figoni. By the time Fouts left after the 1972 season, he held 19 school records, foretelling the prolific passing offenses of years to come at Oregon, and proved to be one of the biggest names in the Ducks' fine tradition at quarterback.

"Fouts had an amazing presence in the huddle," said Don Reynolds, a running back with the Ducks from 1972 to 1974. "You hear about guys who are field generals, and that was Fouts.

He was extremely in control, a dominating presence in the huddle. It was very impressive."

That 1970 season began with little indication that Fouts would be a star. He was the backup to veteran Tom Blanchard, who was tagged for full-time duty despite a history of knee problems. Then, in Oregon's first game of the year, against California in Portland, Blanchard again suffered a knee injury, and in came Fouts.

The setting was Civic Stadium in Portland, a night game with lights illuminating the field. On the first passing attempt of Fouts' career, he lofted a laser down the field to sure-handed veteran receiver Bob Newland—who promptly lost the pass in the lights. "I dropped the first pass Fouts threw," Newland (1968–70) said. "And I have heard about that forever."

All was forgiven by evening's end, after Fouts led the Ducks from behind for a 31–24 win over the Golden Bears. It wouldn't be the last comeback Fouts led that season, or the most memorable.

That distinction belongs to Oregon's midseason trip to UCLA. Fouts ran for two early touchdowns, but later in the game he was knocked out while scrambling to recover a muffed snap. In a role reversal, Blanchard was summoned from the bench to replace Fouts.

Despite a separated shoulder, Blanchard completed one of the plays of the game, a pass to Leland Glass that extended a late drive. There was nearly simultaneous possession between Glass and a defender, but it was ruled a catch for the Ducks. Even more impressive, Glass had been poked in the eye as he released off the line of scrimmage. "He said he saw two footballs coming at him," Fouts recalled. "Luckily he caught the right one."

Still, the Ducks trailed by 19 with 4:38 in the game. There was little reason to think they still had a chance.

Late in the game, Blanchard's shoulder injury proved too much to overcome. Fouts had to go back in and, despite being knocked out earlier, he completed the winning touchdown pass to Greg

Dan Fouts was a standout quarterback during some anemic years for Oregon football.

Specht. Oregon had beaten UCLA 41–40. "That has to be one of the best comebacks of all time," said Bobby Moore, later known as Ahmad Rashad.

For Fouts, it is among the most memorable highlights of his Oregon career. "There was great drama in that game," Fouts said. "The lasting memory is just the screams of disbelief as we were going off the field, from the UCLA people. It was just wonderful."

The UCLA comeback came during a stretch of five wins in six games midway through the 1970 season, and the Ducks were flying

Ducks in the Hall of Fame
College Football Hall of Fame

Name	Position	Years at Oregon	Year Enshrined
J.W. Beckett	halfback/tackle	1913–16	1971
Hugo Bezdek	coach	1913–17	1954
John Kitzmiller	halfback	1928–30	1969
Norm Van Brocklin	quarterback	1947–48	1966
Len Casanova	coach	1951–66	1977
Mel Renfro	halfback	1961–63	1986
Bobby Moore	running back/receiver	1969–71	2007

Pro Football Hall of Fame

Name	Position	Year Enshrined
Norm Van Brocklin	quarterback/coach	1971
Tuffy Leemans	running back	1978
Dan Fouts	quarterback	1993
Mel Renfro	defensive back	1996
Dave Wilcox	linebacker	2000
Gary Zimmerman	guard	2008

high. But then they settled for a tie with Army despite a heroic performance from Rashad, then lost the Civil War 24–9. Still, Fouts became the first Oregon quarterback to surpass 2,000 yards through the air (with 2,390) and he'd set another school record with 16 touchdown passes. Already, he was third on Oregon's career passing list.

The 1971 season also had some promise late in the year, with Fouts and the Ducks 5–4 down the stretch. But California got its revenge to even Oregon's record, and then the Beavers won another Civil War, 30–29. It was the final game for Oregon coach Jerry Frei.

Fouts' final season was played under Frei's replacement, Dick Enright. The Ducks were 4–7, this time needing a late rally to finish with a respectable record. They beat San Jose State and Oregon State to close out the year, and Fouts' remarkable career.

In the end, Fouts threw for 5,995 yards, compiled 5,871 yards of total offense, and completed 37 touchdown passes in three years—all school records. As of 2013 he was still sixth on Oregon's career passing record list, despite a parade of prolific quarterbacks who followed him in Eugene.

Fouts went on to one of the most impressive professional careers of any Duck. A third-round pick of the San Diego Chargers in 1973, he enjoyed a 15-year NFL career in which he threw for 43,040 yards and 254 touchdowns. He retired as the NFL record holder at the time for 300-yard passing games, with 51, and 3,000-yard passing seasons, with six. In 1993, Fouts was inducted into the Pro Football Hall of Fame.

After retiring from the NFL, he went on to a career as a broadcaster. Whenever possible, he'd reference his pride in his alma mater. "People say, 'You're a former Duck,'" Fouts said years later. "And I say, 'Nope. I'm a Duck.'"

43 Willie Lyles and the NCAA

The NCAA began investigating the Oregon football program's recruiting practices in 2011, though it wasn't the first time the Ducks had come under harsh scrutiny by college athletics' governing body.

The 2011 case began with a scouting service operator, Willie Lyles, who from 2008 to 2011 was contracted by the Ducks to provide evaluations of high school prospects. In 2010, the Ducks even paid $25,000 to Lyles' company, Complete Scouting Services.

The problem: When the football team disclosed the material Lyles had supplied, it was largely outdated. On the surface, it appeared the Ducks might have actually been paying Lyles, who had mentoring relationships with prominent Oregon recruits LaMichael James and Lache Seastrunk, to influence those two players to sign with the Ducks. Late in 2012, Oregon's attempts to negotiate a settlement with the NCAA regarding the allegations had stalled, and a hearing before the Committee on Infractions was scheduled for 2013.

That the Lyles scandal reached as far back as 2008 meant it occurred within five years of the Ducks' previous brush with college athletics law.

In January 2003, it was later found, running backs coach Gary Campbell had secured an invalid letter of intent from recruit J.J. Arrington, who had both signed the letter after a midnight deadline and forged his father's signature.

That was the second letter of intent Arrington had signed, after another with California. The Golden Bears raised a stink, the Ducks reported themselves to the Pac-10 Conference, and Campbell was briefly suspended without pay and barred from recruiting. While the Pac-10 considered Campbell's actions to be a secondary violation, the NCAA later termed it a major violation, though it accepted previous penalties handed down, including probation.

The Ducks hadn't been nearly so lucky two decades earlier, their first major NCAA troubles.

In August 1980, the Pac-10 ruled that five teams—Oregon, Oregon State, Arizona State, UCLA, and USC—were ineligible for bowl games that season. The charge: Using players who should not have been eligible, having attained bogus credits for academic work they didn't do.

The Ducks were ruled to have used such players from 1977 to 1979, and so received other punishments from the conference. Oregon forfeited its wins from those seasons, was placed on probation, and surrendered a handful of scholarships. An assistant coach who had been most directly involved, John Becker, resigned.

"As the person in charge, I'm ultimately involved with what happens to our program and accept the responsibility," head coach Rich Brooks said. "I don't disagree with the penalties, but I don't like them either."

A year later, though, the NCAA handed down even tougher penalties. An investigation uncovered that not only had the phony credits been handed out, but Oregon coaches had operated a secret fund to pay for airline tickets for athletes, arranged for free meals for players at local restaurants, and allowed improper use of athletic department telephones for players to make long distance calls. There was even the use of a "paid talent scout," a booster who provided airline tickets for use in recruiting, foreshadowing shades of the Lyles scandal 30 years later.

In all, some 35 violations were found to have been committed from 1977 to 1979. The NCAA in December 1981 put the Ducks on two years' probation, banned them from appearing on television for a year, and docked them seven scholarships in recruiting during the next two years.

Charles Wright, chairman of the NCAA's infractions committee, declared himself "quite concerned with the nature of the violations and the direct involvement of the university's athletic coaching staff in the violations."

Brooks offered to resign early in the process. Oregon officials would not accept it. Still, it was a black eye for the program.

"The phony credits sent academia into a rage," said Ed Swartz, an associate athletic director. "Athletics tried to be bigger than the school itself. You don't circumvent the halls of ivy. Our programs are not bigger than the school—never have been and never will be."

44 Gang Green

On a Lake Tahoe golf course during the summer of 1994, defensive coordinator Nick Aliotti alighted on a nickname that would come to define Oregon's defense that season and set the standard for every other defense that came after it: "Gang Green."

Led by a run-stuffing front line, a pair of sure-tackling line-backers, and arguably the best secondary in the nation, the defense was as responsible for Oregon's run to the 1995 Rose Bowl and its first outright conference championship as anything else.

The Ducks went into the bowl against Penn State ranked 12th in the nation against the run, allowing just 112.4 yards per game. Only two running backs rushed for more than 100 yards against Oregon during the season. In eight conference games, they held four teams to under 100 yards rushing and allowed only 760 total yards on the ground.

Oregon also led the Pac-10 with 19 interceptions and had 27 turnovers all together.

"The defense is the key to this team," Oregon quarterback Danny O'Neil said.

It would be hard to single out a standout unit on the defense. Every part was so important to the whole.

But the most decorated group was in the secondary, among which cornerbacks Herman O'Berry and Alex Molden and strong safety Chad Cota all earned first-team All-Pac-10 honors. Free safety Jeff Sherman led the team with 107 tackles and reserve cornerback Kenny Wheaton led the team with four interceptions and was named second-team All-Conference.

Cota, Molden, and Sherman started all 13 games that season, while O'Berry missed four starts.

Despite his limited play, O'Berry was selected to the Football Writers Association of America's All-American team. Both he and Cota would get picked in the 2005 NFL Draft. O'Berry went in the seventh round to the St. Louis Rams—who were then coached by Rich Brooks—and Cota also went in the seventh round, to the Carolina Panthers.

Molden was drafted 11th overall by the New Orleans Saints in 1996, and Wheaton would go in the third round of the 1997 Draft to the Dallas Cowboys.

The Ducks gave up just eight passing touchdowns and 202 yards per game during the 1994 regular season.

Along the three-man line, nose tackle Silila Malepeai and massive left end Troy Bailey were the mainstays.

Bailey, a 6'3", 270-pound junior, started every game and led the team with 15 tackles for a loss of yardage, including 4.5 sacks. Malepeai, a senior, was the emotional leader of the defense. On the right side, senior Mark Slymen was the starter early in the season but sophomore Mark Schmidt emerged late as an injury fill in and had five sacks in the final eight games.

The linebacking corps was a stout group led by the duo of juniors Jeremy Asher and Rich Ruhl, who combined for 200 tackles that season. Like Asher and Ruhl, outside linebacker Paul Jensen started every game for the Ducks.

In the middle was sophomore Reggie Jordan, a 6'3", 240-pound blitzing specialist who led the team with seven sacks.

The defense had its breakout performance in the fourth game of the season when it picked off three passes and allowed just six points in the final three quarters of Oregon's 40–18 win against Iowa at Autzen Stadium.

The following week, Gang Green fueled the Ducks' first win against USC at the L.A. Memorial Coliseum in 23 years with a nine-sack performance and held the Trojans scoreless after the first quarter in a 22–7 victory.

It was a similar story against Cal two weeks later. The Golden Bears scored in the opening four minutes but never again, as the Ducks went on to win 23–7.

Then of course there was the victory against Washington, when the Ducks held running back Napoleon Kaufman to just 101 yards on 23 carries and Wheaton set the course for the future of Oregon football with his pick-six in the final minutes.

The next week, against No. 11 Arizona, the defense allowed just 191 yards against the Wildcats, including 39 in the second half as the Ducks rallied for a 10–9 win.

Oregon then capped the regular season with a 17–13 win against Oregon State in the Civil War. The Beavers were held to 284 yards, including just 63 passing.

In Pac-10 play, the defense allowed opponents an average of just 6.1 points per game in the second half.

Just as Aliotti had predicted that summer, Gang Green was indeed a painful experience for those who faced it.

45 2013 Fiesta Bowl

De'Anthony Thomas set the early tone, head coach Chip Kelly went out a winner, and Oregon made its legion of fans wonder if maybe the Ducks were playing in the wrong bowl game after they pasted highly regarded Kansas State in the 2013 Fiesta Bowl (just two years earlier, the site of the BCS National Championship Game).

Playing in their fourth straight BCS bowl game, the fifth-ranked Ducks came away winners for the second consecutive season and secured their third straight 12-win season with a 35–17 win against the seventh-ranked Wildcats at University of Phoenix Stadium in Glendale, Arizona

It wasn't the BCS National Championship Game, which the Ducks were essentially knocked out of thanks to a gut-wrenching 17–14 overtime loss to Stanford in the second-to-last game of the regular season, but any lingering disappointment for not making the title game disappeared on the Fiesta Bowl's first play.

That's when Thomas, a dynamic, big-play-waiting-to-happen sophomore, returned the opening kick 94 yards for a touchdown. It was Oregon's longest play in its bowl game history.

The running back with sprinter's speed was barely touched as he quickly found a crease and blazed down the Oregon sideline and crossed the goal line like a sprinter cutting through the finish line.

After a two-point conversion rush by defensive end Dion Jordan, the Ducks went up 8–0 just 12 seconds into the game.

The Kansas State fans, who far outnumbered Oregon's in the overall crowd of 70,242, were silenced; it appeared even the Wildcats themselves were stunned.

For Thomas, it was mission accomplished.

"I felt like my role in this game was to be a momentum builder and a game changer," Thomas said after the game. "Once I saw that edge, I wanted to get to the end zone as fast as I could so I could celebrate with my teammates."

Thomas wasn't done, and neither were the Ducks.

Later in the first quarter, Thomas took a screen pass from quarterback Marcus Mariota and went 23 yards for another touchdown. The 5'9", 176-pounder got the last few yards the hard way, dragging three Kansas State defenders into the end zone for a score that put the Ducks up 15–0.

It was a rude welcome for the Wildcats, who were playing in their first BCS bowl game since 2004 and, like the Ducks, had missed out on a shot at the championship game after losing late in the season.

Boasting a Heisman Trophy finalist in quarterback Collin Klein and with legendary coach Bill Snyder patrolling the sidelines, Kansas State came into the game 11–1 and with a reputation for disciplined play.

But an uncharacteristic mistake gave momentum back to Oregon after the Wildcats had cut their deficit to 15–10 late in the second quarter. Kansas State was going for it on fourth-and-1 at the Oregon 18-yard line when a false start penalty pushed them back to the 23. Kicker Anthony Cantele missed on a 40-yard field-goal attempt, giving the ball back to the Ducks with exactly 1:00 left to play in the half.

Five plays and 77 yards later, Mariota capped a 46-second drive with a 24-yard touchdown pass to Kenjon Barner, giving the Ducks a 22–10 lead at the break.

Mariota, who threw for 166 yards and two TDs, and rushed for 62 and another score, was named the offensive MVP. Barner also rushed for 143 yards in his final game for Oregon.

Linebacker Michael Clay was the defensive MVP. The senior had nine tackles and a sack as the Ducks held Klein to 181 total yards.

It was also the final game of the Chip Kelly era at Oregon. The fourth-year head coach, who went 46–7 in Eugene, would take a job with the NFL's Philadelphia Eagles just two weeks after the game, ending the most successful coaching stretch in Oregon history.

The victory also validated Oregon's—as well as its legion of fans'—belief that if not for its misstep against the Cardinal in November, it would have played in its second BCS National Championship Game in three seasons.

46 Cliff Harris

For sheer entertainment value, few players in Oregon football history have been as compelling as Cliff Harris. He was a big-play machine and the most quotable guy ever to play for the Ducks, but he was also a tragic figure who never could stay out of trouble for long.

The best and worst of Harris were on display right from the start. He was a U.S. Army All-American out of Fresno, California, one of the most decorated recruits in his class, and yet his arrival at practice in the fall of 2009 was delayed by an issue with his prep transcript. In a bit of foreshadowing, he also brought to Oregon a misdemeanor obstruction charge from an altercation he had with a police officer at his high school. The incident began when the officer took issue with a hat Harris' brother was wearing.

Then, when Harris did join the Ducks, he told his new teammates at a meeting: "My name is Cliff Harris, and I'm here to lock shit down." It was brash, crass, and ultimately something Harris backed up. Vintage Cliff Harris.

Oregon's coaches were constantly trying to tighten the reins on their young star. Harris' talent was undeniable, but he was slated to redshirt in 2009 before being pressed into duty following injuries to seniors Willie Glasper and Walter Thurmond. Good enough to start in 2010, Harris was delayed in that regard too, until an injury to Anthony Gildon forced the staff's hand again.

For as much trouble as he could be off the field, Harris was magic with the football in his hands. He returned an interception 76 yards for a touchdown at Tennessee early in his sophomore year, and later picked off celebrated Stanford quarterback Andrew Luck

Unpredictable off the field, Cliff Harris was a stalwart part of the Ducks' defense and special teams.

twice. Harris once told a reporter he was "the cheese on top of the nachos," and sometimes it was hard to argue with him.

"Somebody said it ain't braggin' if you do it," said Oregon running backs coach Gary Campbell, who helped recruit Harris. "And I think that's his attitude: 'I may say something that you don't like, but that's what I intend to do.' And inevitably he does.

At California in 2010, Harris made perhaps the biggest play of his college career. With the Ducks struggling to establish their offense, a rarity under Chip Kelly, Harris returned a punt for a touchdown in the 15–13 victory. "Tell you what, he's a big-time player," UO receiver Jeff Maehl said. "He continues to make plays when we need them most."

It was Harris who deemed the 2011 BCS National Championship Game "the Natty," which caught on quickly with Oregon and its fans. He also jokingly referred to Oregon State as "little brother" prior to the Civil War in his sophomore year, which earned him a talking-to from Kelly, and prompted Harris to pass up interview requests for several weeks.

Then, in the title game against Auburn, Harris intercepted one Cam Newton pass and nearly picked off another in Oregon's 22–19 defeat. By the end of the season, Harris had returned a school-record four punts for touchdowns and was named a consensus All-American.

Over the off-season, the *Sporting News* called Harris "the best cornerback in the game [and] the best return man in the game." Harris said the immaturity of his youth was in the past, entering his junior year. "I feel like it's my time now," Harris said. "I'm not a young guy out there no more. So I've got to show an example and be a role model."

That comment, made in the spring, would come back to haunt him. In June, Harris was arrested for driving 118 miles per hour on an Oregon highway, with quarterback Darron Thomas in the passenger seat. The officer who pulled them over thought he smelled marijuana, and asked Harris about it. "We smoked it all," Harris responded, one more memorable quote for the bulletin board.

The traffic violation—the latest on a driving record that included some $5,400 in fines in Oregon and California to that point—earned Harris a suspension from Oregon's opener against LSU. With Harris unavailable to return punts, a backup was called upon; the Tigers scored a touchdown when they stripped the backup and returned the fumble for a score.

Once Harris returned, eased back into the lineup just as he had been to start his career, he was never far from the spotlight. He had a momentum-changing interception in a win over Arizona State, but also was tackled in the end zone for a safety at Colorado, which kept the UO defense from posting a shutout.

Then, in October, Harris was pulled over again, cited for driving with a suspended license. He was suspended from the team—again. A month later, in Fresno, Harris was found to be carrying marijuana when he was stopped by police. After that last transgression, Kelly dismissed him from the Oregon football program.

Harris' legacy included a 16.2-yard punt-return average, the best in school history. Unfortunately, he's remembered more for what he said and mistakes he made off the field.

47 Mariota's Debut

The Marcus Mariota era at Oregon opened with a bang and ended with an MVP trophy for the redshirt freshman and a 12–1 record for the Ducks.

In between, the 6'4", 211-pound laid-back leader from Hawaii built a record-setting résumé and was named first-team All-Pac-12.

Not bad for a first-time starter.

Mariota redshirted in 2011 and then beat out Bryan Bennett for the No. 1 spot, which was vacated by Darron Thomas when the junior put his name into the NFL Draft.

Mariota gave fans a taste of what he could do with his performance in Oregon's 2012 spring game that included an 82-yard touchdown run and 202 passing yards.

Then on September 1, against Arkansas State at Autzen Stadium, in his first college game, Mariota thrilled the crowd of 56,144 with a dazzling debut.

Against the Red Wolves, Mariota completed 18-of-22 passes for 200 yards and three touchdowns in less than two quarters of action.

"The kid looked pretty good, didn't he?" Oregon offensive lineman Carson York asked afterward.

Mariota's most telling statistic, however, was the seven touchdowns on the first seven possessions for the Ducks. They built a 50–3 lead midway through the second quarter.

"Marcus really had command of our offense and it truly showed today," Oregon coach Chip Kelly said. "I am happy with his performance. Marcus showed a great deal of poise out there, it was really fun to watch him play tonight."

It only got better.

Mariota went on to have one of the greatest seasons by a quarterback in school history. He threw for 2,677 yards, 32 touchdowns, and just six interceptions, and rushed for 752 yards and five scores.

He even *caught* one pass for a touchdown.

By the end of the season, Mariota had set school records for completion percentage (68.5) and total touchdowns (38). He stands second on the UO single-season list for passing touchdowns and total offense (3,429), and third in pass efficiency (163.23).

Granted, Oregon's pace of play and radically different style of offense might make statistical comparisons to previous eras tricky.

If nothing else, Mariota was the best quarterback for Oregon—the best package of pass and run threat—since Dennis Dixon in 2007.

Mariota also showed a remarkable ability to make dramatic progress from week to week. He had five interceptions through six games in 2012, but just one more the rest of the season.

Along the way, Mariota was praised by coaches and teammates alike for his uncanny composure.

"He's far beyond his years," running back Kenjon Barner said in an interview just before the 2013 Fiesta Bowl. "He's young, but he's really not. You don't expect a freshman to do what he does, on the field or off the field. You expect him to make mistakes, you expect him to be frantic in some situations; that's just not Marcus."

Mariota credited his island upbringing for his relaxed demeanor, which helped him navigate the high expectations of taking over an offense that had been the driving force behind three straight BCS bowl games.

"This is the kind of person I am," he said at the Fiesta Bowl pregame press conference. "I think if I were ever to credit something it would be the way I was raised. Hawaii, it's funny, [is] so slow and relaxing. I feel that's kind of taken me to my core."

Mariota showed his resolve best in the Ducks' 62–51 victory against USC at the Los Angeles Memorial Coliseum that November when he completed 20-of-23 passes for 304 yards and four touchdowns.

One week later he threw for 377 yards and six touchdowns in a 59–17 win against California in Berkeley.

He also rushed for 135 yards against Arizona State in a 43–21 win at Sun Devils Stadium, the first true road game of his career.

Then in the Fiesta Bowl victory against Kansas State, Mariota threw for 166 yards and two touchdowns and rushed for 62 yards and another score to earn Offensive Player of the Game honors.

It was the perfect ending to a nearly perfect debut season.

48 The Great Escape

The 2010 team was working on its perfect season when it rolled into Berkeley, California, in mid-November.

The Ducks were 9–0 and absolutely mauling opponents. Their average margin of victory was 37 points and they were averaging 54.7 points per game.

There had been no hurdles to clear, no bumps in the road, nothing to slow Oregon in its quest for an undefeated season and a spot in the BCS title game.

Then they played the California Golden Bears, which were 5–4 at the time and struggling through what would ultimately be a 5–7 season.

And yet, on this night, the high-octane Ducks were brought to a halt in Strawberry Canyon and their dreams nearly dashed.

The most explosive offense in the nation was held to just one touchdown, and Heisman Trophy contender LaMichael James rushed for a then-season-low 91 yards.

Instead of pouring on the points as usual, Oregon needed a punt return for a touchdown, a missed field goal by Cal, an eye-opening performance from its defense, and in the end, an extended, game-killing drive in the fourth quarter when the Ducks' up-tempo offense slowed to a crawl to run out the clock to secure the victory.

It was the type of knockdown, drag-out battle the Ducks hadn't been in all season, escaping with a 15–13 victory to secure their sixth 10-win season in school history.

"Man, that was a battle for sure," Oregon wide receiver Jeff Maehl said. "They came with a game plan and stuck to it."

Oregon, on the other hand, had to flip its script late.

The Flop

Oregon's 15–13 win against California on November 13, 2010, also became known for the flop by Golden Bears nose tackle Aaron Tipoti and the subsequent suspension of Cal defensive line coach Tosh Lupoi.

Early in the game, with the Oregon offense starting to pick up steam, Tipoti was caught on camera staring over at the sideline between plays—and then suddenly dropping to the ground with an apparent injury.

Lupoi, who left Cal for Washington in 2012, was eventually banned for a game by Cal head coach Jeff Tedford after admitting he instructed Tipoti to fake an injury.

It wasn't the first time a player was suspected of faking an injury in 2010 to slow down the high-powered Ducks, whose frenetic pace left opposing defenses gassed and unable to substitute players in and out.

Earlier in the season a similar scenario played out at Autzen Stadium against Stanford, when linebacker Chase Thomas was grounded on the turf with an apparent left ankle injury.

After limping off the field, Thomas raced back onto the field to thunderous boos after sitting out just one play.

The offense had been shut out in the first half; Oregon's only points came off a 64-yard punt return by Cliff Harris midway through the second quarter. The following two-point conversion gave the Ducks an 8–7 lead they took into halftime.

Oregon defensive end Kenny Rowe recovered a fumble by Cal running back Shane Vereen on the opening drive of the second half, giving the ball to the Ducks at the Golden Bears' 29-yard line.

It took one play for Oregon quarterback Darron Thomas to connect with Maehl for a touchdown, putting the Ducks up 15–7. But that score, 31 seconds into the third quarter, would be Oregon's last.

Cal scored its only other touchdown later in the third quarter when Thomas, pinned deep in Oregon territory, fumbled into the end zone on a strip and the Golden Bears' Derrick Hill recovered the ball for the score.

Cal appeared to take the lead when Giorgio Tavecchio kicked a 24-yard field goal on the opening play of the fourth quarter. But the play was nullified by a procedure penalty—on Tavecchio, who said the kicking team's rhythm was disrupted by the noise of the visiting Oregon fans in the back of that end zone.

The ball was moved back five yards and Tavecchio was wide right on his next attempt.

Each team had the ball once more before Oregon took over with 9:25 to play at its own 20 and proceeded to run out the clock with an 18-play, 65-yard drive.

Kenjon Barner rushed six times for 30 yards on the drive, and James rushed seven times for 26 yards. James' final carry was for seven yards and gave the Ducks a first down at the Cal 12-yard line, and they were able to kneel for the final two plays.

"Coach Kelly told us in the huddle before we went out there that this was going to be the drive of the year, this was going to be the drive we were going to remember. 'Go out there and put it away,'" Thomas said.

Not to be forgotten was the defensive effort by the Ducks, who held the Golden Bears to just 193 yards and one offensive touchdown.

"I thought our defense played outstanding all game long," Oregon coach Chip Kelly said. "We felt confident the whole time. That's a confident group of guys in that locker room."

49 2010: A Tumultuous Off-Season

Ironically enough, Chip Kelly commanded near-universal respect from his players during his four years as Oregon's head coach, elevating the overall character of the team by recruiting solid young men, encouraging community service, and harshly punishing his players' transgressions.

It is ironic because the beginning of the Kelly regime with the Ducks certainly didn't signal a dramatic uptick in character.

Start with Kelly's first game as head coach. After one of the worst offensive performances in recent UO history, running back LeGarrette Blount punched a Boise State player and had to be dragged from the field by assistant coach Scott Frost, who extracted Blount from an altercation with a fan. All of that took place on a nationally televised Thursday night game, commanding the attention of the talk shows throughout Friday, with the bulk of college football's opening weekend having yet to have been played.

The Ducks spent the rest of the fall putting the incident behind them. They seemed to have done so in impressive fashion, with quarterback Jeremiah Masoli and running back LaMichael James leading them to their first Rose Bowl appearance in 15 years.

Then, the 2010 off-season dawned. Within weeks, the Ducks had disgraced themselves repeatedly, their fans were embarrassed, and Kelly's leadership was in question.

A timeline of events:

- Late January: A fraternity house reports the robbery of some personal electronic equipment, and implicates two football players. One of the fraternity members chases down one of the accused, later identified as receiver Garrett Embry, to retrieve a small video projector.

- On the same night, place-kickers Mike Bowlin and Rob Beard are involved in a fight, which resulted in Beard requiring surgery to repair damage to his nose. One week later, walk-on defensive end Matt Simms is cited for simple assault in a retaliatory incident, and is soon after dismissed from the team. Beard is later charged with misdemeanor assault and serves a one-game suspension for the incident; Bowlin leaves the team.

- A day after Beard is formally charged, in mid-February, James is briefly jailed on domestic abuse charges following an incident with an ex-girlfriend. Though he ultimately is convicted of only misdemeanor physical harassment, James serves a one-game suspension.

- A few days later, linebacker Kiko Alonso is cited for driving under the influence of intoxicants—shortly after a team meeting to address the series of off-field incidents. Alonso is later suspended for the season, which receiver Jamere Holland crudely denounces in a Facebook posting, prompting his own dismissal from the team.

- In early March, linebacker Josh Kaddu is cited for being a minor in possession of alcohol, which would have been a minor blip on the off-season police blotter if not for everything else. It comes a few days after university president Richard Lariviere was compelled to issue a statement calling the football team's behavior "unacceptable."

- On March 12, the bombshells: Both Masoli and James appear in court, and Masoli pleads guilty to second-degree burglary stemming from the January frat-house incident, prompting a season-long suspension by Kelly. Earlier in the day, James pleaded guilty to one minor charge stemming from his arrest, and is suspended for Oregon's opener against New Mexico. "I apologize to our fans and to the faculty at the University of Oregon," Kelly says. "This is not what we're all about."

- And finally, in June, Masoli is stopped by police on a traffic violation, and marijuana is discovered in the car's glove box. Two days later, he is dismissed from the team. "I had a plan in place for him to follow, and if he didn't follow it, he was gone," Kelly said. "He didn't follow it, so he's gone." Masoli later transferred to Mississippi.

In the car during the traffic stop was backup quarterback Darron Thomas. How did the Ducks respond to their winter of discontent? Thomas led them to the first undefeated regular season in modern school history, and Oregon faced Auburn for the BCS Championship in January 2011.

As Kelly's tenure progressed, the Ducks had a few minor transgressions, but by and large avoided major incidents, with the exception of cornerback Cliff Harris. It took a couple of years, but by the time Kelly departed in January 2013, the stain of the 2010 off-season had been washed away completely.

50 Barner Rushes to Record

The 2012 season: the year Kenjon Barner moved out of the shadows and into the record books.

And all it took was the single greatest individual rushing performance in Oregon history.

In a game that included a handful of eye-popping individual performances, especially from Oregon quarterback Marcus Mariota and USC wide receiver Marqise Lee, it was Barner who stood high above the rest.

Running back Kenjon Barner rushes straight into the Oregon record books against the USC Trojans on November 3, 2012.

The senior from Riverside, California, steamrolled the Trojans for a school-record 321 yards and five touchdowns on a career-high 38 carries in a 62–51 Oregon win at the Los Angeles Memorial Coliseum on November 3.

The win was the 12th straight for the Ducks—a streak that would reach a school-record 13 one week later against California—and Barner's performance would launch him into the forefront of the Heisman Trophy race, and eventually, as one of three finalists for the Doak Walker Award.

"Everybody just did their job tonight," Barner said after the game. "When we communicate and we execute properly, it's hard to stop us. Tonight was just one of those nights we were hitting on all cylinders."

No one more so than Barner, who eclipsed LaMichael James' single-game rushing record by 33 yards.

Oregon scored the first touchdown just more than one minute into the game and led the rest of the way. But the Trojans stayed on the Ducks' heels until the end. Barner did his part to keep Oregon out front, with scoring runs of 27, 5, 9, 5, and 22 yards, respectively. His long run of the game was 41 yards—and he also caught two passes for 26 yards.

"I definitely know when it's one of the better performances, and this certainly was one of his," said longtime Oregon running backs coach Gary Campbell, who has coached all but one of the Ducks' top-10 career rushing leaders, and 17 of the 19 best single seasons by Oregon running backs. "And I knew he was capable of it."

Barner had already built a solid career backing up the incomparable James for three seasons. Heading into his senior season, the 5'11", 195-pound converted defensive back had rushed for 1,856 yards and 20 touchdowns and amassed 3,825 all-purpose yards—ninth all-time at Oregon.

As a redshirt freshman he set the school record with 1,020 yards as a kick returner with an average return of 24.9 yards. He made his first start in the 2010 season opener and scored five touchdowns in the first half of a 72–0 win against New Mexico. As a junior he rushed for 939 yards and 11 TDs with four 100-yard games, while in a reserve role and also missing two games with an injury.

However, until his game at USC, Barner might have been most remembered for a play that could've ended his career. Midway through his sophomore season against Washington State in Pullman,

Top-10 Single-Game Rushing Performances

1. Kenjon Barner, 321 yards, 11/3/2012, at USC
2. LaMichael James, 288, 9/24/2011, at Arizona
3. Onterrio Smith, 285, 10/27/2001, at Washington State
4. LaMichael James, 257, 10/2/2010, vs. Stanford
5. Jonathan Stewart, 253, 12/31/2007, vs. South Florida
6. Jonathan Stewart, 251, 10/20/2007, at Washington
7. Bobby Moore, 249, 9/18/1971, vs. Utah
8. LaMichael James, 239, 10/30/2010, at USC
9. LaMichael James, 227, 9/18/2010, vs. Portland State
10. Tony Cherry, 227, 9/21/1985, at Stanford

Barner was knocked unconscious fielding a kickoff, taking a scary blow to the helmet delivered by Cougars safety Anthony Carpenter.

With his family on the field and his shell-shocked teammates—including some openly weeping—waiting on knees nearby, Barner lay motionless for several minutes before finally he was loaded onto a stretcher and put into an ambulance on the field. Barner was hospitalized for several days.

He was out for nearly a month and missed two games before returning November 6 against Washington. He finished the year with 551 yards rushing and 1,040 all-purpose yards.

Entering his senior season, Barner was finally the No. 1 running back for the first time in his career, and he didn't disappoint. He finished the season with 1,767 yards, the second-best mark in school history, capped by a 143-yard performance in Oregon's 35–17 Fiesta Bowl win against Kansas State. He also scored on a 24-yard pass reception in that game. His 3,623 career rushing yards are also second most in school history.

"He wanted to prove himself, that he could be the guy," center Hroniss Grasu said.

He finished his career with the second most career all-purpose yards, with 5,848. He also had 50 career touchdowns.

51 Stanford the Dreamkiller

Oregon vs. Oregon State is a century-old, bitter, in-state rivalry that divides families and ruins friendships.

Washington is Oregon's pretentious foe to the north, an archnemesis that Oregon fans have detested for decades but secretly wanted to be like (minus the Husky fans of course) not too long ago.

And yet, there has really only been one team that's continuously been a thorn in Oregon's side, a team with a history of breaking Ducks fans' hearts, of dashing dreams, ruining perfect seasons, and blowing up potential BCS championship bids, and it is neither the Beavers nor the Huskies.

The Ducks' first loss of the 1964 season, after a 6–0 start and rise to No. 7 in the national poll? Stanford.

The only blemishes during 2001's and 2012's almost-magical one-loss seasons? Stanford.

The team that kept the Ducks from a Rose Bowl repeat in 1995 with an unthinkable upset at Autzen Stadium? Stanford.

Oregon's only losses in Pac-12 play in 2009 and 2012? Stanford.

The team that killed the Ducks' 23-game home winning streak in 2001 and ended their school-record 13-game winning streak in 2012? Stanford.

See the theme?

The Cardinal lead the all-time series against Oregon 45–30–1, even though the Ducks won 10 of the last 13 games through 2012. However, two of those three losses were devastating gut punches.

In 2012, the Ducks were just two wins away from completing a perfect regular season and earning their second trip to the BCS title game in three seasons.

Oregon, ranked No. 1 in the country at the time, just had to get past Stanford at home then beat the Beavers the following week in Corvallis and it was 'Hello Orange Bowl!'

It didn't happen, as the Cardinal came into Autzen and beat the Ducks 17–14 in overtime, ending Oregon's NCAA record of 23 straight games with 30 or more points.

With mobile quarterback Kevin Hogan providing a changeup to Stanford's power offense, the Cardinal took an early lead, then tied the game on a controversial touchdown catch by tight end Zach Ertz with 1:35 remaining. Ertz was initially ruled out of bounds as he fell to the turf with the ball, but replay officials overturned the call. Stanford kicker Jordan Williamson atoned for a fourth-quarter miss by drilling the game-winner in overtime.

Oregon kicker Alejandro Maldonado missed field-goal attempts in the third quarter and overtime, but the biggest "what if?" moment for the Ducks came in the first quarter, when Marcus Mariota broke free for what could have been a 92-yard touchdown run but was stopped at the Stanford 15 when De'Anthony Thomas, with a chance to make a play, failed to block the last defender. The Ducks failed to score in the red zone and were unable to grab the early momentum.

"It hurts so much because we've invested so much," a somewhat stunned coach Chip Kelly said afterward, later adding, "You'd love to have some words that could kind of take the pain out of it, but there aren't any."

In 2001, the Ducks were off to a 6–0 start to the season when Stanford came to town and rallied for 21-unanswered points in the fourth quarter to win 49–42.

It was a mind-numbing loss for the Ducks, who had two punts blocked, including one late in the fourth quarter that set up a 19-yard touchdown drive by the Cardinal to make it 42–35. Stanford recovered its ensuing blooped kickoff and quickly scored, making it 42–41 after the extra point was blocked.

The Ducks fumbled on their next drive, and with 1:10 remaining, Stanford recovered, and then drove for the winning score.

"It's difficult to lose in that manner," Oregon coach Mike Bellotti said. "The most important thing is not that you get knocked down, it's whether you get back up."

Oregon did, winning the rest of its games that year, including an emphatic Fiesta Bowl victory against Colorado.

But just as the case was in 2012, when the Ducks also went on to win the Fiesta Bowl, one loss to Stanford was all that prevented Oregon from reaching the championship game.

52 2010: A Perfect Regular Season

Led by its "blur" offense and an underappreciated defense, Oregon cruised through the 2010 regular season undefeated en route to its first and only BCS title game appearance, in which the Ducks were finally tripped up by Auburn on a last-second field goal.

During its run to 12–0, the Oregon offense averaged an NCAA-leading 49.3 points and 537.5 yards per game and beat opponents by an average margin of 30.9 points. The Ducks scored 79 touchdowns and rushed for 3,646 yards—an average of 303.8 per game and 6.1 per carry.

The defense recorded two shutouts and held three other teams to just 13 points.

Along the way, Oregon was challenged just one time, in a 15–13 win against California. Otherwise, no opponent came within 17 points of beating the Ducks.

September 4: 1–0
Oregon 72, New Mexico 0

Despite first-time starters at quarterback and running back, the Ducks had no problem squashing the Lobos at Autzen Stadium. One week after being named the starter, Darron Thomas threw for 220 yards and two touchdowns and Kenjon Barner, who filled in for the suspended LaMichael James, rushed for 147 yards and scored five touchdowns in the first half. Cliff Harris also returned two punts for touchdowns in the second quarter and the defense held New Mexico to 107 total yards.

September 11: 2–0
Oregon 48, Tennessee 13

The Ducks scored 45 unanswered points—including 35 in the second half—to blow out the Volunteers in front of 102,035 fans at Neyland Stadium in Knoxville. LaMichael James, after sitting out Oregon's opener, rushed for 134 yards and sparked the Ducks in the second half with a 72-yard highlight-reel scoring run to break what was a 13–13 tie at halftime. Cliff Harris also scored on a 76-yard interception return and Kenjon Barner scored on an 80-yard punt return.

September 18: 3–0
Oregon 69, Portland State 0

The visiting Vikings, a Football Championship Subdivision team, were no match for the Ducks. LaMichael James rushed 66 yards for a touchdown barely one minute into the game, and Oregon finished with 528 yards on the ground, including 227 from James. It was the second shutout for the defense, marking the first time Oregon had two shutouts in one season since 1964.

September 25: 4–0
Oregon 42, Arizona State 31
On a night when the offense wasn't clicking—only 385 yards—the defense recorded seven turnovers to prevent the Sun Devils from pulling an upset in Tempe despite their 597 yards of offense. Trailing 24–14 late in the second quarter, the Ducks finally got rolling with Darron Thomas throwing for one touchdown and rushing for another in the final 2:21 of the first half to lead 28–24 at the break. Two more quick scores in the third quarter made it 42–24, and ASU couldn't keep up.

October 2: 5–0
Oregon 52, Stanford 31
In a top-10 matchup featuring No. 9 Stanford vs. No. 4 Oregon at Autzen Stadium on national television, the Ducks rallied from a 21–3 first-quarter deficit to pin a blowout loss on the Cardinal. LaMichael James rushed for 257 yards and three touchdowns, Darron Thomas rushed for 117 and threw for 238 and three TDs, and Oregon outscored Stanford 28–0 in the second half after trailing 31–24 at halftime.

October 9: 6–0
Oregon 43, Washington State 23
The third-ranked Ducks got off to a slow start against the Cougars on a cold day in Pullman, and lost quarterback Darron Thomas and running back Kenjon Barner to injuries during the game. But trailing 14–8 in the first quarter, LaMichael James put Oregon up with an 84-yard touchdown catch-and-run, Cliff Harris added to the lead with a 67-yard punt return to make it 22–14, and backup quarterback Nate Costa led three scoring drives.

October 21: 7–0
Oregon 60, UCLA 13
The Ducks entered the Thursday night home game ranked No. 1 in the nation for the first time in school history—and proceeded to live up to those lofty heights with a beatdown of the Bruins. The Ducks led 32–3 at halftime and didn't give up a touchdown until there was 1:53 left in the game.

October 30: 8–0
Oregon 53, USC 32
The 24th-ranked Trojans appeared to have figured out how to keep up with the Ducks by the time they took a 32–29 lead at the Coliseum in Los Angeles early in the third quarter. Then Oregon followed with 24 unanswered points to post another blowout win. LaMichael James rushed for 239 yards and Darron Thomas threw for four touchdowns.

November 6: 9–0
Oregon 53, Washington 16
Despite being shut out in the first quarter for the first time all season, the Ducks still scored more than 50 points for the third straight game, scoring four unanswered touchdowns in the final 18 minutes of the game to pad their lead. A then-record Autzen Stadium crowd of 60,017 was on hand to see LaMichael James rush for three touchdowns and Kenjon Barner play for the first time since suffering a concussion against Washington State.

November 13: 10–0
Oregon 15, California 13
For the first time all season, the Ducks were challenged by an opponent. The Golden Bears held the offense to just one touchdown and a season-low 317 yards, though Cliff Harris helped with a 64-yard punt return for a touchdown, and the defense held Cal to

just 193 yards. Oregon secured the win with an 18-play, 65-yard drive that ate up the final nine and a half minutes of the game.

November 26: 11–0
Oregon 48, Arizona 29
In their final home game of the season, the top-ranked Ducks trailed the No. 20 Wildcats 19–14 at halftime (only their second time trailing at the half all season) before outscoring Arizona 34–10 in the second half to win big. Josh Huff put the Ducks up for good with an 85-yard run on their first possession of the second half and Darron Thomas threw for three touchdowns and rushed for a fourth.

December 4: 12–0
Oregon 37, Oregon State 20
The Ducks, still ranked No. 1, went into Corvallis for the Civil War needing one last win to secure a spot in the BCS National Championship Game. They delivered. LaMichael James rushed for 138 yards and two touchdowns, Kenjon Barner rushed for 133 yards and also scored twice, and the Oregon defense had four interceptions as the Ducks wrapped up its first undefeated regular season.

53 2000 Holiday Bowl

Based on the eyeball test, Oregon had no hope.

At the time of the 2000 Holiday Bowl, the Ducks were still a team on the rise, recognized as a solid contender year in and year out in what was then the Pac-10 Conference, but yet to have crashed the party of elite national powers. In their bowl game after the 2000 season, the Ducks would face just the sort of program they hoped to become: Texas.

What ensued was one of the most thrilling postseason games in school history, a statement victory for the Oregon football program and a memorable night for Joey Harrington.

"It wasn't just any game," defensive lineman Saul Patu recalled of his final appearance with the UO football team. "We were playing Texas, who has a good tradition, and everyone was predicting that we'd get beat. We'd seen those guys [the week of the game], and they had this walk to them, like, 'Man, this is going to be a walk in the park.'...We felt like we had something to prove to the world—that we were here in Eugene, Oregon, we're the Ducks, and we're not a slouch."

Half the battle for Harrington was shaking off his performance in Oregon's regular-season finale. The junior quarterback had thrown five interceptions and lost a fumble in Oregon's Civil War loss, which denied Harrington his dream of a Rose Bowl appearance, and sent hated rival Oregon State off to the Bowl Championship Series.

But there was still much to play for. A win over the Longhorns would give Oregon 10 wins in the regular season for the first time ever, and serve as a stepping stone to a 2001 campaign in which the Ducks returned most of their key parts and figured to have what was then a rare shot at entering the national championship picture.

With all of that on the table—the high stakes, the chance to make a statement, the opportunity for redemption—Harrington seized the moment. He enjoyed a historic night the likes of which has seldom been seen in college football's annals.

The Ducks started with a bang. If there was a Civil War hangover, it had long before lifted. Harrington threw a short touchdown pass to his friend and tight end Justin Peelle as Oregon took an early lead. And then, later in the quarter, came one of the more memorable highlights in UO history, still to this day.

With the Ducks at Texas' 18-yard line, sophomore wide receiver Keenan Howry lined up split to the left, then motioned all the way into the backfield. Harrington pitched the ball to Howry, who ran to his right while Harrington bootlegged out to the left, against the pursuit of the Texas defense. Howry lofted a pass that Harrington caught at the 10-yard line before stumbling his way toward the goal line and then falling into the end zone.

He had failed in the effort to keep his balance, but had succeeded in giving the Ducks a 14–0 lead in the first quarter over the mighty Longhorns. "That was a heck of a catch, let's be honest," Harrington said later, tongue somewhat in cheek. "Slow that thing down on video, you'll see that it was fingertips. There was some hand-eye coordination there. But in terms of foot-eye coordination, I needed to work on that."

Texas was not about to get blown out, and stormed back with three touchdowns in the second quarter for a 21–14 halftime lead. But the Ducks tied it early in the third quarter on a 55-yard touchdown reception by Maurice Morris, and reclaimed the lead when Harrington completed the touchdown trifecta by running for a nine-yard score early in the fourth quarter.

Harrington had become the third player in Holiday Bowl history to score rushing, receiving, and passing touchdowns in the same game. The feat wouldn't be repeated at Oregon until 2012, when redshirt freshman Marcus Mariota did it against Arizona State.

"Overall," Harrington said, "that was the perfect way to remedy—as much as you could—what had happened against Oregon State."

Texas answered Harrington's rushing touchdown by returning the ensuing kickoff to tie the game 28–28 with 9:25 left. But that was the only breakdown by Oregon in the second half, as the Ducks went on to a 35–30 win after conceding a late safety to the Longhorns.

A victory with massive implications at the time, Oregon's upset of Texas was surpassed in the ensuing decade, when Bowl Championship Series appearances became the norm and wins against traditional powers such as Michigan, Oklahoma, and Tennessee became commonplace.

But Harrington's triumphant night lives on in Oregon lore, thanks in large part to that stumbling touchdown on a pass from Howry. "You look at all the guys on that Texas team, and at every position they had first-round NFL Draft picks," Howry said. "But we went out as a team and really stuck it to them."

54 1994: Ducks Sack Troy

Weeks before Kenny Wheaton's transcendent interception against Washington propelled the Ducks to their first Rose Bowl in 37 years, Oregon established itself as an unlikely Pac-10 title contender with the most improbable victory of its program-changing season.

With their starting quarterback, starting tailback, and top cornerback sidelined with injuries, the Ducks went to Los Angeles and manhandled the mighty USC Trojans in the 1994 conference opener.

The 22–7 victory was Oregon's first win at the L.A. Memorial Coliseum since 1971.

The Ducks improved to just a 3–2 regular-season record with the win, but they showed they had the heart, talent, and depth to make a run at the Pac-10 title.

Quarterback Tony Graziani was the star of the day, throwing for 287 yards and a touchdown against the Trojans.

Graziani was forced into the role of starter the previous Monday when Danny O'Neil had to have surgery for a staph infection on the ring finger of his passing hand.

Graziani—who struggled against Portland State during a relief appearance in the season opener a month earlier, rushing for –21 yards and throwing for just 58—showed no nerves against the No. 19 Trojans.

On Oregon's first drive, Graziani, a 6'3", 210-pound sophomore from nearby Newport Beach, California, completed 3-of-5 passes for 43 yards to set up the first of Matt Belden's three field goals on the day for a 3–0 lead.

Up 10–7 midway through the second quarter, Graziani connected with receiver Cristin McLemore on a 19-yard touchdown strike and the Ducks took a 16–7 lead into halftime.

"I expected Tony to play well but I was a little amazed at and admired how well he played," coach Rich Brooks said. "He isn't bothered by too much. He's a loosey-goosey kid and it didn't bother him at all to come in here and play Southern Cal. He is obviously a leader."

He wasn't alone. Senior reserve running back Dino Philyaw filled in for starter Ricky Whittle, who was out with a hamstring injury, and rushed for a career-high 123 yards, including a spectacular 49-yard touchdown run in the first quarter that put Oregon up 10–0 and really set the tone for the upset.

"I always felt like the 1994 USC game was the moment when that season turned [around]," said Philyaw, a second-year junior college transfer from North Carolina. "Nobody gave us a chance whatsoever. That was the turning point. When we went down there and beat them with the young guys stepping up, getting their first real shot, it changed everything. USC doesn't give anybody respect, they thought it was just a stat game, [Trojans receiver] Keyshawn Johnson told me that in the tunnel, 'It's a stat game.' I never forgot that, I responded, 'Yeah it will be, *for me.*' I wasn't afraid of USC.

I hadn't grown up watching them. I saw [North Carolina] and [North Carolina State] as a kid. I wasn't being disrespectful, but USC's history didn't mean anything to me. I'm from the South. It doesn't make any difference to me."

Graziani and Philyaw were handling their business on offense, and the defense was keeping USC out of the end zone, even without All-American cornerback Herman O'Berry, out with a knee injury.

The Trojans' only score came on a seven-yard pass from Rob Johnson to Keyshawn Johnson near the end of the first quarter.

In the end, Oregon outgained USC 478 to 347 in overall offense and the Ducks held the Trojans to a net of 31 yards rushing, aided by nine quarterback sacks for a loss of 60 yards.

"I'm very proud of these young men," Brooks said. "This team rallied around Tony Graziani, and Tony did a good job of keeping his poise and holding a young offensive team together out there."

55 Black Mamba Arrives

The *Sports Illustrated* cover story declared him THE FASTEST MAN IN FOOTBALL, and two years into his Oregon career, De'Anthony Thomas had provided plenty of fodder to back up that assertion.

Just ask Wisconsin. Or Kansas State. Or anybody in the Pac-12 Conference. In two seasons with the Ducks, Thomas had already solidified his place among the program's most electric superstars ever. "I'd like to take credit for coaching him," Oregon head coach Chip Kelly said after Thomas' three-touchdown performance in the 2012 season opener against Arkansas State. "But we just line him up and let that kid go."

"The Fastest Man in Football," DeAnthony Thomas does his thing against Kansas State in the 2013 Tostitos Fiesta Bowl, returning the opening kickoff for a touchdown.

Despite his youth, the Ducks lined Thomas up in all sorts of ways when he joined the team. He was a backup running back as a freshman in 2011, but also the team's second-leading receiver, out of the slot, earning Pac-12 co-Offensive Freshman of the Year honors. Thomas was also the All-Conference kickoff return man, a freshman All-American, and the Ducks' co-MVP.

All that production earned Thomas some preseason Heisman buzz entering the 2012 season, although teammates Kenjon Barner and Marcus Mariota eventually grabbed more prominent spots in the race. Though Thomas did quite well, averaging 7.6 yards per carry and scoring 11 touchdowns on 92 rushes, leading the Ducks with 45 receptions, and serving as the primary kickoff and punt returner most of the season. No surprise that, entering the 2013 season, the Heisman Trophy buzz was audible again.

But more than his statistics, Thomas is defined by his highlights. His value isn't so much in the accumulation of his contributions over the course of a game, or a season, but rather in his ability to change the momentum of a game with one single touch. He had just two rushes in the Rose Bowl as a true freshman, but scored two touchdowns against Wisconsin, of 91 and 64 yards. He set the tone for the Ducks' Fiesta Bowl win over Kansas State a year later by returning the opening kickoff 94 yards for a touchdown, the longest play of any kind in Oregon's postseason history.

Later in the quarter he made it two straight BCS bowl appearances with two touchdowns.

Just by signing with Oregon, Thomas had provided the Ducks with a major victory before he ever stepped on campus. The Los Angeles native was a five-star prospect and a high school All-American, considered a future star whether he played running back, wide receiver, or cornerback. His hometown USC Trojans were considered the favorite to nab the prospect—until he stunned the college football recruiting world by attending his signing-day press conference in Ducks gear. "Oregon is in it to win it and it's where I knew I wanted to be," Thomas said in announcing his decision.

He wasted little time in making an impact, scoring in his collegiate debut, a 2011 season-opening showdown with LSU in Dallas. He scored three touchdowns against Cal, and then had 262 yards against Washington State, with a 93-yard kickoff return for a score and a swing pass that he turned into a 45-yard touchdown by zig-zagging down the field and nearly corkscrewing a hapless Cougars defender into the turf.

By his sophomore year, Thomas saw his opportunities to return kicks greatly reduced, as opponents chose to pooch kickoffs instead. Better to surrender good field position to Oregon's explosive offense, they figured, than risk Thomas taking one to the house—a lose-lose situation if ever there was one. Overall, Thomas' numbers dipped a bit as a sophomore; his average rush, reception, and return yards all diminished from the year before.

But what never changed was his potential to make a highlight-reel play every time he touched the ball, as both Wisconsin and Kansas State memorably found out in bowl games, setting the stage for Thomas' Heisman Trophy campaign in 2013.

56 Howry's Return in the Rain

Oregon's 2001 season ended with a victory in the Fiesta Bowl against Colorado and what was then a program-best 11–1 record.

But it wasn't an easy ride. The Ducks won five games that season by a touchdown or less, and four by a field goal or less.

Those close games all featured at least one game-changing play that at the time seemed as if it would be remembered as the best play of the season.

Such was the case with Keenan Howry's punt return for a touchdown against Oregon State in a 17–14 Civil War victory to end the regular season.

After a crushing loss to Stanford midway through the season derailed the Ducks' chances to play for a national championship, Oregon absolutely had to beat the Beavers on the first day of December to secure a spot in a BCS bowl game.

It was a cold, rainy, windy late afternoon at Autzen Stadium and the Ducks trailed 6–3 early in the fourth quarter when Howry saved the Ducks' season with his 70-yard return, giving his team a lead it wouldn't relinquish.

Howry fielded a short (37 yards), low kick from Oregon State punter Carl Tobey at the Oregon 30-yard line and ran straight up the middle of the field. After picking up a key block from senior walk-on linebacker Ty Tomlin on OSU long-snapper Noah Happe, Howry was free and clear the rest of the return.

"It was a line-drive kick and all I had to do was get to the hole," Howry said. "When I broke through, I could hear the crowd, and I looked at the [video board] to make sure no one would catch me. That play right there, it doesn't get any bigger than that. What a tremendous feeling."

The score gave the Ducks a 10–6 lead with 14:36 left to play, ignited the home crowd, and gave Oregon all the momentum it needed to finish off the Beavers and secure its first outright Pac-10 championship.

"Oregon State was controlling the game, but we were all thinking just one big play could turn it around," Howry said. "I was lucky it turned out to be a punt return. It's special any time you do something to help your team win a championship. Those don't come along too often."

Thanks to some stellar blocking, Howry didn't have to do much other than catch the punt and run through a huge hole.

"You talk about everybody doing a great job," said Robin Ross, Oregon's special teams coordinator at the time. "I'll use this for clinics. It's a perfectly blocked play."

The key block was made by Tomlin, who took out Happe, a 6'5", 231-pound linebacker.

"My goal was to knock him off the ball [after the snap] and push him back," Tomlin said. "But he's a pretty big guy, so he actually kind of threw me out of the way. When he threw me, I thought, *Uh-oh, now I have to go get him.*

"I knew that if I got to the right spot, Keenan would play off it, and that's what happened. Right when he [Happe] turned, I was able to knock the crap out of him."

Oregon State fans have long disputed the block as being illegal, and it did initially look to be a block in the back. But Ross and

Tomlin both challenged that claim because the block propelled Happe forward.

Either way, no flag was thrown and Howry cut through the rain and into the end zone.

"I was looking at the fans and trying to take it all in," Tomlin said. "I thought, *It's over now*. It was one of my better moments in college football. It's a good way to go out: home game, last game, to make a play like that."

57 George Shaw and Ducks in the Draft

Despite all the success Oregon football has experienced in recent decades, the Ducks are far from a pipeline to the NFL Draft. Of the four schools ever to make four straight BCS bowls, Oregon's draft history pales next to those of USC, Miami (Florida), and Ohio State.

The selection of Dion Jordan and Kyle Long in the first round in 2013 gave Oregon 14 all-time first-round selections. But Oregon can boast one relatively rare distinction: A player who was taken No. 1 overall.

In 1955, the Baltimore Colts made George Shaw of Oregon the very first pick in the NFL Draft. After Shaw, the Ducks to go the earliest were Jordan and quarterbacks Akili Smith, in 1999, and Joey Harrington, in 2002—all third overall. Shaw, Smith, and Harrington all experienced the same frustrations at the professional level.

A native of Portland, Shaw became Oregon's next star after the graduation of Norm Van Brocklin in 1948. Shaw became the first man to lead the Ducks in passing three straight years, setting a school record with 1,358 yards in 1954.

Oregon's First-Round Draft Picks

Name	Position	Year	Pick	Team
George Shaw	QB	1955	1	Baltimore Colts
Jim Smith	DB	1968	12	Washington Redskins
Ahmad Rashad	WR	1972	4	St. Louis Cardinals
Tom Drougas	T	1972	22	Baltimore Colts
Russ Francis	TE	1975	16	New England Patriots
Mario Clark	DB	1976	18	Buffalo Bills
Chris Miller	QB	1987	13	Atlanta Falcons
Alex Molden	DB	1996	11	New Orleans Saints
Akili Smith	QB	1999	3	Cincinnati Bengals
Joey Harrington	QB	2002	3	Detroit Lions
Haloti Ngata	DT	2006	12	Baltimore Ravens
Jonathan Stewart	RB	2008	13	Carolina Panthers
Dion Jordan	OLB	2013	3	Miami Dolphins
Kyle Long	OL	2013	20	Chicago Bears

His versatility was unparalleled. Entering 2013, Shaw still held school records with 13 interceptions as a defender in the 1951 season, and 18 for his career. He also kicked off, punted, handled place kicks, and was a punt returner.

Shaw was also Oregon's first two-sport All-American, in both football and baseball. "Baseball was more fun for me," he said, "but I was better at football." And even though the New York Yankees offered him a $10,000 signing bonus out of college, Shaw opted to sign with the Colts after they selected him first overall in 1955.

So began a career in which Shaw was repeatedly overshadowed at every stop he made. He started with the Colts initially, but suffered a broken kneecap and was replaced by one Johnny Unitas. Though just a rookie in 1956, Unitas took quarterbacking duties over for good.

"I developed second-stringitis," Shaw said. "I began to doubt myself. When you sit on the bench game after game, you start to lose interest. Johnny's the same age I am, and I knew if I stayed with the Colts, I'd spend my life on the bench."

Shaw requested a trade, and it was granted in 1958, to the New York Giants. There, he sat behind Charlie Conerly. His last NFL stop was in Minnesota, where Fran Tarkenton was the starter. In 71 NFL appearances, Shaw completed 405-of-802 passes for 5,829 yards and 41 touchdowns.

Shaw remained Oregon's only first-round pick until 1968, when Jim Smith went 12th overall to the Washington Redskins. The Ducks had two players selected in the first round in just one draft prior to 2013, 1972, when Ahmad Rashad went fourth to St. Louis and tackle Tom Drougas was taken with the 22nd pick by Baltimore.

That 1972 class featured six Ducks—though the draft lasted 17 rounds then. There were also players from Oregon selected in 1976—two in the 17th round.

In the modern era, with the draft cut down to fewer than 10 rounds, Oregon had six players selected in both 2002 and 2009. Harrington topped the 2002 group, joined by running back Maurice Morris, cornerback Rashad Bauman, tight end Justin Peelle, linebacker Wesly Mallard, and cornerback Steve Smith.

Oregon's 2009 class included defensive backs Patrick Chung and Jairus Byrd and center Max Unger—all future Pro Bowl players taken in the second round—as well as linemen Fenuki Tupou, Ra'Shon Harris, and Nick Reed.

58 From the PCC to the Pac-12

The Pac-12 Conference has been building its reputation as the most dominant force in college athletics for nearly a century. From its early days as the Pacific Coast Conference to its latest incarnation, the conference has always been a national power, winning 453 NCAA team titles—the most of any conference—through the end of the 2012 calendar year and living up to its nickname as the "Conference of Champions."

On December 2, 1915, during a meeting at the Imperial Hotel in downtown Portland, Oregon, the roots of the Pac-12 were first laid when representatives from the University of Oregon, Oregon Agricultural College (now Oregon State), the University of Washington, and the University of California formed the PCC.

Play began in 1916, and over the following decades the conference has evolved, changed names, added schools, subtracted schools, and extended its national reach through several expansions and now its own television network.

Along the way, Oregon has been a steadfast member, with the exception of one brief stretch during the 1960s.

Two years after that meeting in Portland, the conference added Washington State, then Stanford in 1918, USC and Idaho in 1922, Montana in 1924, and finally UCLA in 1928 to make it a 10-team conference.

That's where things stood for 26 years—with the six schools from the Pacific Northwest competing in one division and the four California schools in the other.

But Montana left in 1950, and the PCC stayed at nine teams until it disbanded in 1959 following pay-for-play scandals at Cal, USC, UCLA, and Washington.

Oregon went its own way at that point and didn't have any conference affiliation from 1959 to 1963.

That changed in 1964, when Oregon and Oregon State were added to the Athletic Association of Western Universities (AAWU), joining Cal, Stanford, USC, UCLA, Washington, and Washington State.

Pac-12 Championship Game

The conference expanded in 2011 to become the Pac-12, and along with it came the conference championship game for football.

On December 2, 2011, Oregon, champions of the North Division, played UCLA, the representative from the South, for the conference title and an automatic Rose Bowl berth.

The game was held at Autzen Stadium, though the Pac-12 did everything it could to make it look like a neutral field, even replacing stadium announcer Don Essig.

However, it didn't look much different once the Ducks took the field. LaMichael James, in his final home game, rushed for 219 yards and three touchdowns to lead Oregon to a 49–31 victory. Darron Thomas, also in his last home game, threw for 219 yards and three touchdowns as the Ducks improved to 11–2.

With the addition of the two Oregon schools, the AAWU officially changed its name to the Pacific-8 Conference in 1968.

The Pac-8 had only one bowl affiliation during its first eight years, not that it mattered to the Ducks, who had just one winning season in the early days of the conference, when they went 6–4–1 in 1970.

The conference expanded inland in the late 1970s when it poached Arizona and Arizona State from the Western Athletic Conference to form the Pac-10 in 1978.

Oregon won its first Pac-10 title in football in 1994 and another in 2001, 2009, and 2010. The Ducks also shared the title in 2000 with Washington and Oregon State.

Then in 2011, under the guidance of commissioner Larry Scott, the conference took its boldest step to date, bringing in Utah and Colorado to form the Pac-12 and announcing it would create the Pac-12 Network, a 24-hour, seven-day-a-week television network that would focus entirely on the conference, ensuring that every football game including a Pac-12 team would be televised.

With the expansion came two football divisions. The North consists of Oregon, Oregon State, Washington, Washington State, Cal, and Stanford. The South is USC, UCLA, the two Arizona schools and the two newest members—Utah and Colorado.

Road Trip!

Life on the West Coast makes following the Ducks on the road a bit more challenging than it is in other parts of the country. The distance between Eugene and the 11 other Pac-12 cities can be daunting. Yet between the warm climates of Arizona, the natural beauty in Colorado and Utah, or a weekend spent in Seattle, Los Angeles, or the Bay Area, a Pac-12 road trip is well worth the hassle.

Arizona

Arizona Stadium (Tucson, Arizona)

Capacity: 51,811

Miles from Autzen Stadium: 1,342.5

Why you should go: This has arguably become the most hostile environment for Oregon in recent years. Who can forget the "ZonaZoo" student section storming the field prematurely in 2009, a game Oregon won in overtime. Half the seats offer a sweeping view of the nearby Santa Catalina Mountains, as well as the campus and city skyline. The pregame buildup leading up to most home games can be spent enjoying a tailgate or Fan Fiesta, then taking seats for a desert sunset behind the west facade of the stadium before welcoming the cooler evenings.

Arizona State

Sun Devil Stadium (Tempe, Arizona)
Capacity: 71,706
Miles from Autzen Stadium: 1,238
Why you should go: There could be a worse way to spend a hot desert night than by taking in a game at Sun Devil Stadium before hitting the equally happening Mill Avenue District a few blocks away for drinking and dining afterward. The stadium, which has hosted a Super Bowl and was once the home of the NFL's Arizona Cardinals, definitely has a pro feel to it. Built between a pair of buttes, the stadium is deep and high. Be prepared for a climb in getting to your seats.

California

Memorial Stadium (Berkeley, California)
Capacity: 63,186
Miles from Autzen Stadium: 521.7
Why you should go: Whether you get a seat in Memorial Stadium or attempt to take in the view for free from "Tightwad Hill," game day in Strawberry Canyon is always worth the trip. The venue reopened in 2012 after a $321 million seismic retrofit and renovation. For those who don't know, the stadium—modeled after the Roman Colosseum—was built directly over the Hayward Fault. With a nod to its history, the renovation kept intact the two big cracks at the top of the bleacher wall where the fault has shifted concrete over time.

Colorado

Folsom Field (Boulder, Colorado)
Capacity: 53,613
Miles from Autzen Stadium: 1,263.8
Why you should go: The view of the Flatirons is breathtaking from inside the stadium, which sits more than a mile above sea level.

Boulder is also a fantastic college town near Denver with ample nightlife offerings. And did we mention they have a real buffalo named Ralphie who runs across the field before first- and second-half kickoffs? It's an awesome sight.

Oregon State

Reser Stadium (Corvallis, Oregon)

Capacity: 45,674

Miles from Autzen Stadium: 43.2

Why you should go: To fully experience a true rivalry, you must venture into enemy territory every once in a while. You might be surprised by what you find. Reser is one of the few on-campus stadiums in the Pac-12 so there is a very collegiate feel to the game-day experience there that you don't get at, say, massive Sun Devil Stadium. Not to mention, it's not such a bad place to watch a game since being renovated in 2005—and you're only an hour from home if you live in Eugene.

Southern California

Los Angeles Memorial Coliseum (Los Angeles, California)

Capacity: 93,607

Miles from Autzen Stadium: 862.8

Why you should go: All the tradition and pageantry that makes college football so unique exists at USC. It starts with the trumpet call as the marching band takes the field while playing "Conquest." Then there's Traveler, the mascot horse who trots around the field with a Trojan warrior on his back after USC touchdowns. The stadium is located in Exposition Park, a 160-acre site that also includes the Memorial Sports Arena, Natural History Museum, California Science Center, Exposition Park Rose Garden, California African American Museum, and the Expo Center.

Stanford

Stanford Stadium (Stanford, California)

Capacity: 50,000

Miles from Autzen Stadium: 563.3

Why you should go: To bolster the visitors' cheering section. The 2005 renovation transformed Stanford Stadium into a smaller but more beautiful venue. Too bad it's so lifeless once inside. Opposing teams' fans can definitely make their presence felt here. And given Oregon's history against the Cardinal, the Ducks could always use the help when down on the Farm.

UCLA

Rose Bowl (Pasadena, California)

Capacity: 91,936

Miles from Autzen Stadium: 858.4

Why you should go: First, because it's the Rose Bowl. Of course, it's a completely different experience for a UCLA home game than it is for the Granddaddy of Them All, the stadium far from full and the atmosphere not as electric. But the San Gabriel Mountains still make a phenomenal backdrop and it's still Southern California, so chances are great of catching a game on a sunny day when it's gray and raining back in Eugene. Tailgating on the golf course is must-do, as is a walk around the outside of one of the most historic venues in college football.

Utah

Rice-Eccles Stadium (Salt Lake City, Utah)

Capacity: 45,017

Miles from Autzen Stadium: 783.3

Why should you go: This has been a challenging place for opposing teams to play since its $50 million remodel in 1998, though through 2012, the Ducks had yet to visit for a conference game. The stadium is regularly above capacity on game days and the home crowd has a reputation for being very loud. If any atmosphere in the Pac-12 resembles Autzen Stadium, this is it. The stadium also served as the site of the opening and closing ceremonies for the 2002 Winter Olympics. The Olympic cauldron remains just outside the stadium gates.

Washington
Husky Stadium (Seattle, Washington)
Capacity: 70,000
Miles from Autzen Stadium: 287
Why you should go: To taunt a Husky, of course. The Ducks haven't lost at Husky Stadium—or at home—since 2003. This once bitter rivalry has turned one-sided. And with the Husky Stadium renovation complete for the 2013 season, it's time to schedule a trip to Seattle. Husky Stadium has always been an awesome place to attend a game. It has great tailgating opportunities, great views of Lake Washington, and now closer views of the field with the removal of its track.

Washington State
Martin Stadium (Pullman, Washington)
Capacity: 33,522
Miles from Autzen Stadium: 464
Why you should go: The smallest venue in the Pac-12 can also be pretty lively when conditions are right. There is something about the long trip to the Palouse that makes wins slightly more elusive, no matter how good the Cougars are in any given season. Between 2000 and 2012, the Ducks were 7–2 in their nine trips to Pullman, but six of those games were decided by an average of 6.3 points.

60 Transfer RBs Keep Program Rolling

From Tony Cherry in 1985 to Kenjon Barner in 2012, the Ducks have fielded an NFL-caliber running back—or two—in nearly each season.

That list includes players such as the incomparable LaMichael James and Jonathan Stewart, who both made tremendous impacts as freshmen on their way to rewriting the Oregon record book, as well as players like Barner, Derek Loville, and Jeremiah Johnson, whose career totals were built over four years of significant contributions.

It also includes a large number of two-year transfers, starting with Dino Philyaw in 1993 and ending in 2010 with LeGarrette Blount.

However, for one seven-season stretch, four different transfers helped transform the Ducks from a team that missed a bowl game in 1996 to Fiesta Bowl champions in 2001.

They were:

Saladin McCullough

Career: 1996–97

Bio: Transferred from El Camino (California) Junior College in 1996 after a sophomore season that included 1,829 all-purpose yards.

Lasting legacy: In 1997 he became the first Oregon player since Bobby Moore in 1971 to lead the Pac-10 in rushing, with 1,193 yards. It was just the sixth 1,000-yard season for an Oregon rusher.

Memorable moment: In his final game, McCullough rushed for 150 yards on 17 carries in a 41–13 win against Air Force in the 1997 Las Vegas Bowl. His 76-yard touchdown run put the Ducks up 13–0 barely two minutes into the game.

Reuben Droughns

Career: 1998–99

Bio: An Oregon recruit out of Anaheim (California) High School, Droughns instead went to Merced Junior College where he rushed for more than 1,600 yards as a sophomore. He was considered the No. 1 JC running back in the nation when he recommitted to the Ducks.

Lasting legacy: When his career ended, Droughns held five of the Ducks' top-11 single-game rushing performances off all time, and four of the Ducks' 10 200-yard rushing games. He finished his career with 2,058 yards and 18 touchdowns in just 16 games.

Memorable moment: He rushed for 202 yards in his debut against Michigan State at Autzen Stadium and averaged 164.8 yards in his first five games as a junior before a broken fibula ended his season.

Maurice Morris

Career: 2000–01

Bio: The South Carolina native and transfer from Fresno City College picked Oregon over USC in a heated head-to-head battle. Morris set the junior college career rushing record with 3,708 yards in 20 games.

Lasting legacy: Morris became the first Oregon player to rush for 1,000 yards in back-to-back seasons. He had 1,188 in 2000 and 1,049 in 2001. The Ducks went 21–3 with two bowl wins in Morris' two seasons. At the time, his career total of 2,237 yards was fifth-best all time.

Memorable moment: A spectacular 49-yard touchdown run against Colorado in the 2002 Fiesta Bowl. Morris got to the edge, raced down the sidelines, and appeared to be tackled at the Colorado 21. But he went down on top of linebacker Joey Johnson, bounced up without hitting the ground, and sprinted into the end zone to give the Ducks a 28–7 lead.

Reuben Droughns is among the running back standouts who found success at Oregon as a transfer.

Onterrio Smith

Career: 2001–02

Bio: The Sacramento prep phenom played one year at Tennessee before being dismissed and transferring to Oregon, where he redshirted in 2000.

Lasting legacy: Rushed for 1,058 yards and seven touchdowns in 2001, when he and Maurice Morris (1,049) became the first duo in Oregon history to each run for 1,000 yards in the same season. Finished his career with 2,199 yards and 19 touchdowns and was just the second Oregon player to have two 1,000-yard seasons. He left after his junior year for the NFL Draft.

Memorable moment: As a sophomore, Smith set the then-single-game rushing record with 285 yards against Washington State, and had seven straight 100-yard games to open the 2002 season before being derailed by an injury.

Before McCullough arrived in 1996, the Ducks had just five 1,000-yard single-season rushers in their history. Following Smith's final season, they had 11. During that seven-year stretch, Oregon played in six bowl games, winning four, and won a Pac-10 championship.

61 Keeping It in the Family

On the day Chip Kelly was promoted to head coach of the Oregon football team in the spring of 2009, he was asked how the Ducks might be different under his leadership.

Kelly was sitting beside the man he was replacing, Mike Bellotti, who, like Kelly, had once been Oregon's offensive coordinator before becoming head coach. Now, Bellotti was moving into the athletic director's chair, allowing the Ducks to keep the highly sought-after Kelly in Eugene.

Kelly, always quick with a quip, thought for a second about differences between himself and Bellotti. "I talk faster than Mike," Kelly offered. Later, he provided a more serious response. "I just went from being in the passenger seat to driving the car, but nothing else is going to change," Kelly said.

In truth, there were numerous noticeable differences between Bellotti and Kelly. But the Ducks' desire to keep Kelly in the fold continued the tradition of promoting top assistants to the head coaching job that began decades earlier and continued after Kelly's departure.

When Mark Helfrich was promoted to succeed Kelly in 2013, he was the third straight Oregon head coach to have been promoted from offensive coordinator. And he was the sixth head coach of the Ducks' last seven to have worked in Eugene as an assistant before ascending to head coach.

The exception to that trend was Rich Brooks, the former Oregon State player who took over the Ducks in 1977 and left in 1995 after leading the Ducks to the Rose Bowl. He was replaced by Bellotti, who had been Oregon's offensive coordinator during the previous six seasons, coaching a pro-style offense unafraid to attack downfield.

Bellotti transitioned the Ducks to a spread offense under new coordinator Gary Crowton in 2005. Crowton left after two years and was replaced by Kelly, who became recognized as one of the scheme's true virtuosos. Kelly became a hot commodity on the national coaching scene almost immediately. The Ducks considered him for a promotion after his first year in Eugene, when Bellotti was considering a jump to UCLA. And when Syracuse came calling for Kelly's services a year later, the athletic department executed the transition plan it had put in place in order to keep Kelly in Eugene, moving Bellotti to AD and Kelly up to head coach.

One of Kelly's first—and only—hires was Helfrich, as offensive coordinator and quarterbacks coach in 2009. Helfrich spent four years in that job, and similarly impressed his bosses early on; when Kelly considered jumping to the NFL in 2012, Helfrich was the pick to replace him. Once Kelly ultimately left a year later, Helfrich became the third Oregon coach promoted from the offensive coordinator's office.

Like Kelly, he used his sense of humor to respond to questions about how the program might change under his leadership. "I won't wear a visor," Helfrich said in reference to Kelly's signature headwear. "I'll eat more vegetables," he joked.

But the offensive coordinator promotions weren't a new phenomenon. Rather, they continued a recent tradition that had only been broken with Brooks' hiring.

Legendary head coach Len Casanova retired after the 1966 season, and was replaced by Jerry Frei, who had been an Oregon assistant dating all the way back to 1955. Dick Enright joined Frei's staff in 1970, then replaced him as head coach in 1972. And Don Read was an assistant for both of Enright's years as head coach before replacing him in the top job in 1974.

To be sure, some of those earlier promotions yielded minimal success, considering the program struggled to find consistency in the 1970s. But after Brooks won 45.6 percent of his games from 1977 to 1994, things took a dramatic upswing. Bellotti won 67.8 percent from 1995 to 2008, and Kelly won 86.8 percent from 2009 to 12.

No pressure, Coach Helfrich.

62 Mickey Bruce Turns Down Bribes

In 1960 Len Casanova took his Oregon team halfway across the country in late September for a game against mighty Michigan.

No sooner had the Ducks' plane landed in Ann Arbor than one of the most bizarre chapters in program history began, complete with bribery and corruption charges, senate hearings, and the face-to-face fingering of a notorious gangster by an Oregon player.

Mickey Bruce was a pre-law student from San Diego and a decent two-way player for the Ducks, lining up as both a halfback and defensive back. His career was cut short by a shoulder injury his senior season in 1961, but as a junior, he led the Ducks with six interceptions, which also ranked fifth in the nation.

Off the plane in Ann Arbor, Bruce was approached in the airport by a man named David Budin, a 27-year-old schoolteacher from Brooklyn who claimed to have a mutual friend in former Oregon basketball player Jim Grenadi.

Budin asked for tickets to the football game and Bruce sold him a pair of $6 tickets for $50 (apparently not an NCAA violation in 1960).

Later that night at the team hotel, Budin approached Bruce again, this time with two professional gamblers who offered Bruce $5,000 to help ensure the Wolverines won by at least eight points. Michigan was a six-point favorite.

The gamblers also told Bruce they would pay him $100 per week for the rest of the season if he'd phone them in Miami Beach each Monday and give them injury reports on the Oregon team. They then offered Bruce a $5,000 bonus if he could bring Oregon quarterback Dave Grosz into the arrangement, for which Grosz would also receive $5,000.

Bruce told the gamblers he would meet them back at their hotel on the morning of the Michigan game to finalize plans. He then immediately went and told Casanova and Oregon athletic director Leo Harris about the meeting. Harris contacted the FBI, while Casanova met with the team to see if anyone else had been approached.

Michigan state police accompanied Bruce to the gamblers' hotel room the next day, but the pair was already gone. Police did arrest Budin, though he later paid a $100 fine and was released.

Bruce played as usual against Michigan that afternoon and even had an interception, but the Ducks still lost 21–0. Casanova later said the episode shook the team's focus, and they played miserably.

The episode didn't end there.

In September 1961, Bruce was summoned to Washington D.C., to testify before a senate committee investigating gambling in college sports. Bruce, then just 20 years old, told the committee about his experience in Michigan and then literally pointed to a man sitting to his left, identifying him as one of the gamblers who attempted to bribe him a year earlier.

The man: Frank Rosenthal, a notorious gangster credited with creating the sports-book industry in Las Vegas. He was famously portrayed (though the character's name was changed) by actor Robert De Niro in the 1995 Martin Scorsese movie *Casino*.

Rosenthal pled the Fifth Amendment.

And still the episode wasn't over.

Two months later the Ducks were headed to Ohio State for a game in Columbus. But the Wayne County, Michigan, district attorney's office wanted Bruce to come up to Detroit at that time and file an official complaint about the 1960 incident so they could go ahead with a prosecution. Bruce, who was injured and not planning on making the trip, refused.

"As far as I'm concerned, this thing should have been dead a month after it occurred," Bruce said. "Instead, I have been plagued with this thing for more than a year."

Despite the urgings of Casanova and Harris to change his mind, Bruce held his ground and the matter was finally over.

Bruce went on to have a long career as a lawyer in San Diego. He died of cancer on March 27, 2011.

In 1981, Mickey Bruce received the Leo Harris Award, presented to an Oregon letterman who has been out of college for 20 years and who has demonstrated continued service and leadership to the university. Other Harris winners include Bill Dellinger, Dan Fouts, Tinker Hatfield, Alberto Salazar, Dave Wilcox, Ahmad Rashad, and John Robinson.

63 Kenny Wheaton: More Than the Pick

He will forever be remembered for the Pick, and while Kenny Wheaton's interception against Washington was no doubt the most memorable moment of his career at Oregon, it was far from the only highlight in the cornerback's distinguished career with the Ducks.

In three years playing in Eugene, from 1994 to 1996, Wheaton earned All-Pac-10 honors three times, and a second-team All-America distinction twice. He led the Ducks in interceptions all three seasons, led the conference as a sophomore, and became the first Oregon player ever to pass up his senior season and enter the NFL Draft.

Wheaton demonstrated a flair for the dramatic. His 97-yard interception return to seal a program-changing win over the Huskies in 1994 was only one example.

Earlier that season, as a redshirt freshman, Wheaton had a memorable debut. Stung by Oregon's decision to redshirt him, and

Sure, he made the Pick, but Kenny Wheaton was also a dominating tackler too.

the departure of the coach who had recruited him, Denny Schuler, Wheaton had considered transferring in the 1994 off-season, but his patience finally paid off in Oregon's win at USC on October 1 of that year.

To this day, Wheaton considers it the best game he ever played—which included a handful of tackles and also a miraculous interception of USC quarterback Rob Johnson. "The best play I ever made," Wheaton has called it, after the nickel back broke on a pass to a slot receiver and somehow came up with possession.

The upset of the Trojans provided both a signature moment in the Ducks' drive to the Rose Bowl and also some much-needed validation for Wheaton—that he could indeed be the impact player he thought himself to be, even if he hadn't been given the chance to show it up until then.

It was three weeks later that the Ducks hosted Washington and came away with a 31–20 win, capped by Wheaton's interception return. The Huskies were on the doorstep of a game-winning touchdown when Wheaton jumped an out route, avoided two would-be tacklers at midfield, and cemented his place in UO football lore. "It is a little weird being identified so closely by just one play," he said. "I love it, but at the same time it took me years to understand that the true Oregon fans understand that Kenny Wheaton had done more than make that one play."

Indeed, Wheaton was far from finished making big plays for the Ducks. He had five interceptions as a sophomore in 1995 to lead the Pac-10 conference. Playing alongside future NFL standout Alex Molden, Wheaton blossomed as a full-time starter. Perhaps his most memorable play of that year was a 71-yard interception return for a touchdown against Pacific, when he sensed something was up on a short-yardage play, broke across the field to provide double coverage on Molden's man, and picked off a pass. "Instincts told me there was no way they were trying to run the ball," Wheaton said. "They were going to try and get a big play." Instead, he turned the tables.

For Wheaton, the 1996 season was frustrating on numerous fronts. Oregon went just 6–5 and missed the postseason, which was particularly frustrating after playing in the Rose Bowl and Cotton Bowl his first two years. The Ducks struggled on defense, with their third coordinator in Wheaton's three years, and had an unsettling lack of continuity. And Wheaton by then had a reputation as a defensive back not to be tested, thus he rarely got a chance to add to his interceptions total since quarterbacks looked the other way. With nine through two seasons, Wheaton entered his junior year on track to tie the school record with 18 for his career; instead, he intercepted just two passes as a junior.

At that point, with the chance to turn pro and give back to two hardworking parents, Wheaton bid good-bye to Eugene. He was selected in the third round of the NFL Draft by the Dallas Cowboys, and played three years in the league before going on to a highly successful career in Canada. "Did my professional career turn out the way I would have liked it to?" he asked. "No, by no means. But I have no regrets." He'd accomplished plenty at Oregon, and much more than just a single play known forever more as the Pick.

64 Pat Kilkenny

Plenty of donors at plenty of schools have given plenty of money to the teams they love. Few have given as much of themselves as Pat Kilkenny.

Prior to February 2007, Kilkenny was an enthusiastic former Oregon student who had turned a small insurance firm into a billion-dollar business—and in turn donated an estimated $6 million to the Ducks. But in early 2007, Kilkenny began to devote much more than money to Oregon. He became the school's athletic director, during a critical era in UO football history.

It was on Kilkenny's watch that Chip Kelly was identified as Mike Bellotti's eventual successor as head football coach. And it was on Kilkenny's watch that a formal succession plan was put in place, while Oregon's explosiveness on offense had suitors lining up to interview Kelly about jobs elsewhere.

Kilkenny, by then deeply involved with the Ducks' financial bottom line but still at heart one of the program's biggest fans, wasn't about to lose his man. "I just think the guy is a moon shot," he said. "And it's not because he's just a brilliant offensive guy. He's this leading-edge thinker who has this football toughness. And that doesn't come in the same package very often. Most of those 'mad scientists' aren't tough."

Raised in the eastern Oregon town of Heppner, Kilkenny attended the University of Oregon in the early 1970s, but left before graduating. He bought a small insurance firm, Arrowhead General, and eventually built it into a giant in the industry; it now does more than $1 billion in business per year.

Kilkenny eventually developed into one of the Ducks' most devoted donors, and forged a friendship with megadonor Phil Knight that later served him well. He held a seat on the board of the university's fund-raising foundation. On Kilkenny's wedding day, he and his new bride attended an Oregon football game.

Among the endeavors Kilkenny helped fund was a buyout of athletic director Bill Moos' contract. Efforts to replace aging McArthur Court with a new basketball arena had stalled under Moos, and a change was initiated.

Where did university administration turn to manage a department with a quickly expanding budget? To Kilkenny himself. "This is a great place," he said upon being hired. "I'm one of the luckiest people in the world to have this job."

At times during the next two years, he might not have felt the same way. One of Kilkenny's earliest major ventures was to reinstate Oregon's baseball program, in the process cutting wrestling and ushering in a new women's program, competitive cheerleading. Wrestling fans were heartbroken, and the addition of cheerleading was met with derision in some circles, but Kilkenny weathered the storm. "He could be on a beach taking it easy," men's basketball coach Ernie Kent said after Kilkenny's first year on the job. "But here he is, in the trenches with us."

To house the new baseball team, Kilkenny made a major donation to the $15 million project, which was ultimately dubbed PK Park—his initials, and also those of Knight. Under Kilkenny's watch the department made a major investment in its baseball coach, George Horton, and the baseball team quickly became nationally competitive. A similarly dramatic change atop the women's basketball program, when Kilkenny hired his friend, former NBA coach Paul Westhead, did not work out as well.

But if Kilkenny's top priority was to see the new basketball arena through to completion, then he was a success. He helped secure a $100 million donation from Knight that was used to backstop the department so it could borrow money to fund construction of what became Matthew Knight Arena.

When Kilkenny finally stepped down in the summer of 2009, replaced by Bellotti, the department's budget had exploded under his watch. The new coffers reflected the money the football team was suddenly generating, but also the investment necessary to sustain that success in football, which funded pretty much everything else at Oregon. An economic downturn had struck the country during his tenure, too, and the Ducks were still pinching pennies to avoid turning a loss in any given year.

When he departed, though, Kilkenny returned to the job he most loved: attending Oregon sporting events. One of the team's biggest fans, he just happened to have unique insight into the inner workings of the athletic department during two years in its biggest office.

65 Fright Night

It was Halloween night 2009, the USC Trojans were in town, ESPN's *College GameDay* was in town, and the game was scheduled for a national broadcast.

Simply put, there was no bigger game in the country that day.

And as the *Register-Guard* wrote, first-year Oregon coach Chip Kelly took it all in stride."

"How did Kelly react to circumstances that might have been a pressure cooker for some? He rose before dawn Saturday, went to the *GameDay* set, secretly donned the head of Oregon's Duck mascot for the cameras, then removed it for the cameras to reveal his identity, sending the crowd into spasms of joy.

"Facing the biggest test of his young coaching career, Kelly couldn't have appeared more relaxed. And 12 hours later, the nation saw why."

On a night when an Autzen Stadium–record crowd of 59,592 eschewed trick-or-treating to watch No. 10 Oregon and No. 3 USC face off, the Ducks handed out the finest treat of all: a 47–20 thumping of the Trojans.

The loss was USC's worst under coach Pete Carroll, whose teams had won seven straight Pac-10 championships and a national title.

Meanwhile, the Ducks improved to 7–1 overall and 5–0 in conference play, and stayed on track for their first Rose Bowl appearance in 15 years.

Standing Room Only

Autzen Stadium's official capacity is just 54,000, but there have been plenty of times during the Ducks' 89-game home sellout streak (active through 2012) when attendance far exceeded what Autzen could actually hold. Standing-room-only tickets have become a tradition at Autzen, allowing spectators to cram into the bleacher seats or watch from along the upper rim of the stadium. Here are the top 10 Autzen Stadium attendance records:

	Opponent	Attendance	Date
1.	Arizona State	60,055	October 15, 2011
2.	Washington	60,017	November 6, 2010
3.	Arizona	59,990	November 26, 2010
4.	USC	59,933	November 19, 2011
5.	Stanford	59,818	October 2, 2010
6.	Oregon State	59,802	November 26, 2011
7.	Oregon State	59,597	December 3, 2009
8.	USC	59,592	October 31, 2009
9.	Arizona State	59,379	November 3, 2007
10.	UCLA	59,376	December 2, 2011

"To beat USC, it's tremendous, just because of the type of reputation that their football program has and the kind of coach that [Carroll] is," Kelly said.

Oregon fans came to the game decked out in special black "Fright Night" T-shirts with a duck-and-crossbones motif. After the win they stormed the field and hoisted quarterback Jeremiah Masoli into the air.

"My ears are still ringing," Kelly said. "There is no place like this in college football. Our crowd definitely answered tonight."

It was certainly a scary night for the USC defense.

Oregon redshirt freshman LaMichael James had the best game of his young career with 183 yards, and Masoli also ran for 164 yards and threw for 222 yards.

And they did it against a USC defense that had consistently been among the best in the country under Carroll. The Ducks recorded season highs of 613 yards of total offense and 391 rushing yards.

"We got run out of here," said Carroll, whose defense came into the game as the fifth-best nationally against the run, allowing opponents an average of just 79.9-yards per game.

Oregon's 47 points were its most ever against the Trojans, and the most USC ever allowed under Carroll, surpassing the 42 by Fresno State in 2005. The Trojans had also not lost a game by more than a touchdown since their 27–16 loss to Notre Dame in 2001.

The blowout was slow to develop, with wide receiver Jamere Holland snaring a 17-yard pass from Masoli with 1:49 left in the second quarter that gave the Ducks a 24–17 lead at halftime.

The two teams traded field goals early in the third quarter to keep it a one-touchdown lead for Oregon.

Then the Ducks blew the game open, scoring the final 20 points on touchdown runs by James and Kenjon Barner, and two field goals by Morgan Flint.

"After halftime, after we kept rolling in the third quarter, you could see it in their faces," Masoli said. "They weren't really talking as much, weren't communicating as much on defense. And on offense, that's when you can tell you kind of have the game."

The Oregon defense also tightened in the second half, coming one field goal away from a shutout. The Trojans amassed just 134 yards and seven first downs in the second half.

Said USC freshman quarterback Matt Barkley, "I never thought this could happen."

66 Kevin Willhite: The First Five-Star

Long before the significantly hyped Jonathan Stewart and Haloti Ngata became Ducks, and well before the more recent signing-day coups of five-star phenoms De'Anthony Thomas and Arik Armstead, there was Kevin Willhite, a prep All-American running back from Sacramento who shocked the college football world when he committed to Oregon in 1982.

Willhite was widely considered the nation's top recruit at the time, a can't-miss prospect with blazing speed and a solid pedigree (his older brother Gerald Willhite had been a star at San Jose State and was a first-round draft pick of the NFL's Denver Broncos).

During his prep career at Rancho Cordova High, Willhite rushed for 4,901 yards and 72 touchdowns. As a senior he was named the national high school player of the year over, among others, running back legends Bo Jackson and Marcus Dupree.

He came to Oregon with so much hype, coach Rich Brooks tried to temper fans' enthusiasm and expectations from the start.

"We're not expecting miracles from him," Brooks said on signing day. "He's a good, young back but how he does and when he does it is up to him…. Certainly he's the most highly recruited and touted player we've ever signed."

But even as Brooks preached patience, the Oregon fan base was electrified by the signing of Willhite, who most thought was going to be the savior for a Ducks team coming off a dismal two-win season. At the first meeting of the Oregon Club in Portland after signing day, 250 boosters packed a location set up for 75.

Landing Willhite was such a significant moment that the *Register-Guard* named his signing as the No. 2 sports story of the year for 1982.

Instead, Willhite's story became just another cautionary tale about the overhyping of a recruit and the unfair expectations put on a player who has yet to put on a college uniform.

Willhite's recruiting story had some odd twists, as he was committed to Washington heading into signing day but let Oregon coaches know he wasn't completely sold on being a Husky. Willhite was also an elite sprinter, and the idea of playing football and also running track for the Ducks appealed to him greatly.

So on the morning of signing day in 1982, Oregon assistant Jim Skipper and Washington assistant Al Roberts sat in Willhite's living room and waited for him to emerge from the bathroom. When he did, he was wearing an Oregon hat.

But it would be two years before he ever played for Oregon. After tearing his hamstring in a high school track meet as a senior, Willhite redshirted his first year in Eugene—much to the fans' chagrin.

Willhite made his Oregon debut in 1983 and fumbled on the first carry of his career. His first season was marred by minor injuries and questions about his toughness and work ethic.

He opened the 1984 season as the fourth-string tailback and it was junior college transfer Tony Cherry getting all the attention and carries. Willhite's weight had ballooned from 190 to 216, and he eventually started getting plays at fullback.

That's where he started as a senior in 1986, and in his final game against Oregon State, he rushed for 66 yards and blocked for Derek Loville and Latin Berry.

"Kevin's gone through some difficult times, both personally and physically," Brooks said after Willhite's career ended. "If he hadn't had that 'greatness' label coming in… there have been a lot of guys with the greatness label who didn't turn out so great. He was overrated coming out of high school. Kevin's done the best job that he can do. If he'd come out of high school without the label, people would probably think he'd become a pretty good fullback for our team. Which he has."

In his four seasons, Willhite carried the ball just 182 times for 731 yards and two touchdowns.

"I was a pretty good player who left Sacramento and learned there are other people who are just as good," Willhite said during an interview in his senior season. "Sometimes a setback will help you grow up.... I should have been a millionaire by now, but I'm not."

67 Musgrave's Magic

During Bill Musgrave's junior season in 1989, the Ducks were like the mythical phoenix, a once-proud program rising from the ashes of two decades' worth of mediocrity to return to the postseason. From defeat, Oregon found the will to win. That spirit would serve the Ducks well again in 1990.

For all the joy the 1989 Independence Bowl season produced, Oregon entered the off-season still stinging after a missed opportunity at Brigham Young that November. The Ducks were up 33–16 at one point in the third quarter, but Ty Detmer drove BYU the length of the field in the final two minutes to cap a wild 45–41 Oregon loss in which Detmer and Musgrave set an NCAA record with 959 combined passing yards.

A rematch was scheduled for 1990 in Eugene, and the Ducks vowed to be ready. "In the five years I went through spring ball at Oregon, I don't recall us ever game-planning for a specific team until 1990," All-Conference defensive end Peter Brantley said. "In spring ball we worked on the BYU game plan, fall camp we worked on the BYU game plan. We wanted revenge bad."

The 1990 season began for Oregon with wins over San Diego State and Idaho. But then the Ducks lost their Pac-10 opener,

22–17 at Arizona. Musgrave was stopped just short of the goal line while trying to scramble for the game-winning touchdown, but he was hampered by an ankle injury he'd suffered in practice the night before.

Thus, entering the game on September 29, 1990, when No. 4 Brigham Young came to Autzen Stadium with Detmer putting together what would become a Heisman Trophy season, the Ducks were frothing at the mouth. And the Cougars paid the price.

After the 32–16 win, Musgrave became Oregon's career passing leader, surpassing his predecessor, Chris Miller. Detmer, meanwhile, was sacked five times, and threw five interceptions. "The defensive line just dominated them all day," said Ducks defensive back Daryle Smith, who picked off three passes. "They had to throw a lot, but it worked in our favor because our secondary was really up for the task."

Losing to a Western Athletic Conference team in 1989 hadn't gone over well with the Ducks. They got their revenge. "It was probably the most satisfying win we had during my time there," Brantley said. "Everybody was just getting back to campus and classes starting, so it was really cool to start off the school year avenging a loss we felt like we really shouldn't have had."

At the time, there was no doubt it would be the most memorable win for Oregon in 1990. Then, UCLA came to town on November 3. The Ducks were 6–2, marching their way back to the postseason, and the Bruins were enduring a .500 year. But in the fourth quarter, Tommy Maddox had UCLA up 24–13.

Musgrave was playing his final game at Autzen Stadium, where he was 18–1 entering the matchup, and he wouldn't go down without a fight. He had the Ducks driving toward the UCLA goal line when he threw a fourth-down pass that fell short of receiver Anthony Jones. Flags flew—defensive back Dion Lambert was penalized for pass interference. "He was playing bump-and-run and a bump threw me off balance," Jones said. "I wasn't sure it was pass interference, but the referee threw the flag."

The penalty advanced the ball 11 yards, and fullback Juan Shedrick scored from the 2-yard line. The Ducks tacked on a two-point conversion, and then trailed by a field goal, 24–21.

Maddox threw for 332 yards and three touchdowns on the day, with two interceptions, but the Bruins got conservative when trying to milk their lead. It backfired, and UCLA went three-and-out. Musgrave, who had thrown for just 224 yards with a touchdown and an interception, had his opening.

A 24-yard punt return by Brian Brown got the Ducks into UCLA territory. A screen pass to Sean Burwell brought the ball to the 17-yard line. And then, on third-and-9 from the 16, Musgrave found tight end Vince Ferry for the go-ahead touchdown. "Vince went down into the corner by the cheerleaders and caught a ball right in the cover-two honey hole," Musgrave said. "He just made a fantastic catch. And I wasn't the best pure thrower, but that ball came out of my hand pretty clean. It kind of frozen-roped there in the air. It looked like a Chris Miller pass to me: The ball didn't have a lot of arc to it, but it was clean, and it got from A to B in a hurry."

UCLA still had two minutes left. But a sack and three incompletions followed, and the Ducks had one of their more memorable comebacks in Autzen Stadium history—and their first-ever victory over the Bruins in the stadium, which opened in 1967.

The phoenix had risen, indeed.

68 Go to *College GameDay*

"If my wife and kids are watching, pack your bags. We're moving to Eugene, Oregon.... This is heaven."
—ESPN *College GameDay* analyst Kirk Herbstreit,
September 29, 2007

Rankings and bowl games aside, nothing announces your team's relevance on the national scene like hosting a visit from ESPN's *College Football GameDay*.

The weekly live show, which films on location at the best matchup or most important game of each week, puts your team, your campus, and your game in the national spotlight for two straight days.

Between 2007 and 2012, no school had more visits from the ESPN traveling road show than Oregon, which hosted *College GameDay* six times during that time period.

"[On] other places that are regular stops on the tour there is a concern about complacency," *GameDay* anchor Chris Fowler said after taping a show in Eugene in 2010. "Are they going to get pumped up? Is the student body going to feel that the attraction has worn off?

"We did not have to worry about that in Eugene. The fact that people showed up so early, hours and hours before the show was very flattering, and it really says more about their passion for their team and this program and their school than just seeing people do a TV show. I think it's reflective of the spirit here."

Oregon was part of *College GameDay*'s first live broadcast from the West Coast when the show made the trip to Los Angeles for the Ducks' game against UCLA on October 17, 1998.

The second time *College GameDay* came west was for another game between the Ducks and Bruins, this time at Autzen Stadium on September 23, 2000.

As of the 2012 season, Oregon had hosted *College GameDay* seven times—the ninth-most of any school and the second-most for a Pac-12 school. (USC has hosted nine times.)

Counting away games and bowl games, *College GameDay* has been present at an Oregon game 15 times.

The show didn't return to Eugene until 2007, for No. 11 Oregon's game against No. 6 Cal. Both teams were 4–0, and three weeks earlier the Ducks had opened eyes when it dismantled Michigan 39–7 in the Big House in a nationally televised matchup.

The enthusiasm of Oregon's fans blew away the ESPN crew.

"By the time [host] Lee Corso made his much-anticipated prediction Saturday morning, Oregon fans already had established Eugene as one of the favorite stops for ESPN's *College GameDay* crew," wrote the *Register-Guard.* "At 8:59 AM, Corso, the popular over-the-top TV analyst, picked up a hidden Duck mascot head and pulled it over his head, echoing the prediction he made seven years ago in the pregame show's only previous visit to Eugene.

"The crowd of about 6,000 roared. Even on a dark and damp morning, the energy was contagious.

Analyst Kirk Herbstreit's "heavenly" assessment must have been a prevailing opinion, because the show was back in Eugene just five weeks later when the fourth-ranked Ducks took on Arizona State.

It was a rare repeat performance for the show, which typically films in a different city each week.

"It's a great scene for Oregon football right here," Corso said after the show. "And that's a great compliment to the Oregon football fans, the fact that they have passion for their team and they come back out there."

Still, there were concerns of overkill, Fowler admitted, and it didn't look good on Friday, when he didn't sense much excitement around Eugene. That all changed when he arrived for a production meeting at 5:00 AM on Saturday.

"There was already a big crowd, and you could see the big line of headlights going back in the dark and it really gave us a great feeling," Fowler said. "It was kind of a surreal scene. You walk out and it's dark and foggy and you can see the Day-Glo yellow stuff sticking out, and at the end, Autzen is back there through the fog. We got a lot of comments from people the first time we were here about how great the backdrop and the crowd was. It definitely comes through on TV, and it's not the same everywhere we go."

After skipping Oregon in 2008, the show returned to Eugene for one game in each of the next four seasons.

69 Gary Zimmerman

While the era of the 1970s and early '80s was a lean time for Oregon football, it didn't lack for a few big-name players. None was more marquee than Gary Zimmerman.

Until Zimmerman's senior year with the Ducks, there were few signs that head coach Rich Brooks and his assistants were developing a future Pro Football Hall of Famer. Zimmerman wanted to play defense in college, and did so for one year, as a junior. But he blossomed as a senior on the O-line, and was named the Pac-10 Conference's top offensive lineman before going on to a 12-year NFL career with the Minnesota Vikings and Denver Broncos that featured seven Pro Bowls, a Super Bowl title in 1998, and election to the Pro Football Hall of Fame in 2008.

"He had enough aggressiveness for the defensive side of the ball, but he understood how to block people, and he was a big,

Shown here at his induction ceremony among the Class of 2008, Gary Zimmerman is one of six former Oregon players enshrined in the Pro Football Hall of Fame.

strong guy," said Michael Gray, an Oregon defensive lineman in 1981–82 and later an assistant coach with the Ducks. "To this day, when I talk to guys about switching sides of the ball and they fight it, I tell them about Gary Zimmerman and how a lot of times [staying put] works out for the best."

Zimmerman grew up in Los Angeles and actually dreamed of playing at Washington, but the Huskies didn't have a scholarship available for him. He did know one thing: He had no interest in sticking around the big city. "I was looking to get away from that scene," Zimmerman said. "Eugene definitely fit the bill there."

An offensive lineman and linebacker in high school, Zimmerman ultimately picked Oregon because the Ducks promised him a chance to start on defense. He later came to realize he lacked adequate foot speed to play linebacker in the Pac-10, but when Zimmerman first walked into the Oregon locker room and saw a high-numbered offensive lineman's jersey hanging in his designated stall, it didn't sit well with him. "They had pulled the old switcheroo on me," he said. "At first I was pretty upset. But I made the best of it, and it all worked out in the end."

Zimmerman made it onto the field as a freshman in 1980, playing some special teams and as a backup lineman. His real education came during the middle of the week, against one of the more unheralded defensive linemen in Oregon's history. "I learned a lot from playing against Vince Goldsmith in practice—mainly that you didn't want to be in his way," Zimmerman said. "He was crushing people. That was quite an eye-opener coming from high school."

As a sophomore, Zimmerman earned a few starting assignments. Then coaches approached him about that position change. He moved to defense as a junior, and "stunk it up," to use Zimmerman's words. "I must have stunk," he concluded, "because they moved me back to offense."

It was a good decision. Zimmerman developed into the conference's best blocker as a senior, though the Ducks struggled to a 4–6–1 record capped by the infamous Toilet Bowl. In all, Zimmerman enjoyed just one winning season at Oregon, his freshman fall of 1980, but he retained cherished memories of toiling with teammates in the weight room, relaxing with them at a local fishing hole, or going Dumpster diving for old shoes the athletic department threw out, in those days before players were lavished with all sorts of gear.

Though his career ended with that scoreless tie against the Beavers, Zimmerman takes particular pride in having never lost to rival Oregon State, having been a part of three wins in his first three years. "That's something that's gone by the wayside, because the guys now don't seem to take the rivalry as serious as we did," Zimmerman said. "Back then it was kind of like the Super Bowl for us." And Zimmerman would know that feeling, having gone on to play in one 15 years after leaving Oregon.

70 Onterrio Smith

The Ducks had plenty of comebacks during their program-changing 2001 season. But for the first and only time during that 11–1 campaign, No. 11 Oregon needed a bounce-back win when it went into Pullman, Washington, as underdogs for a game against No. 14 Washington State.

Oregon was coming off a potentially devastating loss at home to Stanford and desperately needed a victory to keep alive its chances to win the Pac-10 title and play in its first BCS bowl game.

The Ducks came through, beating the Cougars 24–17, but it took what was at the time the program's greatest single-game rushing effort—from a second-string transfer running back—to do so.

Onterrio Smith, a sophomore playing in his first season for the Ducks, rushed for 285 yards and three touchdowns, breaking the record of 249 yards set by Bobby Moore 30 years earlier. It was just the 11th 200-yard game in Oregon history.

Smith also had 342 all-purpose yards to break the record of 338 held by both Moore and receiver Keenan Howry, Smith's teammate at the time.

Smith didn't get the first of his 26 carries until five minutes into the second quarter, but he quickly made up for lost time, rushing for 27 yards on his first carry of the game during the Ducks' second possession of the quarter.

He finished the drive with five carries for 47 yards, including a memorable eight-yard touchdown run on which he flattened a Washington State defender at the 4-yard line before plowing into the end zone to put Oregon up 7–3.

Smith went into halftime with only 56 yards, but set the tone for a spectacular second half with a 41-yard touchdown on the opening drive of the third quarter. He made it a two-touchdown lead for the Ducks when he went 73 yards untouched late in the fourth quarter to put Oregon up 24–10.

He finished with 229 yards in the second half, 151 of them in the fourth quarter.

It was a performance for the ages for Smith, who transferred to Oregon after being dismissed from Tennessee after his freshman season. Smith redshirted in 2000 and was averaging only 10.8 carries and 70.8 yards through the first seven games of 2001 as the primary backup to Maurice Morris.

Smith had shown glimpses of his abilities weeks earlier when he had 131 yards and two touchdowns in a win against Arizona. But when the Ducks needed a breakout performance from Smith, in a game Oregon had to win, he delivered.

"Onterrio Smith got no easy yards Saturday," wrote *Register-Guard* sports columnist Ron Bellamy. "Not one of those 26 carries wasn't important. Not one of those 285 yards didn't matter. He got them in one of the hardest-fought Oregon victories in a recent history that has included some thrillers. He got them when the Ducks needed every first down and touchdown. He got them when he had to be exhausted and when the football was slick with rain, and when the Cougars were trying, in vain, to rip it away from him.

"He got them by spinning, by struggling, by darting. He ran over people. He ran away from them. He was tougher to tackle than a truck.... And when it was over...you were left to wonder which run had been the most spectacular."

Washington State's defense came into the game ranked No. 1 in the Pac-10 against the run, allowing just 93.1 yards per game, and the Cougars had surrendered just 652 yards in their previous seven games.

But that didn't stop the Ducks from trying to attack them on the ground. Instead of relying on their passing game led by Heisman Trophy–candidate quarterback Joey Harrington, the Ducks went straight at the Cougars' strength.

Morris led the way early, rushing for 76 yards in the first quarter alone. He would finish with 138 yards on 19 carries before leaving in the third quarter with an injured hamstring.

In the end, the Ducks had racked up 446 rushing yards, breaking the previous school record of 403 set in 1960 against California.

71 Grooming Future Head Coaches

Oregon has a long tradition of promoting assistant coaches into the head job, from Jerry Frei, Dick Enright, and Don Read to Mike Bellotti, Chip Kelly, and Mark Helfrich.

But the Ducks have also been quite generous, too, in grooming assistant coaches to take over other programs. Frei's staffs produced a number of legendary head coaches, and Bellotti helped groom Jeff Tedford and Chris Petersen before they took over Cal and Boise State, respectively.

The most successful Oregon assistant who became a head coach elsewhere was one of the first, John McKay. At USC from 1960 to 1975, McKay won nine conference titles and four national championships. He then moved up to coach the NFL's Tampa Bay Buccaneers from 1976 to 1984.

McKay was 6–2 with the Trojans against Oregon—also his alma mater. McKay played alongside Norm Van Brocklin with the Ducks, and became a UO assistant after graduating.

He spent nine seasons under Jim Aiken and Len Casanova, working with the offense. "Coach McKay was one of those guys who might not pay a ton of attention to you, but you couldn't take that personally," said halfback Jim Shanley (1955–57). "And then when he did pull you aside and deal with you one-on-one, it just meant the world to you."

The final four years of McKay's tenure overlapped with Jerry Frei's early seasons as an assistant under Casanova, whom Frei would replace as head coach in 1967. Casanova also hired John Robinson, an end on Oregon's 1957 Rose Bowl team, who worked 12 seasons with the Ducks and was later a head coach with USC and the NFL's Los Angeles Rams.

Robinson was initially a freshman team coach at Oregon, and later assisted on offense with the varsity. "He was a great offensive coordinator, a great offensive mind," said Bob Newland, who blossomed into one of the most productive receivers in school history in Robinson's offense.

Robinson remained at Oregon through Frei's five years, which featured a remarkable staff of future coaching luminaries. Frei's initial staff included future San Francisco 49ers coach George Seifert, future Cal and Arizona State coach Bruce Snyder—another UO alum—and Robinson, and in 1969 Frei hired John Marshall, who would be a longtime college and NFL assistant.

Seifert and Marshall were initially on the freshman team's staff, where they mentored future star receivers Newland and Bobby Moore, now known as Ahmad Rashad. "He was tough, man, really tough—a great coach, but a tough guy," Rashad said of Seifert, his freshman team coach in 1968. "He was the toughest guy I think I'd ever seen at that point. Coming out of high school I'd never seen anything quite like that. I was fortunate to play for some great guys. I had great coaching influence at that time."

Fast-forward to the '80s, and the staff of Rick Brooks. It included offensive coordinator Bob Toledo, who would go on to serve as head coach at UCLA from 1996 to 2002.

"His ingenuity on offense, bringing in a new scheme—that's what Oregon needed, big-time," said Chris Miller, who had grown up in Eugene before quarterbacking Toledo's offense at Oregon from 1983 to 1986. "Bob came in and brought some excitement to it. We got some pro sets, three receivers and four receivers, stuff we hadn't seen around here as Oregon fans in quite a long time. We lost some games, but we were a lot of fun to watch on offense. He taught me a lot of football."

And more recently, Bellotti hired Chris Petersen to coach receivers when Bellotti was promoted in 1995. Petersen went on to become head coach at Boise State, where he built the nation's model mid-major program—and became a thorn in Oregon's side. From 1998 to 2001, Tedford was offensive coordinator and quarterbacks coach for the Ducks, tutoring Akili Smith and Joey Harrington before moving on to become head coach at Cal.

72 It's All Ducky

His push-ups have become legendary, his fight with the Houston Cougar was a YouTube sensation, and he's appeared in so many commercials for ESPN that he's got to be the first fake-fowl since the San Diego Chicken to have a SAG card.

No one has benefited from the recent success of the football team more than the Oregon Duck, a mascot borne out of a handshake agreement with Walt Disney himself in 1947, and resembling Disney's Donald Duck.

Yet, the path to mascot superstardom has been a long road for the Duck. Along the way, Oregon coaches questioned his toughness, the UO student newspaper wanted him gone, and the athletic department itself, in an ill-fated attempt, tried to partner the pudgy, feathered ham of a Duck with a streamlined, muscular, intimidating version of itself in 2002.

And yet, the Duck has fought off all challengers to become one of the most recognizable mascots in the nation.

In 2011, the Huffington Post College blog ranked the Duck No. 1 among all college mascots, and Fox Sports put him at No. 12. He also participated in the Capital One mascot contest in 2011 and 2012.

"There's something about the Duck that endears people to him," Matt Dyste, director of marketing and brand management for the university told *Oregon Quarterly* in 2012. "He's a little feisty, a little lovable. He crosses the spectrum."

But he wasn't the first mascot the school had, and he almost wasn't the last, either.

Oregon's teams were first known as the Webfoots, a nickname dating back to the 1890s that referred to a group of fishermen from Massachusetts who had been heroes during the American Revolutionary War. When their descendants settled in the Willamette Valley in the 19th century, the name came with them, and a naming contest in 1926 won by Oregonian sports editor L.H. Gregory made the Webfoots name official.

In a 1932 vote, the students affirmed the Ducks nickname over other suggestions such as Pioneers, Trappers, Lumberjacks, Wolves, and Yellow Jackets, and despite protests from the student newspaper.

"Why should a fighting football team, a brilliant basketball five, or other combinations be saddled with the name of a bird that is noteworthy only for its ability to shed water?" wrote *Oregon Daily Emerald* sports editor Harold Mangum during the naming debate. "It's like lining a runner's shoes with lead and expecting him to break records."

Oregon's first live mascot surfaced in the 1920s when "Puddles," a resident of the nearby Millrace, was escorted to football and basketball games by his fraternity-house neighbors, a common scene until the early 1940s.

The Duck made his first appearance at a football game in 1947, the same year Disney approved Oregon using Donald as a likeness.

Jerry Frei, Oregon's football coach from 1967 to 1971, didn't exactly appreciate the lovable version of the Duck, wishing instead for a more intimidating mascot, something with a little more bite to its beak. And basketball coach Dick Harter (1971–78) wouldn't even acknowledge the Duck, insisting instead that all promotional and public relations materials referred to his team and its players as the "Kamikaze Kids," a nickname the basketball Ducks earned through their frenetic, hardnosed playing style.

Then in 1978, the Duck endured another popularity contest when a cartoonist for the *Oregon Daily Emerald* wanted his creation, Mallard Drake, to replace the Donald Duck version as the school's mascot.

But in a vote by the students, Donald won by nearly a two-to-one margin—1,068 to 590—in an election that saw more than twice the typical voter turnout on campus.

In 2002, the Duck faced one last challenger to its throne: a futuristic, chiseled Duck with a menacing face, bulging muscles, and a penchant for backflips who earned the nickname "RoboDuck."

He was "born" at halftime of Oregon's game vs. USC on October 26 of that year, cracking out of a giant egg at midfield in a presentation complete with dramatic music and smoke machines.

Being sensitive to the growing passion the fans had for the Duck, Oregon was careful not to introduce RoboDuck as a new "mascot," instead calling him a new "duck character" intended to complement, not compete, with the current Duck.

He did neither. RoboDuck was never embraced in any capacity, and not long after he emerged from his shell, he was gone.

Unlike the Duck, who nearly seven decades later, still remains the beloved leader of Oregon's flock.

73 The Early Rose Bowls

When Oregon played in the 2010 Rose Bowl and then won the 2012 game in Pasadena, its two appearances in three years were unprecedented in school history.

But not by much.

Though the Ducks experienced a barren stretch during which they reached Pasadena just once from 1921 through 1993, Oregon actually played in two of the first six Rose Bowl games, and represented the West Coast in two straight games.

In 1917, the Ducks beat Pennsylvania 14–0. For the next two years, while World War I was raging, military squads played in the Rose Bowl. But in 1920, Oregon made a return trip, dropping a 7–6 heartbreaker to Harvard.

The 1917 game, played before 27,000 fans on New Year's Day in Pasadena, began inauspiciously for the Ducks. Midway through the second quarter, Penn had a kick blocked but managed to recover, and drove down to the 3-yard line using its powerful rushing attack.

Knocking on the doorstep of the end zone, Penn deviated from a series of runs between the tackles and tried a play to the outside. Oregon's Bricks Mitchell made a tackle for a 10-yard loss, Penn had to settle for a field-goal try that ended up no good, and the Ducks had the momentum.

The star of the game was Shy Huntington, who had three interceptions, the first of which came late in the third quarter. That gave the Ducks possession at their 30-yard line, and they moved the ball efficiently through the air and on the ground, scoring on a 15-yard touchdown pass from Huntington to R.L. Tegert.

Another Huntington interception set up the second score of the game. He picked off a pass near midfield, and Johnny Parsons followed with a 45-yard run to the 1-yard line. Huntington ran for the short touchdown, added his second extra point of the day, and it was 14–0, Oregon.

Huntington's third interception thwarted Penn's final drive of the day, and the Ducks had their first bowl victory. Despite Huntington's heroics, tackle and team captain John Beckett was named player of the game. More importantly, the East Coast was finally forced to concede that the boys out West could play a little football.

That was driven home three years later, when the Ducks made a return trip to Pasadena—this time with Huntington as head coach and his brother, Hollis, as the star player.

The Oregon-Harvard game was decided by defense and special teams; each had a dropkick, or field goal, blocked in the first quarter. The Ducks finally converted in the second, when Bill Steers connected on a kick from 25 yards out.

But the Crimson took the lead later in the period. Quarterback Billie Murray first returned a punt 25 yards before completing two passes to game MVP Eddie Casey to set up a 13-yard touchdown run by Fred Church. Skeet Manerud got the Ducks to 7–6 at half-time on a 30-yard kick.

The Ducks had another kick blocked in the third quarter, however, and both teams missed kicks in the fourth. Oregon's attempt was a 25-yard kick by Manerud; reports suggested the kick was so close, the scoreboard gave the Ducks three points and Harvard players were heading to the sideline in dejection before realizing the kick had been ruled no good.

Oregon lost despite getting 122 rushing yards from Hollis Huntington, who was playing in his third Rose Bowl, having participated with a military team in 1918.

74 The Last Losing Season

One reason the 1994 Rose Bowl season is so revered by Oregon fans is that it marks the start of an unprecedented run of success for a program not previously known for winning.

Prior to 1994, the Ducks had recorded just seven winning seasons in the previous 29 years dating back to 1965, a stretch that included 19 losing seasons.

However, beginning with the 1994 9–4 Pac-10 championship team, Oregon produced winning seasons every year through 2012 with one exception—2004.

And what a forgettable season that was.

It began with a stunning loss at home to Indiana and ended with a humiliating defeat in Corvallis by Oregon State for a final record of 5–6, snapping a run of seven straight bowl games.

In between those bookend losses were just a few highlights for a team that featured 12 players—including quarterbacks Kellen Clemens and Dennis Dixon—who went on to play in the NFL, a 1,000-yard rusher in Terrence Whitehead, and the Pac-10's third-best rush defense.

The season began on an incredibly somber note when prized linebacker recruit Terrance Kelly was murdered in his hometown of Richmond, California, in August, just days before he was to return to Eugene for the start of fall camp. Kelly had already spent most of the summer working out with his teammates, including five who played with Kelly at De La Salle High School.

"It's going to be very difficult to begin a season," coach Mike Bellotti said.

But at least the 24th-ranked Ducks had what appeared to be an easy start to the season, with a home opener against Indiana, which had won just two games in the previous season.

But the Ducks, despite statistically dominating the Hoosiers, couldn't get out of their own way. They turned the ball over seven times, committed nine penalties for 85 yards, and surrendered a kickoff return for a touchdown before eventually losing 30–24. It snapped a string of 21 consecutive nonconference wins at Autzen Stadium dating back to the 1994 season.

Oregon had 495 yards on offense to Indiana's 198 but still trailed 23–0 at halftime. The Ducks managed to get within six points with 8:38 to play—they just couldn't score again.

The next week, Oregon lost 31–7 on the road to Adrian Peterson and No. 2 Oklahoma, then returned home for a win against Idaho, and followed that with a loss at home to No. 21 Arizona State for a 1–3 start to the season.

Then the Ducks found some life, starting with a 41–38 win against Washington State in Pullman that included a 27-point fourth-quarter rally. Wins against Arizona, Stanford, and Washington followed, and suddenly Oregon was 5–3 with three games to go.

But they couldn't finish off their upset attempt against No. 4 Cal and quarterback Aaron Rodgers, losing 28–27 on the road. Then they dropped back to .500 with a surprising loss at home to shorthanded UCLA.

That left the Civil War, one last chance to get bowl eligible against a Beavers team who was also just 5–5 and looking for their own bowl berth.

Instead of seizing the moment, the Ducks crumbled, losing in a 50–21 rout. It remains the most points scored by Oregon State in the Civil War, as well as the largest margin of defeat in the annual game for the Ducks since 1942.

"This was a very frustrating season in a lot of ways, in a lot of respects," Bellotti said in the aftermath of the Civil War. "Sometimes when those happen, it's almost good to be over with [it], so you can say it's done, put in the can, [and say] 'Let's go. We can start the new season.' Having said that, I would have liked to have won this game and [gone] on, obviously."

The oddness of the 2004 season was magnified the following season when the Ducks finished the regular season 10–1 with essentially the same group of players.

75 Jerry Allen

When Jerry Allen was hired in the late '80s as Oregon's radio play-by-play voice, the Ducks' ninth in 15 years, job security obviously wasn't a trait of the position that made it so attractive.

But 25 years later, Allen was among the most prominent faces of Oregon athletics. Players and coaches had come and gone, administrators and other media personalities too, but Allen was still calling Oregon games, giving voice to some of the most memorable moments in Ducks football history.

Now 20 years after the fact, Allen's call of Kenny Wheaton's interception against Washington is still replayed just prior to kick-offs in Autzen Stadium. His exuberant cries that "Kenny Wheaton's gonna score! Kenny Wheaton's gonna score!" are as memorable as the play itself.

"You dream you're going to get a chance to make a call like that, and what you're going to say if you do," Allen said. "And then when it happens it all goes out the window and you lose control, which is exactly what I did. I became in every sense of the word a fan at that moment."

Some broadcasters prefer to play it down the middle; Allen made no secret of his allegiance. He grew increasingly closer to the athletic department over the years, serving as the emcee for official events and hosting an afternoon radio show devoted to Oregon sports.

"He loves the Ducks, he loves his job, he loves his community," said former UO quarterback Mike Jorgensen, Allen's partner for football broadcasts. "He pours his heart out for everything that happens, from daylight to dusk, when it comes to auctions, fund-raisers, everything. He's the Green and Yellow. He truly bleeds green and yellow."

That was never illustrated better than during the 2010 Civil War, when the Ducks finished off a perfect regular season by beating Oregon State in Corvallis and clinched a Bowl Championship Series berth. Allen couldn't hide the emotion in his voice as he called the final seconds: "And [Darron] Thomas takes the snap...and the field is rushed by players...and the fans want to come out but won't be able to, but they'll celebrate in the stands as the team heads down to the end zone. And fans everywhere...114 years they've waited... two...one.... It's official: Oregon is gonna be in the BCS National Championship Game! Can you believe the magical season this has become? And it's not over! And somewhere down in that humanity, a soaking-wet Chip Kelly is talking to the media about his team and what they've accomplished. Unbelievable to have been a part of this."

He reflected on the moment later. "As a professional broadcaster, I lost control, and you hate to do that," Allen said. "But that was just my genuine emotion."

"He is Oregon," said Joe Giansante, the television voice of UO athletics for several years before briefly serving as an administrator under athletic director Pat Kilkenny. "Whether it's a commercial or a Duck thing or his morning show, he has become Oregon.... Walking with him for a day, Jerry Allen is never not working for Oregon. Whether it's at the fair, or going to lunch, or at the grocery story, he's always working for Oregon, because he's so recognizable with the program.

"People need to understand what a toll that takes. That's tough, to have your job be your identity to hundreds of thousands of people, and yet he does it with such grace, and such humility, and he cares a lot about it."

To be sure, Allen is not without scrutiny in Eugene. Besides his outward enthusiasm for the Ducks, he can be overly critical of officiating, particularly when calling men's basketball games. And he often gets so caught up in describing action that he omits crucial details for long stretches, including the score and the time left in a game.

Some of it hits home, but Allen makes no apologies. "It's kind of like a family," Allen said. "I'm one of them. Sometimes I get a little too defensive. Sometimes I need to keep my mouth shut and let fans vent and say what they want to say, and not try to defend them.... You get to be very good friends with the coaches and even, in the short years they're here, the players. You have feelings for them. You care about them as people."

76 The Electric Samie Parker

It was only fitting that the most productive receiver in the history of Oregon football had his most productive day in his final game.

Samie Parker, a slick and speedy pass catcher from Southern California, capped his career with a record-setting performance in the 2003 Sun Bowl against Minnesota with 16 catches for 200 yards and two touchdowns in a 31–30 loss to the Golden Gophers.

With those totals, Parker not only set Sun Bowl records for catches and receiving yards, but he also set Oregon school records for receptions in a game, season, and career.

He also set the Oregon career record for receiving yards and moved into second place for single-season receiving yards.

"It was exciting I was able to do that," Parker told Eugene's *Register-Guard* after the game. "I just felt the flow of the game was coming to me, and I was making plays."

Parker's sixth catch of the first quarter tied Bob Newland's single-season record of 67 receptions. Parker eclipsed that mark

Receiving Records

Samie Parker remains the Oregon record-holder in game, season, and career receptions, as well as career receiving yards. But he now has some company in a couple of those categories. Jeff Maehl, a converted defensive back, ended his career after the 2010 season by joining Parker atop the record books with 178 receptions, including a record-tying 77 as a senior. Like Parker, Maehl capped a sensational senior season with a strong showing in a bowl game. Maehl caught nine passes for 133 yards in the BCS title game loss to Auburn, ending his year with 1,076 yards and 12 touchdown catches.

with his first catch of the second quarter and pushed his total to 77 by the end of the game.

He set Oregon's career record for receptions on the final play of the third quarter with his 174th career catch, and then in the fourth quarter Parker caught a 25-yarder that gave him 178 catches and 2,761 yards.

"Finally we got him healthy," Oregon quarterback Kellen Clemens said at the time. "He had fresh legs from Christmas, and he was out to prove a point today and he did. He was unbelievable. He was everywhere."

Parker had been slowed for much of the season by an ankle injury, and in October of that year his stepfather was shot to death in Long Beach, California.

But the senior still found a way to be productive with his 77 catches for 1,088 yards and seven touchdowns. He had four 100-yard receiving games during the season, capped by only the seventh 200-yard receiving game in Oregon history in the Sun Bowl, which also included touchdown receptions of 17 and 40 yards.

No one should have been surprised when Parker came up big in a bowl game for the Ducks. Throughout his career, Parker thrived in the postseason, beginning with his performance in the 2002 Fiesta Bowl victory against Colorado.

Samie Parker celebrates a touchdown catch on the road against the Bruins in October 2003.

In that game, Parker torched the Buffaloes with then-career highs of nine receptions for 162 yards.

"It was Samie's night," fellow Oregon receiver Keenan Howry said of the Fiesta Bowl. "He made big plays. He stepped up in a big game. He got open and made catches. Samie is a great receiver and not many people know it."

The secret was probably out early in the second quarter when Parker teamed up with quarterback Joey Harrington for one of the most pivotal plays of the game.

With the game tied 7–7, Harrington hit Parker in stride for a 79-yard scoring strike to give the Ducks a 14–7 lead. They led the rest of the way en route to a 38–16 win.

Parker, who doubled as a sprinter on the Oregon track-and-field team, was the fastest player on the team that season with a 4.36-second 40-yard dash. His speed was on display on his long touchdown play, as he blew past double coverage and had four yards of separation and no one in front of him when Harrington's pass landed in his hands.

That pass play was both the longest in Fiesta Bowl history and the longest ever allowed by Colorado.

The following season, Parker had four catches for 43 yards and a touchdown against Wake Forest in a 38–17 loss in the Seattle Bowl.

He ended his career with 29 catches for 405 yards and four touchdowns in three bowl games. Parker did play as a freshman in the 2000 Holiday Bowl, but he was injured rushing for seven yards on Oregon's very first play and missed the rest of the game.

Parker was drafted in the fourth round of the 2004 NFL Draft by the Kansas City Chiefs and played four seasons for them.

77 Hugo Bezdek and the Early Hall of Famers

When Chip Kelly left Oregon in 2013 having won 86.8 percent of the games he coached, he held a record for winning percentage by an Oregon coach who stayed at least three years on the job.

To find the previous record holder, one needs to go back nearly a century, to the tenure of Hugo Bezdek, the first of seven Ducks inducted into the College Football Hall of Fame and one of several key contributors to the early years of Oregon football history.

The Ducks played their first game in the spring of 1894, and for the next few decades played a schedule heavy on regional rivalries, such as Oregon Agricultural College (later Oregon State) and Willamette University, along with athletic clubs and even Native American tribes. Over the first 19 seasons of Oregon football, the Ducks had 16 coaches. One of those was Bezdek, who coached the team in 1906, left after a year, and then returned in 1913 for one of the most successful coaching runs in school history.

Bezdek was of Czech descent, and played at the University of Chicago under legendary coach Amos Alonzo Stagg, who recommended Bezdek for the Oregon job in 1906. The Ducks went 5–0–1 that season, allowing just 10 points, but Bezdek decided to go to medical school the following year.

That foray was short-lived, and Bezdek returned to coaching soon after, eventually landing back in Eugene in 1913. Three years later, he led the Ducks to one of the best seasons in their now-long history. Oregon was 7–0–1 in 1916, allowed 14 points in one game, three in another, and pitched shutouts in the other six, and went to the Rose Bowl. There, the Ducks beat Pennsylvania 14–0. It remained their lone Rose Bowl victory until Kelly led the Ducks over Wisconsin in Pasadena to cap the 2011 season.

Bezdek was credited with bringing innovations such as the forward pass and training-table meals to Oregon, but he left after the 1917 season, having compiled a career record with the Ducks of 30–10–4 (.727 percent).

The captain of that Rose Bowl team was J.W. Beckett, a halfback and defensive tackle who also made his way to the College Football Hall of Fame. Beckett rushed for 100 yards in the Civil War to cap that regular season, and the next year he played for the Mare Island Marines, which also won in Pasadena, with Beckett as captain.

But the star of the 1917 Rose Bowl was C.A. "Shy" Huntington, who ran for one Oregon touchdown, passed for another, and had three interceptions—a Rose Bowl record that stood for decades. "We ran into a batch of football that was a cross between a zip of forked lightning and the roll of a fast freight," Penn coach Bob Folwell is reported to have said afterward. "We were licked by a better team. Just let it go at that."

Huntington replaced Bezdek as Oregon's coach in 1918, and a year later he led them back to the Rose Bowl, becoming the first man to both play and coach in the game. One of his seniors in 1919 was Huntington's younger brother, Hollis, who ran for 122 yards in a 7–6 loss to Harvard in which the Ducks missed a third field-goal attempt that would have given them the victory.

Oregon's next College Football Hall of Famer was tailback and defensive back John Kitzmiller, who played from 1928 to 1930. "The Flying Dutchman," as he was known, scored 14 career touchdowns. A teammate, Bill Bowerman, the Ducks' legendary future track coach, called Kitzmiller "one of the most elegant halfbacks in the history of football."

In Kitzmiller's playing career the Ducks won 23 of 30 games, two of those defeats coming late in 1929 after he had been sidelined by a broken leg. Twice a member of the All-Pacific Coast team, Kitzmiller played one season professionally before returning to Oregon as an assistant coach.

Those early greats of Oregon football, Bezdek, Beckett and Kitzmiller, were later joined in the College Football Hall of Fame by quarterback Norm Van Brocklin, head coach Len Casanova, halfback Mel Renfro, and receiver Bobby Moore (Ahmad Rashad). Van Brocklin and Mel Renfro were also inducted into the Pro Football Hall of Fame, along with Oregon alums Dan Fouts, Dave Wilcox, Gary Zimmerman and Alphonse "Tuffy" Leemans.

Most of those names are quite familiar to those who follow Oregon football. The exception might be Leemans, who began his college career with the Ducks in 1932, then enrolled at George Washington, where he ran for 2,382 yards in his career. Leemans led the NFL in rushing as a rookie with the New York Giants in 1936, was named All-NFL in 1936 and 1939 and was inducted into the Pro Football Hall of Fame in 1978.

78 Go to Pre's Rock

The night before Oregon's season opener against New Mexico in 2010, coach Chip Kelly gave a speech to his team that touched on legendary UO distance runner Steve Prefontaine.

It was Prefontaine's style to lead wire to wire, to always run as hard as he could, and to always run to win. Kelly told the Ducks how Prefontaine absolutely disdained the runners who sat back, waiting until the end of the race to take the lead with a big push.

The next day, Oregon went out and beat the Lobos 72–0 to begin what would become a 12–0 regular season, earning the Ducks a spot in the BCS National Championship Game.

You don't think a distance runner has anything to do with football? At Oregon, "Pre" has everything to do with everything.

Pre's spirit is not just the driving force within Eugene's track-crazy community, but it also helps define the Oregon athletic department. Pre has also been called the "soul of Nike" by cofounder Phil Knight, the Ducks' most significant booster.

That is why a trip to Pre's Rock is a must-do for any fan of Oregon.

Along a basalt rock wall on Skyline Boulevard in Eugene, situated on a steep, curved sliver of forestland in the hills above the Oregon campus, with views of the Willamette River below, is a shrine to America's greatest distance runner.

It was here on May 30, 1975, the 24-year-old Prefontaine died after he crashed into the wall while driving his MGB convertible after leaving a party. The car flipped and rolled on top of Pre, trapping him underneath.

"That rock endures as a place to remember Pre—not simply his death, but how his all-out, run-for-the-tape life says something about us," wrote the *Register-Guard's* Ron Bellamy. "About how much we respected the proud, gutty kid from Coos Bay, who ran always to win. About how intensely we mourned his death.... About how we've found inspiration in Pre."

At the time of his death, Pre held seven American records in distance running between 2,000 and 10,000 meters, and was called his sport's most popular athlete in the world by *Track & Field News*.

"It's the end of an era," Eugene mayor Les Anderson said the day of Pre's death.

Pre wasn't just a great runner, NCAA champion, and Olympian, he was also well known for his battles with the Amateur Athletics Union and the strict control they held over athletes. He also was instrumental in the start of Knight's Nike when it was transitioning away from being known as Blue Ribbon Sports in the early 1970s.

From NikeInc.com about the birth of its brand:

"With a new logo, a new name and a new design innovation, what BRS now needed was an athlete to endorse and elevate the

One of Oregon's favorite sons, Steve Prefontaine competes in the 1972 Olympic Games. Pay tribute to Pre by visiting his memorial at the site of his death.

new Nike line. Fittingly for the company founded by Oregonians, they found such a young man from the small coastal town of Coos Bay, Oregon. His name: Steve Prefontaine.

Pre challenged Blue Ribbon Sports to stretch their creative talents. In turn, he became a powerful ambassador for BRS and Nike after he graduated from Oregon, making numerous appearances on behalf of BRS and sending pairs of Nike shoes to prospective runners along with personal notes of encouragement."

In 1997, 22 years after his death, a two-foot-high, half-ton stone monument that bears Pre's face was placed at the rock wall.

Beneath his name is etched this tribute to Pre:

FOR YOUR DEDICATION AND LOYALTY TO YOUR PRINCIPLES AND BELIEFS. FOR YOUR LOVE, WARMTH, AND FRIENDSHIP FOR YOUR FAMILY AND FRIENDS. YOU'RE MISSED BY SO MANY. AND YOU WILL NEVER BE FORGOTTEN.

79 Bill Byrne

The tenure of Bill Byrne as Oregon's athletic director from 1984 to 1992, before he moved on to Nebraska and then Texas A&M, was marked by remarkable expansion for the department.

The Ducks opened fund-raising offices across Oregon, added an in-house radio and television network, and played a role in the establishment of a state lottery NFL pick 'em game that benefitted colleges on both the academic and athletic sides. Byrne completed a $4 million addition of sky suites and a press box in Autzen Stadium, installed grass football practice fields across the street, and built the $12 million Casanova Center administrative building.

"He's accomplished more maybe than any athletic director in Oregon history," said football coach Rich Brooks, Byrne's successor as AD. "He was persistent, optimistic, and clearly the right man at the right time to salvage Oregon athletics and bring respect and dignity back to the program."

Along with all of that, however, Byrne was also a visionary willing to take risks, including two that have become the most memorable aspects of his tenure. One was successful, one was not; each was audacious.

The first home football game at Oregon during Byrne's tenure was a visit from Long Beach State to open the 1984 season. He didn't see much of the game; he spent much of it in the bowels of Autzen Stadium, trying to help maintenance crews identify a plumbing problem that had stopped all the toilets from flushing.

No, Autzen Stadium wasn't quite the marquee facility in those days that it would become 15 years later. And Byrne soon after concocted a plan to fix that.

Within a year, Byrne proposed a novel concept: a dome on Autzen Stadium. The initial cost was pegged at $7.5 million, with the project estimated to end up at $15 million after the facility was enhanced with offices and configured to allow basketball games to be held there too.

A dome would increase attendance—and thus ticket revenue—for football games, get the team out of often sloppy late-season weather, and be an attractive item to highlight in recruiting.

"I'm convinced that with a dome our crowds would increase and so would our home-field advantage, and with that our chance to win," Brooks said. "I don't think that can be overemphasized, that in addition to all the financial advantages, it would give us a better chance to win than we've had before."

Almost immediately, the problem hit roadblocks, most significantly those related to fund-raising. University president Paul Olum required that money for the dome not affect academic fund-raising. That ultimately proved to be too much for the project to overcome, and the idea was essentially scrapped in 1986.

That fall, the Ducks went 5–6 in football, their fifth losing season in six years. But in 1987, Oregon won six games, and the Ducks did so again in 1988. The program seemed to be on the cusp of turning a corner behind Brooks and quarterback Bill Musgrave, and the Ducks finally broke through in 1989, going 7–4.

As a reward, the Ducks were offered a spot in the Independence Bowl. The caveat: Byrne had to commit to buying 14,000 tickets, which could then be resold to Oregon fans. The game was to be played in freezing conditions in Shreveport, Louisiana. The Ducks faithful hadn't been able to celebrate a bowl bid since 1963, but 14,000 was a lot of tickets. Byrne rolled the dice.

"I think it proved sometimes you have to spend money to make money," Musgrave said. "Bill Byrne really kind of speculated on the football program and almost underwrote the trip. Everything blossoms from that point, but he got our foot in the door there. It really kind of launched the entire program."

Oregon fans came through and rallied to Shreveport. The Ducks beat Tulsa 27–24. They were back in a bowl again in 1990, and once more in 1992. Since the 1994 season, Oregon has only missed the postseason twice. Byrne's decision to gamble on the purchase of those 14,000 tickets helped pave the way.

"We showed our fans followed our team," Brooks said.

80 Salvaging the 2007 Season

It wasn't often that a Chip Kelly offense with the Oregon Ducks was made to look helpless. The exception was November 24, 2007, at UCLA, the lowest point in what was a disheartening end to a magical UO football season.

The final month of the 2007 regular season was one of the more dramatic stretches in recent Oregon football history. It began with Dennis Dixon's final act in a UO uniform in Autzen Stadium, against Arizona State, and the knee injury that he aggravated two weeks later at Arizona, which ended his career.

A week later, the Ducks were shut out by the Bruins—the only time in the Kelly era when they were held scoreless. A rotating cast of quarterbacks hurt the Ducks again the next week in an overtime loss to Oregon State on December 1, although the Ducks rallied behind Justin Roper for a win in the Sun Bowl. For a team once in the thick of the national championship and Heisman Trophy races, it was a nice consolation prize—particularly considering what the Ducks had endured in November.

Dixon was originally injured November 3 against the Sun Devils. The Ducks had 11 days off before playing at Arizona, and Mike Bellotti did everything he could to mask the severity of the quarterback's knee injury: a torn ACL. Dixon was adamant about playing, and Bellotti allowed it.

"He did well through practice for a week, so we felt comfortable letting him try to go and see what he could do," team medical adviser Dr. Robert Crist said. "With the understanding that if he had an episode, he would tell us immediately and pull himself out." Dixon didn't have to say anything, though. Later in the first quarter at Arizona, after a miraculous 39-yard touchdown run, Dixon was scrambling in the pocket when his knee buckled. His college career was over.

Senior backup Brady Leaf took over against the Wildcats, and gamely kept the Ducks in it despite suffering a serious ankle injury himself. But the Ducks, ranked No. 2 at the time, lost 34–24. Not only was Dixon's Heisman campaign over, but so was Oregon's title shot. And it got worse.

In the first quarter at UCLA, on November 24, Leaf suffered another ankle injury and left the game. With running back Jonathan Stewart also gimpy, redshirt freshman quarterback Cody Kempt was under constant pressure from the Bruins' defense. Classmate Justin Roper later replaced Kempt; in total, the three quarterbacks went 11-of-39 for 105 yards, with three interceptions and five sacks. "When those new guys came in, we went after them," UCLA defensive end Bruce Davis said. "We made sure they weren't comfortable back there. We were hitting them all day."

Never mind that Oregon's defensive effort against the Bruins had been Herculean. The sexy offense that had bamboozled Michigan two months earlier had disappeared completely. The Ducks never even got into the red zone at UCLA, much less scored. It was a crushing collapse.

"We had a chance to do something really special this year," UO defensive coordinator Nick Aliotti said. "We, collectively, had a chance to do something. It's sad.... It's an interesting game. I think without a doubt we were one of the best teams in the country this year. Without a friggin' doubt, we were one of the best teams in the country."

The inexperience at quarterback might have contributed to more folly in the finale against Oregon State. The Ducks, behind Roper at quarterback after Kempt suffered a concussion, had a chance to win at the end of regulation, but had a mix-up between the offense and special teams that resulted in a rushed—and missed—field-goal attempt. Offensive line coach Steve Greatwood, who coached the field-goal team, took the blame for sending the unit out one play early, before Roper could spike the ball and stop the clock.

The Beavers won in the second overtime. The Ducks, who once looked damn near unbeatable, had lost three in a row, their starting quarterback lost to injury in all three defeats. "The more you think about it," UO cornerback Jairus Byrd said, "it's like it's not real."

The Ducks finally awoke from their bad dream in, of all places, El Paso, Texas. Finally granted enough time to prepare a new quarterback for a game plan tailored to his strengths, Kelly coached Roper to a four-touchdown performance in a 56–21 win over South Florida. "We knew what we could do still," junior center Max Unger said. "It was just a matter of getting the new guys into the system. It's tough, it takes more than a couple weeks of practice to get it done."

Oregon football had something to celebrate again to cap the 2007 season, during which some of the highest highs in program history were followed by the lowest lows, including that dark November when they hit rock bottom in Los Angeles.

81 Go to the Spring Game

The span between January and September can be long and dreary for college football fans, who have very few chances to get a fix during those eight months.

There's the excitement of signing day in February and the adrenaline rush that comes with the start of fall camp in August, and of course, there's the annual spring game in between.

At Oregon, the spring game has turned into a must-see event in recent years.

Though the Ducks have recently treated it more like a scripted scrimmage than an actual game, it hasn't stopped fans from treating the day as if it were just another sunny Saturday in the fall.

Tailgating in the Autzen Stadium parking lot gets rocking and the Moshofsky Center is open for business. However, the price of admission has typically been free with the donation of nonperishable items to the local food bank.

Oregon's success on the field has obviously resulted in larger crowds and increased interest in the Ducks' spring game.

In 2010, with Oregon coming off its first Rose Bowl appearance since 1995, the spring game drew a then-record crowd of 25,211.

"We had that when we played 'SC!" quipped Ahmad Rashad, who played at Oregon from 1969 to 1971 and was an honorary coach for the 2010 game.

It was also the first year then-coach Chip Kelly turned the spring game into what became an annual tradition honoring the United States military personnel and their families.

A four-hour fan festival with the theme "Support our Troops and Families" preceded the game in the Mo Center and the Ducks wore special camouflage uniforms for the game.

The genesis for the tribute was in part a funeral attended by Kelly earlier that year for "huge Duck fan" U.S. Army Sgt. Joshua Lengstorf of Yoncalla, Oregon. Kelly was struck by the fact that the 24-year-old Lengstorf was not much older than most of Oregon's players.

"It puts it in perspective: what we do and why we're allowed to do what we do," Kelly said. "There are people overseas in every branch of the military fighting for our freedom. I don't want to say we take it for granted, but we go about our daily lives and do what we do, and forget about those people.

"I thought, what can we do? What small token can we do to recognize them?"

Players gave their jerseys to troops immediately after the game, a tradition that continued through 2013.

"I want those guys to connect, whether it's some rudimentary version of pen pals or whatever," Kelly said.

For the 2011 game, a record crowd of 43,468 poured through the gates of Autzen Stadium. From the raucous pregame festivities in the parking lot to the electric mood in the stands, it was clear that Oregon's run to the 2011 National Championship Game had fans clamoring for football.

"They love their Ducks," defensive coordinator Nick Aliotti said.

The 2012 spring game was even bigger, as 44,129 filled the stands to watch the Rose Bowl champions do their thing.

Oregon's spring game also began to draw national interest; the 2010, 2011, and 2012 games were all broadcast live on ESPN2.

The popularity of the spring game hasn't always been so rabid. In 2009, with the Ducks coming off a win in the Holiday Bowl, only 12,400 attended the game—though it was also played in pouring rain.

The spring game was once used as a showcase for Oregon football throughout the state. From 1998 to 2002, the game was played outside of Eugene three times.

The 1998 game moved to Volcanoes Stadium, a 5,000-seat, single-A minor league baseball park in Keizer, Oregon. In 2001, the Ducks played in front of 7,110 at Hillsboro Stadium near Portland, and in 2002, while Autzen Stadium was being remodeled, Oregon played in Portland at PGE Park in front of 12,524.

Nowadays, it's hard to imagine the Ducks playing the spring game anywhere other than Autzen Stadium.

It's also hard to imagine a more perfect way to cure the off-season blues than by spending an afternoon at the spring game.

82 Taken Too Soon: Terrance Kelly and Todd Doxey

In the summer of 2004, the Oregon football team experienced the sort of internal tragedy that seems unspeakably cruel for a group of young men just leaving their teenage years. Then, just four years later, it happened again.

The deaths of Terrance Kelly and Todd Doxey deprived the Ducks of two talented young defensive players who were both considered future stars. They were also men of solid character, and potential leaders who were taken too soon.

Kelly, an All-American tight end and linebacker, was from Richmond, California, a tough neighborhood in the East Bay Area. He attended powerhouse De La Salle High School, where Oregon defensive coordinator Nick Aliotti's brother was an administrator, a connection that yielded several prominent signees for the Ducks over the years.

In 2004, Kelly was one of four Spartans to sign with Oregon, along with receiver Cameron Colvin and defensive backs Willie Glasper and Jackie Bates. Safety T.J. Ward also planned to play for the Ducks, though he would initially walk on because of a knee injury.

Early that summer, Kelly spent a few weeks in Eugene working out with his new teammates. He was back home in Richmond for a few days, prior to the start of fall camp, when the unthinkable happened. A 15-year-old boy from the neighborhood who apparently held a grudge against Kelly, came upon Kelly, 18, late one night while he was sitting in a car and shot him to death.

A few days later, Kelly's funeral was held, and a letter he wrote for his application to Oregon was read aloud. "I am determined not to end up like so many of my peers," Kelly wrote of his desire to escape the rough streets of Richmond.

Oregon coach Mike Bellotti, defensive coordinator Nick Aliotti, and linebackers coach Don Pellum attended the ceremony. "Terrance was an awesome kid," Aliotti told the congregation. "I loved being around him. Not because he was an All-American linebacker at De La Salle. Not because he was going to be an All-American linebacker at Oregon. But because he was an All-American person."

Kelly was also something of a leader among his friends who were joining him at Oregon, none of whom fulfilled his potential. Bates transferred after two years, Colvin struggled with consistency before an ankle injury ruined his breakout senior year, and Glasper had his own senior year ended by a knee injury. Ironically enough, it was the Spartan who walked on, Ward, who enjoyed the best career with the Ducks.

It was prior to Ward's junior year that tragedy struck again. Doxey, who sat out 2007 as a redshirt, was on a summer river-rafting trip with teammates, a longstanding off-season tradition at Oregon. He was one of the last players in the McKenzie River that day, and said a quick prayer with teammate William Wallace before jumping from a bridge.

Doxey told Wallace, "God is on my side," then jumped into the cold, fast-moving water without an inner tube. He began to struggle, was lifeless when pulled out, and died a few hours later.

"This was a really beloved kid," Oregon defensive backs coach John Neal said. "He had character, attitude, drive, instincts—all those intangibles that I can't coach."

To honor Doxey, a different player wore his No. 29 jersey in each of the six home games in 2008. Ward had a season-high 14 tackles when he did so, cornerback Jairus Byrd matched his season-high with nine, and safety Javes Lewis also tied his season-high mark of five, despite being a backup.

At the end of the season, the Ducks played in the Holiday Bowl in Doxey's hometown of San Diego. "Definitely emotions will be running high, but if there's any place we'd want to play a bowl game, for me at least, it would be Todd's hometown," UO receiver Jeff Maehl said. "It'll give his family a chance to see us play and see how much love we have for him, how much we miss him every day. I'm excited to see them after the game, and go out and get a win for him in his hometown." Oregon came through, beating Oklahoma State 42–31.

Following Doxey's death, the Ducks named a team award in his honor. It was given to the player who "best exemplifies the spirituality and dedication of the former UO safety."

"I think it's important to keep Todd's memory alive," Neal said. "It was a life-changing experience for all of us that were deeply involved, and you hope that means it changed us for the better. I don't want to forget about it, and so we're doing some things to really honor that young man and the friends he had, and the character kid he was."

83 Notre Dame Comes to Town

On the third weekend in October 1982, the Hilton Eugene sold out every room it had. Patrons hoping to get a meal in the hotel restaurant or a drink at the bar, had to wait as long as 90 minutes.

It was even crazier at the Valley River Inn, which enjoyed record-setting revenues that weekend. The wait for dinner in the restaurant there was closer to two hours.

What could have possibly caused so many people to flock to Eugene? The presence of the Notre Dame football team, which played one of the biggest nonconference games in Oregon football history at Autzen Stadium on October 23, 1982.

The Ducks entered the afternoon 0–6. The Irish were 4–1, ranked No. 15 by the Associated Press.

An estimated 10,000 Notre Dame fans traveled to see the game, many of whom attended a packed pep rally in Eugene on Friday night. The Marist High School band supplied entertainment; by one estimate, perhaps tongue in cheek, the Notre Dame fight song was requested, and played, 100 times.

Late in the evening, Eugene mayor Gus Keller addressed the pep rally, and tried to make the case for the home team. "If you think you have an easy test tomorrow, God help you," Keller said. The crowd shouted back in response, "He will!"

Notre Dame coach Gerry Faust was more conservative, as might be expected prior to kickoff.

"From what everyone has told us, Notre Dame coming to Eugene is one of the biggest things to hit this area in a long time," Notre Dame coach Gary Faust said. "Oregon may not have won a game and may be underdogs again, but the Oregon coaches will have no problems getting their kids ready to play. With a big crowd behind them, if Oregon comes out and puts up some quick points, that could be all the momentum they need. If we don't establish something early, we'll be in trouble."

He was oh so wrong. The Ducks didn't get off to a good start. Even so, they gave the Irish all they could handle.

Autzen Stadium was packed—the first nonconference sellout in its history, despite forecasts of rain. Early on, the Ducks demonstrated why they were significant underdogs, when their punter muffed a snap, setting up a touchdown for the Irish. Oregon answered with a field goal, and trailed 7–3 after the first quarter.

That field goal was just the second of the year for the Ducks, on nine attempts, and their struggles continued in the second quarter. Two kickers were tried; freshman Tim Wise missed a 48-yard attempt, and Todd Lee missed from 31 yards, after having made his first collegiate attempt in the first quarter, a 37-yarder. Thus, Notre Dame remained up at halftime, though just 7–3, as the Oregon defense held its own and the Ducks dominated time of possession.

In the third quarter, Oregon's special teams woes continued. A punt was partially blocked, and though Oregon coach Rich Brooks protested the call that Notre Dame had recovered before an Oregon player ended up with the ball, the Irish were granted possession. They quickly tacked on another field goal, and it was 10–6.

Finally, early in the fourth quarter, the Ducks got rolling. They drove 80 yards in 10 plays, taking a 13–10 lead on a one-yard touchdown run by Terrance Jones. The Irish tried to respond in kind, but facing fourth-and-10 from the Oregon 18-yard line, Faust elected to have Mike Johnston kick a game-tying 35-yard field goal. "I'd have rather had Oregon win than this," one Notre Dame fan was heard to mutter in the stands.

Faust was unapologetic for having played for the tie. "We've got too much at stake this year to just throw it away. We didn't have much choice," he said.

For the Ducks, there were also mixed feelings. Brooks conceded at least that a tie felt better than a loss. But Oregon had faced one of the nation's most storied programs, and clearly been the better team. "We kicked their butts all day and they are the ones who have to feel lucky to get out of here with a tie," Jones said.

By weekend's end, all those fans who had flocked to Eugene headed home. They weren't in nearly as celebratory a mood. Wondered Liz Fendrich, a Notre Dame fan from Los Angeles who attended the game, "What I can't understand is, how can a team that hasn't won a game look so good?"

84 Mighty Oregon

Original Lyrics for "The Mighty Oregon March":
She is small our Alma Mater,
But she rules with strength and right.
What she lacks in mass and numbers,
She makes up for in her fight.

Oregon is never beaten,
Till the final whistles call.
Who can tell her tale of triumph?
Scores can never show it all.

Oregon, our Alma Mater,
We will guard thee on and on.
Fellows gather round and cheer her.
Chant her glory Oregon.
Roar the praises of her warriors.
Sing the story Oregon.
Down the gridiron urge the heroes,
Of our mighty Oregon.

Rally fellows, stand behind them,
They are doing all they can.
Back the team in sun and shadow,
Back the captain, back each man.
They will carry home the vict'ry,
To old Deady's hallowed hall.
Give the team the best that's in you.
Give your Alma Mater all.

—Composed by Albert Perfect,
Written by DeWitt Gilbert

"The Mighty Oregon March," played after touchdowns, during timeouts, at halftime, and on campus twice every school day, has been Oregon's rousing fight song for nearly 100 years.

At the turn of the 20th century, Oregon was using "On Wisconsin" as its fight song. The dean of the university's music school convinced Albert John Perfect, a musically educated Swedish immigrant living in North Dakota, to lead the Eugene Municipal Band and help organize the student-run band ensemble.

Within months of his arrival in 1915, Perfect had established order in the University Band, agreed to direct a band at Eugene High School, and initiated the Eugene Municipal Band.

On January 7, 1916, at the city band's inaugural performance, Perfect unveiled his latest composition, "The Mighty Oregon March," including lyrics written by Oregon sophomore journalism student DeWitt Gilbert.

With a melody fashioned to fit into the harmony of "It's a Long Way to Tipperary,"—a popular World War I marching song—"The Mighty Oregon March" was an immediate success.

The song has been altered through the years, and its most popular and well-known verse now is:

Oregon, our Alma Mater,
We will guard thee on and on,
Let us gather 'round and cheer her,
Chant her glory, Oregon!
Roar the praises of her warriors,
Sing the story, Oregon,
On to vict'ry urge the heroes
Of our Mighty Oregon!
Go! Ducks! Go!
Fight! Ducks! Fight!
Go!
Fight!
Win! Ducks! Win!

The Oregon football team also seems to have its own version, with the most significant difference found at the end with a reference to the Ducks' hated in-state rival:

We will march, march,
on down the field, fighting for Oregon.
Plough through the foeman's line,
Their strength we'll defy.

We'll give a long cheer for our men,
We're out to win again.
OSU may fight to the end but we will win.

85 Tom Graham

There are many eye-popping numbers in the Oregon record book, no surprise for a team with one of the nation's most explosive offenses throughout the last 20 years.

Few are more ridiculous, however, than the totals Tom Graham put up on defense from 1969 to 1971. There were the 433 career tackles, the 206 during the 1969 season and 41 in the 1971 Civil War; all three marks are still Oregon records.

"I know that seems outlandish," Graham said of his single-game total, when the Beavers continually ran up the middle out of their triple-option scheme. "But I had the bruises to prove it."

The men who played with Graham vouch for the fact his numbers weren't simply the product of overeager statisticians. "In my whole career, he was as dominant as any player I've ever played with, even professionally. Tom made tackles from sideline to sideline," Ahmad Rashad said. "He was our heart and soul. He was something."

Graham played in an era when the Ducks were known for outscoring opponents, if they won at all. But as his seven-year NFL career illustrates, Graham was always one of the best players on the field.

86 Playing at Hayward Field

The popularity of Oregon football has soared to unthinkable heights the past decade, but at its core, Eugene is still Track Town, USA, and Hayward Field remains its beating heart.

With its historic covered grandstands, immaculate infield, and rust-colored running surface, Hayward Field is a legend in the world of track-and-field, widely considered the sport's top venue in the United States.

As of 2012, Hayward Field had hosted five U.S. Olympic Trials since 1972, six U.S. Championship meets, and 10 NCAA championships.

It's hard to spend a sunny spring afternoon sitting in the west grandstand without feeling Hayward Field's spirit and history.

It's equally as easy to forget its original intent.

Hayward Field opened in 1919 as Oregon's new football stadium, replacing the old Kincaid Field, which was near what is now the western edge of campus.

Hayward cost just $7,000 and took two years to build.

The Ducks opened their new stadium with a 9–0 win against Oregon Agricultural College on November 15, 1919.

One report had a crowd of nearly 12,000 at that opening game. The problem was, there were only 7,000 seats.

The *Register-Guard* called it the largest crowd ever assembled in Eugene.

The account from the student newspaper, the *Emerald*, had this tidbit: "Just before the game began, Governor Ben W. Olcott announced to the stands that the new Oregon gridiron had been named Hayward Field by the student body of the University of

Oregon in honor of Trainer Bill Hayward. The veteran trainer received a wonderful ovation from the crowd."

Hayward was *also* the head track coach from 1904 to 1947.

Hayward's original turf survived only the first two seasons, so the team played on sawdust until sometime during the Great Depression, when new sod and a drainage system were installed as part of a WPA project.

"The field held up well after that," former player and coach Shy Huntington told the *Register-Guard* in 1967.

The east grandstand was built sometime before 1925 and eventually horseshoe-shaped covered stands were added at the north end of the field. They were later torn down in 1947 by athletic director Leo Harris, who replaced them with temporary bleachers.

Two years after Hayward Field opened, a six-lane cinder track was installed and the track team moved from Kincaid Field as well.

The opening of Hayward Field spurred the *Emerald* to write about the passing of Kincaid Field:

"With the dedication of the new field, historic old Kincaid has to give way for the accommodation of the rapidly growing University. Many an Oregon football and track victory has been fought out on old Kincaid, many an old Oregon grad, here for homecoming, will find the foundations at a number of sacred traditions taken away."

There didn't seem to be the same level of nostalgic pining when the football Ducks moved from Hayward Field to Autzen Stadium in 1967.

In the final seasons of football at Hayward Field, Oregon regularly played a handful of home games each season in Portland at Multnomah Stadium (now known as Jeld-Wen Field) because visiting teams didn't want to play in Eugene at such a small venue.

From the *R-G*'s Jerry Uhrhammer on November 4, 1966: "Few will be sorry, really, to see Hayward Field fade out of the football picture. Its capacity of 21,000 to 22,000—depending on how closely the fans are jammed together in the bleachers—is small-time in an era when twice as many seats are needed to support a big-time program."

Still, Hayward Field gave Oregon fans plenty of memories in its 47 years as a football venue. Players such as Shy Huntington, Norm Van Brocklin, and NFL Hall of Famers Mel Renfro and Dave Wilcox all played at Hayward Field, as did the 1920 and 1958 Rose Bowl teams. It's also where Len Casanova coached.

But in the end, Hayward Field was forced into "semi-retirement," the *R-G* wrote, reduced to a track-only venue and an unknown future. We should all be so lucky.

87 Bill Moos

Bill Moos' tenure as Oregon's athletic director, from the summer of 1995 through the spring of 2007, was marked by extraordinary expansion—not only of the Ducks' facilities but also their national profile.

But Moos' tenure was tainted, too, most notably by a rift with Nike founder and UO booster Phil Knight that came to a head just prior to Moos' departure.

A former All-Conference football player at Washington State (where he served as AD after leaving Oregon), Moos arrived in Eugene at a fortuitous time. Bill Byrne was the outgoing AD, after getting the facility expansion off the ground through the construction of the Casanova Center and the addition of skyboxes in Autzen Stadium. Mike Bellotti was poised to kick off a hugely successful run as head football coach, and Knight was months away from pledging his increased financial support for the department, which he would do following the Cotton Bowl in January 1996.

But no one who followed Moos' tenure saw him as simply the beneficiary of others' work. He fostered the relationship with Knight that led to the construction of the $14.6 million Moshofsky Center indoor practice facility and the $90 million expansion of Autzen in 2002.

Moos also took dramatic steps to raise Oregon's national profile. He signed a rights agreement with ESPN Regional in 1998, oversaw the marketing of new uniforms and a lavish locker room for the football team, and signed off on a billboard in New York City promoting Joey Harrington's Heisman candidacy.

During Moos' tenure, the athletic department budget more than doubled, from $18 million to $40 million (it would double again in another few years). Upon his departure, he pointed to the construction of the Moshofsky Center as a key development in his tenure.

"That allowed us to compete in recruiting, it allowed us to train our athletes year round, and it created new revenue streams with the stadium expansion," Moos said. "It showed a commitment by the university that played well with our fans and student-athletes and made our competition stand up and take note. We provided our coaches with the resources so that every student-athlete at the University of Oregon can realistically feel they can win a conference championship. That was not the case in 1995."

Wrote *Register-Guard* columnist Ron Bellamy, "When Moos came to Oregon, the Ducks were looking at what other schools had, and wanting that. Now, schools look at what Oregon has, and want that. And it's not as if every football season will produce a championship…but Oregon will always have that chance, thanks to the improvements of the Moos era."

"What Bill was able to do here was change the way we thought about ourselves," wrestling coach Chuck Kearney said when Moos' departure was announced.

But while Moos was lauded for his accomplishments upon leaving, the last few years of his tenure were tainted by controversy. In 2004, he expressed an interest in the AD opening at Washington, Oregon's hated rival. "It has elements of appeal to me both professionally and personally," Moos said. "Having said that, I've got my signature on a wonderful period of time here at Oregon, and that means a lot to me. That would be a tough call."

Needless to say, that flirtation did not go over well with the Oregon faithful—including Knight, it was thought. Coincidence or not, within a month of Moos' initial comments about the UW opening, Oregon's efforts to raise funds and build a new basketball arena—contingent on a large donation from Knight—were shelved.

Moos called the inability to complete that project a major regret of his time with the Ducks. It was, he said, "kind of like a greased pig. I couldn't get my hands around it, and we'd lose it each time, for a variety of reasons."

Knight and Moos were at odds again in 2005, when track coach Martin Smith stepped down. While Oregon's tradition—and Knight's passion—lay in distance running, Smith built a more well-rounded program, and it was thought Knight had influence on Smith's departure. Moos did little to dispel that notion, and when Smith left, Knight said that, "Bill Moos had 10 chances to make the right decision...and missed every one of them. It's hard to be that perfect."

When Moos' departure from Oregon was announced, it was first presented as amicable. "I greatly appreciate the progress that has been made during Bill's tenure as athletic director," UO president Dave Frohnmayer said in his statement. "Bill and I agreed this was a good time to reflect on that progress and look closely at what it will take to be successful over the next decade. Together we reached the decision that now was the appropriate time to make this change."

Later, it was learned Moos received a $2 million buyout, paid for in part by donor Pat Kilkenny, his ultimate successor as athletic director. Moos retired to a ranch near Spokane, Washington, before later taking a job at Washington State. "I know there wasn't any direct influence," Knight said of his role in Moos' ouster. "Indirect, I suppose I made his job a little harder. It may have made Spokane look better faster than it would have otherwise. I don't know."

So fitting: An ambiguous answer to cap the cloudy tenure of Bill Moos with the Ducks.

88 D-Boyz

In 2007, safety Matt Harper gave Oregon's secondary a nickname: the D-Boyz.

The name caught on publicly a year later. Perhaps not coincidentally, the foursome that came to embody that nickname also could make an argument as one of the most impressive position groups in UO football history.

The 2008 secondary featured three holdovers from the 2007 D-Boyz, safety Patrick Chung and cornerbacks Jairus Byrd and Walter Thurmond III. They were joined in '08 by free safety T.J. Ward, and within two years the entire foursome was in the NFL, a remarkable achievement.

The Ducks had featured a stellar group in the secondary in 1994. That year, Alex Molden and Herman O'Berry were the corners and Chad Cota played safety. All three of them became NFL players.

But the D-Boyz, of course, did them one better.

D-Boyz Patrick Chung (15) and Jairus Byrd (32) celebrate with teammate J.D. Nelson (28) after Chung's interception against UCLA in 2006.

Chung, Oregon's leading tackler in 2007 and a 51-game starter over four years, was a second-round pick by the New England Patriots in 2009. Byrd passed up his senior year to enter the draft that same year and was taken in the second round by the Buffalo Bills.

Ward, who led the Ducks in tackles in 2008, was also a second-round pick, by the Cleveland Browns in 2010. His senior season the previous fall was derailed by an injury, as was Thurmond's, though he, too, was drafted, in the fourth round by the Seattle Seahawks.

That the D-Boyz wanted to stand out at Oregon was apparent in 2008's fall camp. Chung used tape to apply the squad's nickname to his shoulder pads. And the unit would drop and do push-ups whenever one of its members screwed up a play in practice.

"We hold ourselves to a higher standard," Byrd said. "Coach [John] Neal does that as well. We just go about our business in a different way.... Every day that we go out there, we know what we can do. And we see if, even in our individual drills, we try to push each other and test each other."

"I trust them," said Neal, their position coach. "And that may be the greatest thing I can say about them. Because they do all the things I ask them to do, on and off the field. We don't have a lot of issues in terms of accountability. On the field they're hard workers, they care, they work all the time. They get it."

The conspicuous nickname raised the bar of expectations for the group, and they didn't always hit it. When they gave up a play in a game, all the attention they'd garnered made it stand out even more.

But there was far more good than bad. Byrd and Ward each had an interception in Oregon's double-overtime win at Purdue in 2008. Later that September, in a win over Washington State, Thurmond had two picks, Byrd recovered a fumble, Ward had a tackle for loss on the game's first snap, and Chung had six tackles in the first quarter alone.

"We haven't been making a lot of plays in the secondary," Chung said. "We always talk about that, that we've got to make a lot of plays. We've got to make every play. We came out and worked hard; when opportunity comes, you have to be prepared, and we were prepared for it."

Byrd, Chung, and Thurmond all made the watch list for the Bednarik and Thorpe Awards in 2008. Two years later, those three, plus Ward, were on NFL rosters, as all four of Oregon's D-Boyz reached football's highest level.

89 The Collapse at Cal

The photo on the front page of the *Register-Guard* sports section the morning of October 3, 1993, said it all: Oregon safety Dante Lewis, on his knees, helmet in hand, head buried in the shoulder of assistant coach Steve Greatwood, who was doing his best to console the distraught player.

Moments earlier, in what was the biggest comeback in the history of the Pac-10 Conference, California had rallied from a 30–0 deficit to beat the Ducks 42–41 at Memorial Coliseum in the league opener.

It was a gut-kick loss for Oregon, which fell to 3–1 and would go on to win just two more games the rest of the season, finishing 5–6. Cal, meanwhile, improved to 5–0 and went on to finish 9–4 and beat Iowa in the Alamo Bowl. If the Ducks had held on to beat the 17th-ranked Golden Bears to remain undefeated, who knows where their season might have gone.

"I'm in shock," quarterback Danny O'Neil said. "I don't know what to say. We put up 41 points and lost."

In one of Oregon's best offensive performances ever (and certainly in the pre-Chip Kelly era), the Ducks recorded 614 total yards, O'Neil threw for 313, wide receiver Derrick Deadwiler equaled the UO single-game record for receptions with 11 and set a new record with 234 receiving yards, and both Ricky Whittle (113) and Sean Burwell (101) rushed for more than 100 yards.

In addition, the defense was rock solid in the first half, holding the Golden Bears to −9 yards rushing and 93 yards overall. They also sacked quarterback Dave Barr five times before halftime.

Then came the collapse.

How do you lead a game 30–7 at halftime and still lose? You allow big plays—and lots of them.

The Golden Bears didn't nickel-and-dime their way to the lead, they flat-out stole it. Cal had one-play scoring drives of 61 and 72 yards, a four-play drive that went 95 yards, and also scored on a 15-yard return of a blocked punt.

"Cal's too good a team not to come back and score some," said coach Rich Brooks, who suffered his 100th loss in 17 seasons at Oregon that day. "The problem was, we gave up too many easy ones instead of making them work for their points. If they'd had to drive down the field for any one of those touchdowns, there wouldn't have been time left for them to come back at the end."

Three of those big plays took place in the third quarter, and yet the Ducks still led 41–27 with roughly five minutes to play.

Then Cal struck with one of its one-play drives, a 72-yard bomb from Barr to Damien Semien to make it a one-score game with 4:53 to play.

Following an Oregon punt, the Golden Bears put the finishing touches on their miraculous comeback with a nine-play, 85-yard, 77-second-long drive that ended with a 26-yard touchdown strike from Barr to wideout Iheanyl Uwaezuoke.

Barr then threw a fade route to wideout Mike Caldwell for the two-point conversion to take the lead with 1:05 to play.

"Losses like this take years off your life," defensive coordinator Nick Aliotti said. "This hurts pretty bad."

Cal's offensive coordinator at the time was Denny Schuler, a former defensive coordinator and player for the Ducks who took no special amount of pride in beating Oregon that day.

"I felt really bad for the Oregon kids because they played well enough to win," he said. "It was tough looking those kids in the eye because of how they were feeling."

Carr finished with 368 yards passing and Cal had 372 yards of offense in the second half alone.

"This ranks right up there as one of the toughest defeats I've had in my life," Brooks said.

90 Stars of the '80s

While the decade of the 1980s was in many ways lean for Oregon (the Ducks didn't break their long postseason drought until 1989) it was not without some standout moments by some standout players.

Depth was not a strength of the program in those days, and a key injury could cripple a team's entire season. But that's not to say Oregon was lacking in star power from several big names throughout the decade.

Following Bobby Moore in 1971, Oregon went another 36 years—until Jonathan Stewart in 2007—with just one All-American on offense. That lone All-American was Lew Barnes, an electric if undersized wideout who was named first-team All-Pac-10 in three straight years and graduated as the Ducks' all-time leading receiver after his All-American 1985 season.

Barnes, who was just 5'8" and 160 pounds, put his talent on display early, leading the Ducks in receiving as a sophomore in 1983. He caught 30 passes for 625 yards that year, the only time in school history that Oregon's leading receiver averaged more than 20 yards per catch.

Barnes was no better than on September 24, 1983, when the Ducks upset Houston. He caught a 53-yard pass for a touchdown and returned a punt 50 yards to set up a field goal. Late in the game, he was on his way to another long gain but fumbled; the ball bounced another 20 yards downfield as players from both sides failed to secure it, but Doug Herman finally recovered for Oregon near the goal line, setting up the winning touchdown by Kevin McCall. "When I lost the ball I said, 'Oh no!'" Barnes said. "It was a big relief to me when Herman wound up with it."

Oregon's tailback at the time was another undersized threat, Tony Cherry. He became the third Duck ever to rush for 1,000 yards when he reached 1,006 in 1985.

That was Barnes' senior season, too, the year he enjoyed his biggest day by catching nine passes for 183 yards and a touchdown against San Diego State. It was the second-highest single-game total in school history at the time—a mark he made on his way to what was then a UO career record of 2,048 receiving yards. "I didn't see as much double coverage in this game as I have; I think they thought their corners were good enough to cover me one-on-one," Barnes said after the game.

Oregon's quarterback that day, Chris Miller, threw for 368 yards, at that point second all-time at Oregon behind the 396 yards Dan Fouts accomplished in a 1970 game. But Miller, an athletic Eugene native who stayed home to play his college ball, outdid himself a year later, throwing for 376 yards in a loss at USC. Miller recalled, "After the game Ted Tollner, who was USC's coach at the time, came up to me and said, 'Son, you just made yourself a whole

Ducks in Japan

In 1985 the Ducks played their final game of the season across the Pacific Ocean against USC in the Mirage Bowl in Tokyo.

It was hardly a memorable experience.

Starting quarterback Chris Miller had to be stretchered off the field after taking a vicious hit out of bounds by Trojans linebacker Rex Moore. Oregon went on to lose 20–6 to finish the season 5–6.

But it wasn't just the game itself that left a bad taste. The substandard accommodations had coach Rich Brooks fuming in the days leading up to the game.

"If I'd known it was going to be like this, we wouldn't be here," said Brooks, who was especially upset the team was put up in a hotel with small rooms and even smaller beds, instead of the luxury hotel he felt they were promised during negotiations.

Then came the game and Miller's injury—a cracked pelvis—in the third quarter that in effect, ended the game.

lot of money.'" Perhaps Tollner was right; Miller was a first-round draft pick the following spring.

Miller threw for what was then a UO single-season record 2,503 yards as a senior and finished his career with 6,681 yards, another record at the time.

As one record-setting career was ending, another was beginning. Running back Derek Loville was a freshman in Miller's senior season of 1986, and by 1989 Loville had become the Ducks' all-time leading rusher, with 3,296 yards. Not the fastest back in a sprint, Loville had ample quickness and was a tough runner.

Loville struggled behind a rebuilt offensive line the first half of his senior year, but on October 21, 1989, he exploded for 203 yards against Arizona State, with touchdowns of one, two and 68 yards. "I guess I showed there's still some hop in my stride," said Loville, whose career-best 215 yards came against Idaho State as a junior.

Loville's career lined up with that of Terry Obee, Oregon's leading receiver in 1987, 1988, and 1989. Ironically enough, though, it's a running play for which Obee is best remembered.

Entering Obee's sophomore season, 1987, the Ducks had lost six straight to hated rival Washington. But they broke through with a 29–22 win in 1987, helped in part by an 82-yard reception on a screen pass to Obee, then made it two in a row in 1988 thanks to Obee's signature moment, a five-yard touchdown run on a reverse that gave Oregon a 17–14 win.

"Coach said it would be a great play to run against Washington, and we've practiced it for a couple of weeks, but when he called it I started getting butterflies," Obee said after the game. Such was the thrill of the chance to beat the Huskies in those days, when the Ducks had some forgettable teams but quite a few memorable players.

91 "Shout"

"Now, waaaaaait a minute!"

What happens when you blend Eugene's most popular place to be on a Saturday afternoon in the fall with one of its most popular contributions to pop culture?

You get nearly 60,000 people singing along to "Shout" between the third and fourth quarters at Autzen Stadium.

Somehow, it took 33 years for Oregon football to incorporate a piece of the movie *Animal House* into its game-day experience, but when it finally did in 2011, it became an instant fan favorite.

"You know you make me want to shout! Kick my heels back and shout! Throw my hands up and shout! Throw my head back and shout! Come on now!"

The song, originally a 1959 Isley Brothers hit, is performed by the fictional band Otis Day & the Knights in the 1978 movie that was filmed almost entirely on the University of Oregon campus.

Numerous major motion pictures have been filmed in Eugene through the years, but none, including two about iconic runner Steve Prefontaine, has been as popular as *Animal House*. The *National Lampoon* comedy starring John Belushi ranks 36th on the American Film Institute's list of 100 great comedies and earned $141 million at the box office.

Following a 2012 in-house survey, the *Register-Guard* had the filming of *Animal House* among the top 20 most significant moments in the city's history.

In the movie, a group of fraternity brothers from fictional Faber College throw a toga party before their house gets shut down. Otis Day & the Knights are there to perform and lead a rousing edition of "Shout."

That scene is now played on Oregon's video screen at the end of the third quarter, starting a massive sing-along in the stadium.

"A little bit louder now! A little bit louder now! A little bit louder now! Jump up and shout now! Jump up and shout now! Jump up and shout now!"

Actor DeWayne Jessie played the role of Otis Day in the movie and the Knights were a collection of Eugene-area musicians. The vocals were actually recorded by Lloyd Williams, and Jessie lip-synched during filming.

However, that didn't stop Jessie from making the most of his newfound fame once the movie came out. Inundated by requests from clubs across the country hoping to book Otis Day & the Knights, Jessie quickly put a band together and hit the road.

He said in a 2012 interview that the offers have never stopped and that he continues to play at fraternity parties and special events.

In 2011, he performed in front of 30,000 Oregon fans at a pep rally in Tucson, Arizona, leading up to the Ducks' BCS National Championship Game against Auburn.

Oregon was able to take its newfound fan-pleaser on the road at the end of the 2011 season when "Shout" was played during the

Rose Bowl game against Wisconsin. "Shout" played at the end of the third quarter as usual, but not until the Badgers got to play their own fan favorite, "Jump Around" by House of Pain.

By the time the game resumed, nearly all the 91,245 in attendance were dancing to "Shout."

92 Playing for the Platypus

On the surface, perhaps it makes sense: an animal that possesses both the beak of a Duck and the body of a rodent.

As college football rivalry trophies go, it's certainly one of the quirkiest—and has a short, strange history to boot. Since 1959, Oregon and Oregon State have ostensibly played for the Platypus Trophy, though at times its whereabouts have been unknown for years at a time.

The trophy was commissioned in 1959 by Oregon's director of public service, Willard Thompson, who picked university art student Warren Spady to carve it out of wood. The platypus is an Australian mammal, one that lays eggs at that, but with attributes of a duck and, arguably, a beaver, it seemed a natural choice.

"It seems appropriate," OSU alumni association communications director Kevin Miller said years later, "that two teams who are seen across the nation as having two of the sillier mascots would have an appropriately silly trophy."

The Beavers scored an upset to first claim the trophy in 1959. Somehow it ended up back in Eugene after a tie in 1960, but Oregon State won it back a year later.

Soon after, the platypus was stolen from a trophy case in a fraternity prank. From 1964 through 1968, the Oregon water polo team used the trophy to mark four championships.

Quarterback Marcus Mariota breaks free for a long run in the second quarter of the 2012 Civil War matchup with the Oregon State Beavers. The Ducks went on to take the game—and the Platypus Trophy.

By 1986, the platypus had come to reside in a trophy case on campus at Oregon. But it was misplaced at some point, only to resurface decades later when members of the athletic department staff were looking through an old storage area.

In the spring of 2008, the Platypus Trophy finally made its way back to Corvallis, after an absence of more than 40 years. The

Beavers had won the Civil War football game the previous fall, but it wasn't until a basketball game the following March that the trophy was handed over by the Ducks.

It wasn't long before the tradition was quickly dropped again. The Platypus Trophy might seem like the perfect way to recognize the victor of a battle between Ducks and Beavers, but nobody seems to want to have much to do with it.

93 Conquering Saban's Spartans

Long before Alabama coach Nick Saban won three BCS championships to cement his status as one of the greatest college football coaches of all time, he brought his 23rd-ranked Michigan State team to Autzen Stadium in 1998 and got manhandled in one of the most memorable season-opening wins in Oregon history.

In front of a record season-opening crowd of 43,634, the Ducks defeated the Spartans 48–14 on a warm September afternoon and debuted an offense that would electrify the country during the first five weeks of the season.

Led by newcomer Reuben Droughns at tailback and senior Akili Smith at quarterback, the Ducks led 34–0 at halftime and 48–0 at the end of the third quarter. The 590 yards gained on offense was the most by Oregon in five years and the sixth most ever allowed by Michigan State.

It remains the worst loss for Saban in his last 13 seasons on a college sideline.

"We looked real good today," Smith said. "It was kind of shocking the way things opened up. Sometimes you just have to say good job to the coaches and that's what I would say it was. They put together this great game plan and as players we just have to go out there and execute."

They certainly did that. The offense averaged 7.6 yards per play and the Ducks scored on their first six possessions. That included touchdown drives of 69, 80, 50, 67, and 89 yards—in the first half.

"We had five months to prepare for these guys, [as] opposed to them having a week to prepare for us," said Smith, noting how the Spartans had opened their season a week earlier against Colorado State. "This is expected of us. When you have that long to prepare for a team, you're suppose to kick their butt, and we did that."

Smith, who wasn't announced as the starter until the day of the game after winning a fall camp battle with Jason Maas for the job, had a spectacular start to a senior season that would end with him being the third overall pick in the 1999 NFL Draft.

Smith completed 15-of-25 for a then-career-high 266 yards and four touchdown passes—all in the first half—to tie the Autzen Stadium record.

In his debut game for the Ducks, Droughns, a junior-college transfer, rushed for 202 yards—then the seventh-highest single-game total in school history—on 17 carries for an average of 11.9 yards per rush. He had touchdown runs of two and 75 yards, and also caught an eight-yard pass for a score.

It was a significantly better performance than that of Michigan State's Sedrick Irvin, a highly regarded junior coming off a 1,200-yard sophomore campaign. But the Ducks held Irvin to just 66 yards and also kept him out of the end zone.

"I had a talk with Reuben Droughns earlier in the week and told him he would be the best back on the field," said Mike Bellotti, who was then in his fourth season as Oregon's coach. "It was just that no one knew it yet except he and I."

The Ducks went on to a 5–0 start that season, averaging almost 51 points in those wins and reaching No. 11 in the Associated Press poll by early October. But a season-ending leg injury suffered by

Droughns in a 41–38 overtime loss to UCLA in Game 6 hurt the Ducks, who went 3–4 the rest of the season, ending with a 51–43 loss to Colorado in the Aloha Bowl.

94 Getting to the Game

If you don't have a parking pass or designated tailgate spot, there is absolutely no reason to drive to Autzen Stadium on game day. You won't get into the parking lot, which has lost nearly half its spots the past six years with the development of PK Park for baseball and Papé Field for soccer and lacrosse. Instead, you'll end up paying a significant price to park in a private lot or you'll just drive around the neighborhood hoping for a spot on the street.

But worry not, Eugene is a small city with an extraordinary amount of bike and walking paths and an exceptional public transportation system. Both will serve you well getting to the game.

Whether you're coming from campus, downtown, or somewhere further out, Autzen Stadium is easy to get to without driving yourself. Here are some options:

Bus

It can't be said enough how easy and convenient the UO DuckExpress shuttle service is for fans wanting to get to Autzen.

With eight locations throughout the Eugene-Springfield area, these shuttles will get you to and from the game for only $6 roundtrip. You can also purchase a season pass for significant savings (in 2012 it was $25 for all seven home games).

Almost all locations have ample amounts of free parking where you can safely leave your car for the game, and the shuttles begin their runs four hours before kickoff, so you can get to Autzen with plenty of time to take in the atmosphere or find friends at a tailgate.

Here are the shuttle locations.

In Eugene:

- Lane Transit District's downtown station. Get breakfast or lunch downtown before the game, then shuttle over. It's also an ideal location if you're in for postgame drinks.
- Lane County Fairgrounds (13th Avenue and Jackson Street)
- South Eugene High School (19th Avenue and Patterson Street)
- Valley River Center (Northwest lot; note: there is limited parking at this location)
- LTD River Road Station (River Road and Beltline)

In Springfield:

- Symantec (555 International Way; the closest location to the hotels near the Gateway Mall)
- LTD Springfield Station (355 South A Street)
- Thurston High School (333 59th Street; this location is the furthest east, making it a perfect stop for fans coming in from Bend, Redmond, or Sisters)

Buses run every 10 to 20 minutes from the eight park-and-ride locations. But remember, return trips are available only at halftime and for 60 minutes after the game.

Walk

It's roughly a mile walk to Autzen from campus and not much further from downtown, and on a warm autumn day, there isn't a better way to get to the game.

The walk from campus—starting at either end of 13th Avenue—takes you across the Autzen Footbridge over a beautiful section of the Willamette River and puts you into the east end of

Alton Baker Park for a quick jaunt through the woods. When the path turns and Autzen Stadium is visible for the first time, it's a spectacular view.

From downtown, take the Peter DeFazio Pedestrian Bridge into Alton Baker Park, cross the parking lot and jump on Pre's Trail—a bark mulch path named after Oregon icon Steve Prefontaine—and follow the crowd to the stadium.

Bike

The same walking paths can be used for biking as well. It'll take just minutes to get from campus or downtown to the stadium on bike, and it won't take much longer from anywhere else once on the Ruth Bascom Riverbank Path System, the 22-mile paved loop that runs parallel to the Willamette River on both sides.

Some local hotels even offer bike rentals, making it an easy option for fans coming in from out of town.

Once you get to the stadium, Oregon offers secured bike parking for $1 per bike in the Duck Pen, which is located right across Leo Harris Parkway, between the Science Factory and the Autzen Footbridge.

Open three hours before kickoff and run by the Eugene Active 20–30 Club, proceeds from the Duck Pen go to local children's charities in Lane County.

Billboard Blitz

Joey Harrington's Manhattan billboard ignited a firestorm of media criticism when it was erected on the side of an NYC building in the summer of 2001.

Despite the negative feedback, Oregon was more determined then ever to push its brand both nationally—with another billboard in New York—and regionally, with smaller but strategically placed billboards in a handful of Pac-10 cities as well as throughout the Eugene and Portland areas.

So one year after Harrington's image graced a seven-story billboard near Madison Square Garden, Oregon was at it again. This time, it was receiver Keenan Howry getting the star treatment with a billboard at 47th and Broadway in Times Square featuring the slogan, WE'RE BACK.

"We made a big splash last year and fortunately were able to back it up (with an 11–1 season and Pac-10 championship)," Bill Moos, Oregon's athletic director at the time, told the *Register-Guard*. "It's not a repeat of what we did last year but a continuation."

Howry's billboard was 53 feet by 172 feet; Harrington's was 80 by 100.

Instead of promoting an individual player's Heisman Trophy candidacy, Oregon was instead attempting to advertise its agreement with the YES (Yankees Entertainment and Sports) Network, which would replay all 12 of the Ducks' 2002 season football games on the East Coast.

"With the success we're enjoying right now with Oregon football, we felt it could be beneficial for us to follow that up with something innovative that's more than just a billboard," Moos said. "Last year's effort, which I think was a tremendous success, stimulated curiosity about Oregon football and the university in general. Rather than let that dry up and blow away, we wanted to refuel it."

Oregon also viewed New York as an untapped market, with no major college football team in the city. Moos figured another billboard and an agreement with YES could create a nice East Coast fan base.

"If we could be so fortunate as to be adopted as their team, we would love it," he said.

There was no way he could hope to get those results from Oregon's other out-of-state billboard blitz.

In 2001, Oregon put up a roadside billboard featuring cornerback Rashad Bauman in San Francisco just off the Bay Bridge for every motorist heading into the city from the east to see.

There was also one in the backyards of two Pac-10 rival schools in Stanford and California.

Oregon also posted a billboard of running back Maurice Morris on Interstate Highway 405 in Los Angeles.

Then in 2002, on the side of the Hotel Figueroa near the campus of USC, Oregon put up a 144-by-90-foot image of receivers Keenan Howry, Jason Willis, and Samie Parker—a trio of players from Southern California who ended up Ducks.

From Oregon's perspective, touting its players and success in such a talent-rich area was a no-brainer. Any team that hopes to contend in the conference needs to recruit well in Southern California, and the Ducks, after consecutive Pac-10 championship seasons, had every intention of staying relevant.

"Certainly it's about recruiting," Oregon marketing director Greg Graziano told the *Los Angeles Times*. "Whether we get kids from L.A. or from San Francisco, or from our own state, we put billboards where there are potential student-athletes."

As expected, the billboards were not well received by the Trojans.

"I feel as if that's an insult," Trojans receiver Kareem Kelly said. "When I saw it, I was shocked."

Kelly and the Trojans got their revenge that October when they beat the Ducks 44–33 at Autzen Stadium.

Kelly and fellow USC receivers Mike Williams and Keary Colbert combined to catch 23 passes for 397 yards and three touchdowns, and vastly outplayed the three players Oregon put on the billboard.

After the game, Kelly, Williams, and Colbert posed for the ABC cameras in the same manner as Howry, Parker, and Willis were depicted on the billboard.

"I don't know if they were trying to promote Oregon football or if they were trying to make a statement," Williams said after the win. "But we wanted to come out and show that our three were better than their three."

96 Pat Johnson's Catch

In 1994, Kenny Wheaton gave Oregon fans the Pick in a win over Washington. Three years later, Pat Johnson added "the Catch" to the rivalry's rich history.

The date was November 8, 1997. Since Wheaton's famed interception, the once one-sided UO-UW rivalry had evened out. Even so, this Husky team was ranked No. 6 in the country, while Oregon came in at 4–4, the Ducks in danger of missing out on a bowl for the second straight year.

The day began well for the visiting team in Husky Stadium. Quarterback Akili Smith, a junior-college transfer in his first year with the Ducks, threw for an early touchdown pass, and Oregon went up 14–0 in the first quarter on a short run by Saladin McCullough, which was set up by a 23-yard Smith-to-Johnson pass.

Smith completed another touchdown pass in the second quarter, to tight end Blake Spence, and the Ducks took a shocking 24–6 lead into halftime. To that point the story of the game was Smith, who demonstrated a remarkable ability to avoid the pass rush in his first full game as the UO quarterback. "He was great," Spence said. "He kept our confidence up and he had tremendous poise. He has come of age as a quarterback now. If he gets in trouble, he stays calm and uses his athletic ability to get away from it."

Washington was playing without quarterback Brock Huard and running back Rashaan Shehee, so the Huskies' woeful early offense perhaps should have been anticipated. But the Dawgs got rolling in the second half with two touchdowns in the third quarter, and added another in the fourth for a 28–24 lead.

The Ducks, meanwhile, went scoreless in the third quarter. One drive ended on a drop by Johnson—not the first time in his career he'd failed to come through in the clutch. "I challenged Pat after that," Smith said. "I told him I'd be coming back to him, and he had to step up and answer the challenge."

The opportunity came in the fourth quarter, when the Ducks had a chance to beat the Huskies back-to-back in Seattle for the first time in more than 30 years, and to beat a Top-10 team for the first time since 1990. However, it would require Johnson to bounce back from the ultimatum he had received from Smith.

"It was no problem," Johnson said. "Not coming from my quarterback. We're close enough we can communicate and not get mad at each other. He said, 'I can't have that out of you.' He told me to quit messing up. I knew he'd come back to me."

The game-winning drive began with a 23-yard completion from Smith to Spence, an underrated member of Oregon's recent tight end lineage. Moments later it was third-and-16 from the Washington 46-yard line, when Smith hit Donald Haynes for a 27-yard completion.

Two plays later, it was again third-and-long. A sack cost the Ducks 10 yards, so they needed 20 for a first down, from the UW 29-yard line.

Washington burned a timeout, which allowed the Ducks to regroup. When the snap finally came, the Huskies blitzed, and Smith had the option of a receiver streaking down either side of the field.

The quarterback looked to his right, where Mel Miller was in man coverage on Johnson. Smith threw toward the right-front corner of the end zone, Johnson dove from the 2-yard line and he hauled in the pass despite being blanketed by Miller.

For Johnson, a senior with world-class speed who was a raw receiver when he arrived at Oregon, it was a redemptive moment.

"Pat Johnson's catch made up for a lot of things over the course of his career," head coach Mike Bellotti said. "He stepped up when we needed him to. Akili's throw was perfect, and the catch was even better."

Johnson admitted he had suffered from a tendency to beat himself in tough situations. After the touchdown that gave Oregon a 31–28 win, he said, "I don't know how to explain it, but there have been so many times over the years I could have made a play like that and just didn't have the confidence. But today I finally beat it. I started crying I was so happy. I knew Akili was going to come to me, and it finally paid off."

97 Where to Get a Brew

From brewpubs to crazy campus scenes to dive bars, Eugene has many and varied options for wetting one's whistle.

Near Autzen Stadium...
McMenamin's North Bank, 22 Club Rd. A prominent franchise of Oregon brewpubs, this one features a scenic back deck overlooking the Willamette River. There are also other options on High Street and East 19th Avenue.

The Cooler, 20 Centennial Loop. Everywhere you look there is either a TV screen or Oregon memorabilia. Beware: it gets packed before and after football games.

O Bar, 115 Commons Dr. A hidden gem located among student housing, it also has some coveted game-day parking spots.

On campus...

Rennie's Landing, 1214 Kincaid St. A reconditioned house, there are various nooks and crannies to settle into during the day, before students pack it to the rafters on Friday and Saturday nights.

Taylor's Bar & Grille, 894 E. 13th Ave. Cheap drinks and a big dance floor entice the evening crowd, and a front deck overlooking the entrance to campus beckons in the afternoon.

The Webfoot Bar & Grill, 839 E. 13th Ave. A new addition to the campus scene, it features a more modern menu than the typical bar food.

Just off campus...

Old Pad, 3355 E. Amazon Dr. The south Eugene bar where Steve Prefontaine once worked.

New Max's Tavern, 550 E. 13th Ave. The feel of a biker bar but with a student clientele.

Good Times Cafe & Bar, 375 E. 7th Ave. Located between campus and downtown, if there's a game on, they'll have it.

Wild Duck Cafe, 1419 Villard St. After a basketball game at Matthew Knight Arena, head across the street for some local flavor.

If you head downtown...

Jameson's Bar, 115 W. Broadway. Located at the heart of Eugene's "Barmuda Triangle."

John Henry's Club, 77 W. Broadway. Catch a band here, or head down the block to shoot pool at *Luckey's Tavern*, another Eugene institution.

Rogue Ales Public House, 844 Olive St. An Oregon brewer that's gained a national reputation.

A Local Touch...

Sam Bonds Garage, 407 Blair Ave.

Ninkasi Brewery, 272 Van Buren St.

98 Where to Grab a Bite

Whether it's game day or otherwise, Eugene's diverse eating options match the city's renowned unique culture.

For fine dining...

Beppe & Gianni's Trattoria, 1646 E. 19th Ave. If you go in December, get the seafood ravioli.

Cafe Soriah, 384 W. 13th Ave. Order the Steak Diane and thank the authors of this book later.

Ambrosia Restaurant & Bar, 174 E. Broadway. A classy dinner spot in the heart of downtown.

Cafe Lucky Noodle, 207 E. 5th Ave. Modern atmosphere and a trendy menu, good for dinner or just cocktails.

Marche, 296 E. 5th Ave. Ste. 128. Located in the Fifth Street Market, it features a menu and ingredients with a local flavor.

Oregon Electric Station, 27 E. 5th Ave. Fine dining and a beautiful bar, with the option of sitting in a repurposed train car.

For a local touch...

Glenwood Restaurant, 1340 Alder St. Just off campus, it's a favorite spot for students, particularly at breakfast and lunch.

Steelhead Brewing Co., 199 E. 5th Ave. A good spot for a hearty meal if there's a game you want to catch on TV.

Turtles Bar & Grill, 2690 Willamette St. Located in the shadow of Spencer Butte at the southern end of town.

Papa's Soul Food Kitchen, 400 Blair Blvd. Comfort food with a Southern flair.

6th Street Grill, 55 W. 6th Ave. Pairs a bustling restaurant with a vibrant sports bar next door.

In the morning…

Brails, 1689 Willamette St. A classic breakfast diner at the edge of the West University neighborhood.

Original Pancake House, 782 E. Broadway. The best option if you want to spot a UO athlete during breakfast.

Off the Waffle, 2540 Willamette St. Belgian waffles made in the Liège style—glazed and yummy.

For a slice…

Pegasus Pizza, 790 E. 14th Ave. Grab a pie upstairs, then head to Fathom's Bar downstairs.

Track Town Pizza, 1809 Franklin Blvd. Located across the street from Matthew Knight Arena and across the Willamette River from Autzen Stadium.

Sy's New York Pizza, 1211 Alder St. Right around the corner from many of the bars, this place is popular among students.

On a student-sized budget…

Burrito Boy Taqueria, 510 E. Broadway. This place is always hopping—particularly just after last call at the campus bars.

Caspian Restaurant, 863 E. 13th Ave. Mediterranean food on bustling 13th Avenue.

Cafe Yumm!, 730 E. Broadway. Hearty and healthy, there are several other outlets around town.

The Jail, 490 E. Broadway. You'll get enough teriyaki and noodles for two meals, at least.

99 UO and UW Deliver Double Zeroes

Oregon and Washington have certainly played plenty of classic games during the long history of their heated rivalry.

But the back-to-back historic humiliations in the early 1970s represent one of the oddest chapters of any rivalry in college football.

Two games, two shutouts, and a whopping 124 total points scored. And two different winners.

On October 27, 1973, the Ducks crushed the Huskies at Autzen Stadium, winning 58–0 in the highest scoring Oregon game since a 97–0 win against Willamette University in 1916. It was also Washington's worst loss since 1921.

"You hope a game like this never happens," said Washington coach Jim Owens, who was under fire back home in Seattle after the Huskies had started 1–6.

"I'd rather beat USC by one," remarked Oregon coach Dick Enright, getting in one last postgame dig.

Almost one year later to the day, the Huskies got their revenge and then some, beating the Ducks in Seattle 66–0, a loss that remains the worst in school history for Oregon.

"It was a beautiful sight," Owens said. "Most of us suffered through that 58–0 game down there."

Rewind to the first matchup. The 1973 game was a laughter from the start, with the Ducks scoring 21 in the first quarter and leading 35–0 at halftime.

"I wasn't sure we'd win until just before game time," Enright said. "Then when the players kicked the doors open and started shoving coaches aside trying to get out. Then I new they were ready."

Just for extra motivation, Enright rode the bus to the game with the defense, to let them know he wasn't convinced they were ready to play.

"He didn't think we were up for it," defensive end George Martin said.

The defense responded with its first shutout since 1968.

Led by linebacker Bobby Green, the Ducks were in the Husky backfield all game long. They stopped 11 running plays for a loss and harassed three different Washington quarterbacks into throwing six interceptions and completing just 4-of-29 pass attempts.

Green said the Ducks knew every time the Huskies were going to throw because freshman guard Charles Jackson tipped off the defense when he cocked his back leg.

"We kept trying to fight," Washington coach Jim Owens said. "You didn't see us standing around out there. But the afternoon just got longer and longer as we didn't produce."

And in case you thought there was any sympathy for the Huskies on the Oregon sideline, you're wrong.

"I was having a gas out there," said Oregon receiver Bob Palm, who held out the ball and taunted Washington defensive back Roberto Jourdan on a 29-yard touchdown run. "It was fun, especially against them. I'd thought about the revenge (for a loss in 1972), I guess that's why I held the ball out at Jourdan. On the next series they said they were going to get me."

They did, but it took a year.

The Huskies clearly had revenge on the mind when the Ducks came to town in 1974, and Oregon running back Henderson Martin acknowledged as much.

"They really came to play," he said. "We just couldn't rise to the pitch they were playing at. The biggest thing, I think, is we were not intense."

Unlike a year earlier, when the Ducks' defense was completely dominant, Washington did what it wanted on offense while Oregon was the team rendered inept.

The Huskies had 508 total yards, including 338 on the ground. They also had 30 first downs to two for the Ducks, who had just 55 yards on 55 plays.

"I'll start apologizing to everybody that's a Duck," first-year Oregon coach Don Read said. "I'm very sorry. Very sorry."

Washington led just 3–0 after the first quarter before turning it on for 21 points in the second quarter and 28 in the third.

"The victory came first," Washington defensive tackle Mike Green said, "but the closer to 60 we got the more we knew we were getting even with them."

100 Don Essig: The Voice

In 1990, the use of umbrellas was banned in Autzen Stadium, to eliminate obstructed views for other fans. Given that the city of Eugene averages some 50 inches of rain per year, this was a significant development.

At the time, nobody could have predicted the biggest implication of the decision. It led to one of the great traditions in recent Oregon football history.

That season, Autzen public address announcer Don Essig sought to reassure Ducks fans who might have felt bothered—all wet? Left out in the cold?—by the decision. Not to worry, Essig announced, "It never rains in Autzen Stadium."

More than two decades later, that is something of a catchphrase for the man who, entering the 2013–14 academic year, had announced nearly 300 football games and some 700 men's basketball games played by the Ducks. Rain or shine, Essig makes that same forecast before every home football game, accompanied by tens of thousands of fans who shout it along with him. "It has nothing to do with the weather," he said. "The feeling you get when you walk in there, it's a sunny experience."

Like Rich Brooks, Essig is that most ironic of Oregon institutions: An Oregon State graduate. Essig graduated from OSU in 1960, and had even been a member of its rally squad. He moved to Eugene three years later, in his early career as a schoolteacher. That fall, he began announcing high school football, beginning a hobby that would continue for a half-century.

In 1967, Essig was serving as the press-box announcer for Oregon State football games. That December, he beat out two other contestants for the right to announce men's basketball games in McArthur Court. A year later, he was on the PA in Autzen Stadium. He has been a constant at Oregon football and men's basketball games ever since. "It has been and is a great ride; a tremendous and unique hobby," Essig said. "It's just about the best hobby anyone could have."

Initially, Essig was paid $50 per football game. He later negotiated a deal to get football and men's basketball season tickets, plus a trip for himself and his wife when Oregon plays in bowl games. He has become, quite simply, a fixture with the Ducks.

Along the way, he's had plenty of milestones.

In a 1968 game against Idaho, Essig's second in Autzen Stadium, he left his mic on and was overheard to say that "the Idaho passing attack isn't worth a crap today." Since then, he has held his microphone in his left hand, with it up to his mouth when he's talking, and by his side when he isn't. In 1974, Essig first worked with spotters Jack Pynes and Stan Hultgren, who would remain by his side for 40 years. In 1984, Essig missed his first and only UO football game in his tenure, due to a herniated disc. In

2009, he was inducted into Oregon's alumni lettermen's organization, Order of the O.

Remarkably, Essig's signature line—"The real weather report is: It never rains in Autzen Stadium!"—spurred a streak of 34 straight home games without rain, in a city that averages seven inches each November. Like all good things, though, the streak didn't last. In 2000, after two straight soggy games, Essig suggested ditching the line. Athletic department officials would have nothing of it.

"From an athletic director's standpoint, one of the more important people in your life is your public-address announcer," former athletic director Norv Ritchey (1970–75) said in 2010, because of that person's "being able to set the stage. We've been very fortunate to have him as a staple of the university and the athletic department. Not only did he perform well, but he grew on the job in the coming years and became increasingly important to the athletic family."

In 2011, Autzen Stadium hosted the first Pac-12 championship game. To preserve neutrality at the field, the conference brought its own personnel, including its own public-address announcer. Essig, however, was permitted one duty: the pregame weather report.

Sources

1. The Pick
Conrad, John. "The Race Is On." *Register-Guard*. 23 October 1994.
Elder, Brian. "15 Years Later, Wheaton Still Proud; Huard Not Losing Sleep." KVAL.
    com. 22 October 2009.

2. The Natty
Jude, Adam. "Mistakes in the Trenches Doom UO Offense." *Register-Guard*. 11
    January 2011.
Jude, Adam. "The BCS Breaks." 12 January 2011.
Moseley, Rob. "Short of Goal." *Register-Guard*. 11 January 2011.

3. The Chip Kelly Era
Domowitch, Paul." Chip Kelly Protégé Tells Eagles Players to Shape Up." *Philadelphia
    Daily News*. 22 February 2013.
Moseley, Rob. "A Beautiful Mind." *Register-Guard*. 19 July 2009.

4. 2012: Bringing Home Roses
Jude, Adam. "Alonso, an Unlikely Hero, Leads Defensive Stops." *Register-Guard*.
    3 January 2012.
Moseley, Rob. "Reflected Glory." *Register-Guard*. 3 January 2012.
The Rose Bowl Game Book. University of Oregon.

5. Uncle Phil
Bellamy, Ron. "For Knight, the Time Was Right to Expand on Charitable Legacy."
    Register-Guard. 22 August 2007.
Bellamy, Ron. "Knight Holds Court." Register-Guard. 4 May 2008.
Moseley, Rob. *What It Means to Be a Duck*. Triumph Books, Chicago, 2009.
Rosenberg, Michael. "Inside College Football." SI.com. 7 January 2011.

6. Joey Harrington: Captain Comeback
Moseley, Rob. *What It Means to Be a Duck*. Triumph Books, Chicago, 2009.

7. Game Changer: Dethroning the Dawgs in 1994
Clark, Bob. "The Last Big Drive Was Oregon's Saving Grace." *Register-Guard*. 23
    October 1994.
Conrad, John. "The Race Is On." *Register-Guard*. 23, October 1994.
McIver, Kelly. "Duck Defenders Did in the Dawgs." *Register-Guard*. 23 October 1994

8. LaMichael James
Branch, Eric. "LaMichael James' Run Not from Danger." *San Francisco Chronicle*.
    1 September 2012.
Moseley, Rob. "After Quite a Rush, James Goes Pro." *Register-Guard*. 7 January 2012.

9. Double OT in the Desert
Jude, Adam. "Masoli, Maehl a Key Combo for UO." *Register-Guard.* 22 November 2009.
Moseley, Rob. "For Ducks, Wildcats, It's Win or Wonder." *Register-Guard.* 21 November 2009.
Moseley, Rob. "Flint's Clutch Leg, Costa's Steady Hand Help Save the Day." 22 November 2009.
Moseley, Rob. "War for the Roses." *Register-Guard.* 22 November 2009.

10. War for the Roses
Bellamy, Ron. "Sweet Roses." *Register-Guard.* 4, December 2009.
Moseley, Rob. "Kelly's Heroes Rally Past Beavers, Reach Rose Bowl." 4 December 2009
Moseley, Rob. "One More for the Rose." *Register-Guard.* 3, December 2009.

11. Mike Bellotti
Moseley, Rob. *What It Means to Be a Duck.* Triumph Books, Chicago, 2009.
Register-Guard. "Today's press conference transcription and photos." RegisterGuard.com. 14 March 2009. http://www2.registerguard.com/cms/index.php/duck-football/comments/todays-press-conference-transcription/

12. Bill Musgrave
Moseley, Rob. *What It Means to Be a Duck.* Triumph Books, Chicago, 2009.

13. Civil War
Moseley, Rob. *What It Means to Be a Duck.* Triumph Books, Chicago, 2009.

14. Dreams Shattered: Dixon Goes Down
Schroeder, George. "In One Painful Move, Dixon's Season Goes From Magic to Tragic." *Register-Guard.* 16 November 2007.
"UO Football Report." *Register-Guard.* 16 November 2007.

15. Dressed for Success
"Oregon Ducks Continue to Assault the Pupils." Deadspin.com. 22 June 2006.
Henderson, John. "If Money Talks, the Oregon Ducks Shot." *Denver Post.* 9 January 2011.
Smith, Michael. "Clothes Make the Brand." *SportsBusiness Journal.* 22 August 2001. http://www.sportsbusinessdaily.com/Journal/Issues/2011/08/22/In-Depth/Branding.aspx

16. Len Casanova: Architect of a Program
Moseley, Rob. *What It Means to Be a Duck.* Triumph Books, Chicago, 2009.

17. Ducks and Dawgs
Ibid.

18. Mel Renfro
Ibid.

19. A Return to the Rose Bowl
Bellamy, Ron. "Oregon Upset Victory Not Unthinkable in Dream Season." *Register-Guard.* 2 January 1995.

Conrad, John. "UO Bows to Lion Kings." *Register-Guard*. 3 January 1995
The Rose Bowl Game Book. University of Oregon.

20. Hail to the Victors
Baker, Mark. "Ducks Dominate the Day." *Register-Guard*. 21 September 2003.
Clark, Bob. "Hail to the Victors." *Register-Guard*. 21 September 2003.
Clark, Bob. "It's D-Day for Ducks, Mighty Michigan." *Register-Guard*. 20 September 2003.
Moseley, Rob. "Burnin' Down the House." *Register-Guard*. 9 September 2007.
Moseley, Rob. "Traditional Test Awaits UO." *Register-Guard*, 8 September 2007.

21. Oregon Football's First Family
Moseley, Rob. *What It Means to Be a Duck*. Triumph Books, Chicago, 2009.

22. The Dutchman
Moseley, Rob. *What It Means to Be a Duck*. Triumph Books, Chicago, 2009.

23. Building an Empire
Henderson, John. "If Money Talks, the Oregon Ducks Shot." *Denver Post*. 9 January 2011.
Sharpe, Andrew. "Oregon, Nike and the Future of College Football." SBNation.com. 22 November 2011
www.goducks.com. Oregon Facilities.

24. Rich Brooks
Moseley, Rob. *What It Means to Be a Duck*. Triumph Books, Chicago, 2009.

25. Autzen Stadium
GoDucks.com, "Autzen Stadium," http://www.goducks.com/ViewArticle. dbml?&DB_OEM_ID=500&ATCLID=205174790.
Hayes, Matt. "No Venue More Intimidating Than Autzen Stadium." *The Sporting News*. 18 McCollough, J. Brady. "Duck, Duck, Lose." *Michigan Daily*. 21 September 2003.
August 2006.
One Click Sports Blog, "Ducks, You Need to Read These," One Click Sports Blog, http://oneclicksportsblog.wordpress.com/2007/09/28/ducks-have-you-read-these/

26. 2001: The First Fiesta Bowl
Bellamy, Ron. "Wild Dreams Coming True." 2 January 2002.
Conrad, John. "It's Oregon's Party." *Register-Guard*. 2 January 2002.
Rodman, Bob. "Top-Dog Debate Rages On." *Register-Guard*. 2 January 2002.

27. Disney's Duck
Bolt, Greg. "No Longer Ducks of a Feather." *Register-Guard*. 4 March 2010.
GoDucks.com. "Tradition and Spirit Groups." www.goducks.com/ViewArticle. dbml?DB_OEM_ID=500&ATCLID=153778
Tallmadge, Alice. "The Duck Abides." *Oregon Quarterly*. Autumn 2012. Vol. 92. No. 1.

28. 2009 Rose Bowl: I Smell Roses
Baker, Mark. "Heartbreaker." *Register-Guard*. 2 January 2010.
Hansen, Chris. "Game of Keepaway Stymies UO Offense." *Register-Guard*. 2 January 2010.

Moseley, Rob. "Gruden Sees Success for UO's Kelly." *Register-Guard*. 2 January 2010.

Moseley, Rob. "Out of Reach." *Register-Guard*. 2 January 2010.

Schroeder, George. "No Reason to Feel Empty After Season Full of Thrills." *Register-Guard*. 2, January 2010.

29. Haloti Ngata: The Most Dominant Duck?

Bellamy, Ron. "Ducks Make Emotional, Religious Connection with Top Recruit." *Register-Guard*. 10 February 2002.

Bellamy, Ron. "Ngata Will Make His Call from the Heart." *Register-Guard*. 28 December 2005.

Clark, Bob. "Ngata's Return Trip Gaining Steam." *Register-Guard*. 12 November 2004.

Moseley, Rob. "Ducks Rally Around Grieving Teammate." *Register-Guard*. 29 December 2002.

30. Returning to the Postseason

Conrad, John. "Oregon Rally Stops Tulsa Cold, 27–24." *Register-Guard*. 17 December 1989.

Conrad, John. "Ducks Come Up Short, Come Up Empty." *Register-Guard*. 30 December 1990.

Conrad, John. "Deacons Wake Up, Bowl Over Ducks." *Register-Guard*. 1 January 1993.

Libby, Brian. *Tales from the Oregon Ducks Sideline*. Sports Publishing, New York. 2011.

31. Win the Day

Bachman, Rachel. "As Oregon 'Wins the Day' Over and Over, Motto Gathers Steam." *Oregonian*. 8 November 2010.

Moseley, Rob. "The Night the Storm Clouds Parted." *Register-Guard*. 28 December 2007.

32. The Punch

Dodd, Dennis. "No Use in Fighting It—Boise State Could Be BCS Title Contender." CBSSports.com. http://www.cbssports.com/collegefootball/story/12155281, 4 September 2009.

Jaynes, Dwight. www.DwightJaynes.com. 4 September 2009.

Jude, Adam. "Blount's Season Ends." *Register-Guard*. 5 September 2009.

Jude, Adam. "No Rest for Ducks' Defense." *Register-Guard*. 4 September 2009.

Moseley, Rob. "Ducks Lose Game, Face." *Register-Guard*. 4 September 2009.

33. The Assistants

Moseley, Rob. *What It Means to Be a Duck*. Triumph Books, Chicago, 2009.

34. Harrington Wills a Win

Bellamy, Ron. "Oregon's Heart in the Right Place." *Register-Guard*. 29 October 2000.

Clark, Bob. "Lost and Found." *Register-Guard*. 29 October 2000.

Conrad, John. "An Incredible Journey." *Register-Guard*. 29 October 2000.

Conrad, John. "Lady Luck Smiles on Ducks." *Register-Guard*. 29 October 2000.

"Oregon Report." *Register-Guard*.

35. Bobby Moore
Moseley, Rob. *What It Means to Be a Duck*. Triumph Books, Chicago, 2009.

36. Midnight Madness
Clark, Bob. "Ducks Open Pac-10 on Right Foot." *Register-Guard*. 26 September 1999.
Clark, Bob. "UO Happy, Not Healthy, After Win Over USC." *Register-Guard*. 27 September 1999.
Hall, Landon. Associated Press. 25 September 1999.
Mims, Steve. "Oregon Refused to Die Late in the Game." *Register-Guard*. 26 September 1999.

37. That BCS BS
Moseley, Rob. *What It Means to Be a Duck*. Triumph Books, Chicago, 2009.
Rohde, John. "Paying the Price: Oregon Coach Caught Lots of Grief About BCS Cancer Comment." *The Oklahoman*. 27 December 2005.
Youngman, Randy. "BCS: Boundless Crazy Scenarios." *Orange County Register*. 22 November 2011.

38. Joey Heisman
Bellamy, Ron. "Like the Billboard said, Harrington is Back." *Register-Guard*. 8 December 2001.
Register Guard, "Ducks Aren't Big Red." *Register-Guard*. 14 August 2001.

40. The Toilet Bowl
Moseley, Rob. *What It Means to Be a Duck*. Triumph Books, Chicago, 2009.

41. Sorry Sooners
Associated Press. "Video Review Leaves Stoops Disappointed." 18 September 2006.
Clark, Bob. "Ducks Block OU's Exit." *Register-Guard*. 17 September 2006.
Clark, Bob. "Ducks Settle Debate: Scoreboard." *Register-Guard*. 19 September 2006.
Clark, Bob. "Pac-10 Punishes Game Officials." *Register-Guard*. 19 September 2006.

42. Dan Fouts
Moseley, Rob. *What It Means to Be a Duck*. Triumph Books, Chicago, 2009.

43. Willie Lyles and the NCAA
Newnham, Blaine. "Ducks Hit Hardest of All by the Pac-10." *Register-Guard*. 12 August 1980.
Newnham, Blaine. "Bigger Than USC." *Register-Guard*. 13 August 1980.
Conrad, John. "NCAA Hands the Ducks Their Bitter Pill." *Register-Guard*. 24 December 1981.
Stahlberg, Mike. "NCAA Slaps UO with Probation, Penalties." *Register-Guard*. 24 December 1981.
Bellamy, Ron. "Oregon's Credibility Takes Direct Hit." *Register-Guard*. 8 July 2004.
Robinson, Charles, and Rand Getlin. "Oregon, NCAA Reach Impasse in Football Investigation." Yahoo! Sports. 19 December 2012. http://sports.yahoo.com/news/ncaaf--oregon--ncaa-reach-impasse-in-football-investigation-215913743.html

44. Gang Green

Dobrosielski, Damian. "Gang Green: Ducks Ride Defense to First Rose Bowl Since '58." *Daily Collegian*. 12 December 1994.

Oregon Rose Bowl Media Guide.

45. 2013 Fiesta Bowl

Clark, Bob. "Barner, a Runner For the Ages, Finishes Fast." *Register-Guard*. 4 January 2013.

Clark, Bob. "Interceptions Play Like a Broken Record." *Register-Guard*. 4 January 2013.

Moseley, Rob. "Lean Machine." *Register-Guard*. 4 January 2013.

46. Cliff Harris

Jude, Adam. "Locking It Down." *Register-Guard*. 29 October 2010.

Jude, Adam. "Mercurial Cornerback No Longer in UO's Orbit." *Register-Guard*. 6 December 2011.

Moseley, Rob. "Dodging them Blues." *Register-Guard*. 14 November 2010.

Moseley, Rob. "No Dwelling on Cliff." *Register-Guard*. 14 April 2011.

Moseley, Rob. "Pumping His Brakes." *Register-Guard*. 23 September 2011.

47. Mariota's Debut

Moseley, Rob. "The Best and the Brightest." *Register-Guard*. 2 September 2012.

Moseley, Rob. "On Pace for a Record Score." *Register-Guard*. 8 November 2012.

Moseley, Rob. "Superior Mariota." *Register-Guard*. 27 November 2012.

Moseley, Rob. "Taking It in Stride." *Register-Guard*. 2 November 2012.

48. The Great Escape

Jude, Adam. "Drive Keeps Perfection Alive." *Register-Guard*. 14 November 2010.

Moseley, Rob. "Beard Seeks Another Chance." *Register-Guard*. 14 November 2010.

Moseley, Rob. "Dodging Them Blues." *Register-Guard*. 14 November 2010.

49. 2010: A Tumultuous Off-Season

Baker, Mark. "The Ducks' Winter of Discontent." *Register-Guard*. 28 February 2010.

Jude, Adam. "Masoli Suspended Entire 2010 Season; James Gets One Game." RegisterGuard.com. 12 March 2010. http://www2.registerguard.com/cms/index.php/duck-football/comments/masoli-suspended-entire-2010-season-james-gets-one-game/

Moseley, Rob. "Masoli Dismissed from Team After Traffic Stop." RegisterGuard.com. 9 June 2010.

50. Barner Rushes to Record

Moseley, Rob. "Afterglow Burns Bright for Barner." *Register-Guard*. 6 November 2012.

Moseley, Rob. "Barner Hangs with Buddy in UO Book." *Register-Guard*. 30 December 2012.

Moseley, Rob. "Barner 'Looks Good' After Scary Hit." *Register-Guard*. 10 October 2010.

Moseley, Rob. "Makin' a Great Trophy Case." *Register-Guard*. 4 November 2012.

51. Stanford the Dreamkiller
Clark, Bob. "Unbeaten No More." *Register-Guard*. 21 October 2001.
Moseley, Rob. "The Road to Glendale." *Register-Guard*. 30 December 2012.
Moseley, Rob. "Sticking Their Landing." *Register-Guard*. 18 November 2012.

52. 2010: A Perfect Regular Season
2010 Oregon BCS Championship Game Media Guide

53. 2000 Holiday Bowl
Moseley, Rob. *What It Means to Be a Duck*. Triumph Books, Chicago, 2009.

54. 1994: Ducks Sack Troy
Conrad, John. "High-Flying Ducks Sack Troy, 22–7." *Register-Guard*. 2 October 1994.
FishDuck.com, "The Era of the Oregon Transfer Running Back." www.fishduck.com/
    2011/10/era-transfer-runningback. 7 October 2011.

55. Black Mamba Arrives
Mims, Steve. "No Catching DAT, or Ducks." *Register-Guard*. 4 January 2013.
Moseley, Rob. "Another Fantastic Finish." *Register-Guard*. 3 February 2011.
Moseley, Rob. "The Best and Brightest." *Register-Guard*. 2 September 2012.
Sports Illustrated. 24 September 2012.

56. Howry's Return in the Rain
Bellamy, Ron. "These Ducks Played Like Champs." *Register-Guard*. 2 December 2001.
Clark, Bob. "UO Weathers OSU." *Register-Guard*. 2 December 2001.
Conrad, John. "Howry Comes Up Big in Biggest Moments." *Register-Guard*.
    2 December 2001.

57. George Shaw and Ducks in the Draft
GoDucks.com. "George Shaw." http://www.goducks.com/ViewArticle.
    dbml?DB_OEM_ID=500&ATCLID=249034
Litsky, Frank. "George Shaw, 64, Backup to Great N.F.L. Quarterbacks." *New York
    Times*. 12 January 1998.

58. From the PCC to the Pac-12
"Four Colleges Form Coast Conference at Very Secret Session." *Oregon Daily Journal*.
    3 December 1915.
Ratto, Ray. "Pac-10 Considers Becoming Pac-12." *San Francisco Chronicle*. 13 August
    2010.

60. Transfer RBs Keep Program Rolling
Bellamy, Ron. "Smith Overcomes Tough Conditions." *Register-Guard*. 28 October
    2001.
Clark, Bob. "Duck Season Opens With a Bang." *Register-Guard*. 6 September 1998.
Clark, Bob. "Morris Picks UO." *Register-Guard*. 1 February 2000.
Clark, Bob. "Old and New Key Ducks' Romp." *Register-Guard*. 6 September 1998.
2011 Oregon Football Media Guide

61. Keeping It in the Family
Moseley, Rob. "With Promotion of Mark Helfrich, UO Coaching Staff Chain Is
    Mostly Unbroken." *Register-Guard*. 21 January 2013.

Register-Guard. "Today's Press Conference Transcription and Photos." RegisterGuard.
com. 14 March 2009. http://www2.registerguard.com/cms/index.php/
duck-football/comments/todays-press-conference-transcription/

62. Mickey Bruce Turns Down Bribes

Bellamy, Ron. "Former Oregon DB-RB Mickey Bruce Dies at 70." *Register-Guard.*
1 April 2011.
Duck Downs. "The Incorruptible Mickey Bruce." http://www.benzduck.com/
journal/2011/3/21/the-incorruptible-mickey-bruce.html.
Harvey III, Paul. "Bribe Try on Duck Gridder Fails Before Michigan Game."
Register-Guard. 30 September 1960.
Harvey III, Paul. "Oregon Footballer Wants to Forget Bribe Attempt." *Register-Guard.*
4 November 1961.

63. Kenny Wheaton: More Than the Pick

Moseley, Rob. *What It Means to Be a Duck.* Triumph Books, Chicago, 2009.

64. Pat Kilkenny

Bellamy, Ron. "On the Money." *Register-Guard.* 10 February 2008.
Bolt, Greg. "Kilkenny Takes Center Court." *Register-Guard.* 15 February 2007.
Schroeder, George. "Kilkenny Reflects on 'Roller-Coaster Ride' at UO."
Register-Guard. 15 February 2009.

65. Fright Night

Bellamy, Ron. "Trojans Wondering What Hit Them at Autzen." *Register-Guard.*
1 November 2009.
Moseley, Rob. "Scary Good." *Register-Guard.* 1 November 2009.
Peterson, Anne. "No Trick, Plenty of Treats for No. 10 Ducks." Associated Press.
31 October 2009.

66. Kevin Willhite: The First Five-Star

Duck Downs. "The Kevin Willhite Story." www.benzduck.com/the-suffer-
ing/2011/3/23/the-kevin-willhite-story-the-last-time-oregon-recruited-the.html.
Newnham, Blaine, and Conrad, John. "Willhite Backtracks to Oregon."
Register-Guard. 10 February 1982.
"1982 Sports." *Register-Guard.* 31 December 1982

67. Musgrave's Magic

FishDuck.com. "Sweet Revenge: Oregon Upsets BYU, Detmer in 1990." 19 October 2011.
http://fishduck.com/2011/10/sweet-revenge-oregon-upsets-byu-detmer-1990/
Florence, Mal. "Bruins Pay the Penalty, 28–24." *Los Angeles Times.* 4 November 1990.
Libby, Brian. *Tales from the Oregon Ducks Sideline.* Sports Publishing. New York.
2011.

68. Go to *College GameDay*

Baker, Mark. "*GameDay* a Big Day For Duck Fans." *Register-Guard.* 29 September
2007.
Bellamy, Ron. "It's Bedlam at *GameDay.*" *Register-Guard.* 3 October 2010.
Hansen, Chris. "Repeat Show Draws Them In." *Register-Guard.* 4 October 2007.
Jude, Adam. "UO Fans Win Over *GameDay* Crew." *Register-Guard.* 30 September 2007.

Schwennesen, Tricia. "Fans Put on *GameDay* Face For Entire Nation." *Register-Guard*. 24 September 2000.

69. Gary Zimmerman
Moseley, Rob. *What It Means to Be a Duck*. Triumph Books, Chicago, 2009.

70. Onterrio Smith
Bellamy, Ron. "Smith Overcomes Tough Conditions." *Register-Guard*. 28 October 2001.
Clark, Bob. "Ducks Back in the Race." *Register-Guard*. 28 October 2001.

71. Grooming Future Head Coaches
Moseley, Rob. *What It Means to Be a Duck*. Triumph Books, Chicago, 2009.

72. It's All Ducky
Baker, Mark. "Robo Gains a Few, Er, Feathers." *Register-Guard*. 11 May 2005.
GoDucks.com. "Tradition and Spirit Groups." www.goducks.com/ViewArticle. dbml?DB_OEM_ID=500&ATCLID=153778
Tallmadge, Alice. "The Duck Abides." *Oregon Quarterly*. Autumn 2012. Vol. 92. No. 1.

73. The Early Rose Bowls
Oregon Football 2012 Almanac, University of Oregon, 2012

74. The Last Losing Season
Bellamy, Ron. "Ducks Season Ends With an Absolute Thud." *Register-Guard*. 21 November 2004.
Clark, Bob. "Ducks Attempt to Move Forward." *Register-Guard*. 15 August 2004.

75. Jerry Allen
Bellamy, Ron. "Ducks Job a Labor of Love for Allen." *Register-Guard*. 27 August 2006.
Jude, Adam. "For Cryin' Out Loud, Allen's Call Memorable." *Register-Guard*. 7 December 2010.

76. The Electric Samie Parker
Moseley, Rob. "Parker Picks Oregon, Not NFL Draft." *Register-Guard*. 16 January 2003.
Moseley, Rob. "Parker's Toughest Route." *Register-Guard*. 14 November 2003.
Rodman, Bob. "Buffs Can't Catch Up with Parker." *Register-Guard*. 2 January 2002.

77. Hugo Bezdeck and the Early Hall of Famers
Athlon Sports. *Game Day: Oregon Football*. Triumph Books, Chicago. 2007.
Libby, Brian. *Tales from the Oregon Ducks Sideline*. Sports Publishing, New York. 2011.

78. Go to Pre's Rock
Mack, Don and Newnham, Blaine. "Pre's Death the End of Era." *Register-Guard*. 30 May 1975.
Bellamy, Ron. "Pre Can't Be Forgotten." *Register-Guard*. 3 October 1975.
Hurt, Suzanne. "Memorial Honors Life of Prefontaine." *Register-Guard*. 14 December 1997.

Moseley, Rob. "A Barner Burner." *Register-Guard*. 5 September 2010.

Nike, Inc. "History and Heritage." http://nikeinc.com/pages/history-heritage

79. Bill Byrne

Withers, Bud. "He Does It All." *Register-Guard*. 14 September 1984.

Clark, Bob. "Byrne's Departure Saddens UO Athletic Staff." *Register-Guard*. 27 June 1992.

Conrad, John. "Will It Cover Most of the Problems?" *Register-Guard*. 6 May 1985.

Duck Downs. "How Bill Byrne Tried to Cover Oregon's Asset." benzduck.com. 20 March 2011.

Libby, Brian. *Tales from the Oregon Ducks Sideline*. Sports Publishing, New York. 2011.

80. Salvaging the 2007 Season

Dohn, Brian. "Preparing for Dixon Pays Off." *Register-Guard*. 25 November 2007

Moseley, Rob. "Beaver Dam Nation." *Register-Guard*. 2 December 2007.

Moseley, Rob. "Dixon's Knee Injury Ends Oregon Career." *Register-Guard*. 17 November 2007.

Moseley, Rob. "Nothing by Thorns for UO." *Register-Guard*. 25 November 2007

Moseley, Rob. "What a Difference a Win Makes." *Register-Guard*. 2 January 2008.

81. Go to the Spring Game

Moseley, Rob. "Camo Can't Disguise the Fun, Pride." *Register-Guard*. 1 May 2011.

Moseley, Rob. "Oregon Honors Troops Throughout Game." *Register-Guard*. 2 May 2010.

Moseley, Rob. "Spring Game's a Special Salute." *Register-Guard*. 1 April 2010.

82. Taken Too Soon: Terrance Kelly and Todd Doxey

Anderson, Curtis, and Rob Moseley. "Doxey Was a Character Guy." *Register-Guard*. 15 July 2008.

Moseley, Rob. "An All-American Loss." *Register-Guard*. 19 August 2004.

Moseley, Rob. "Chung to Carry Doxey's Memory on His Back for Washington Game." *Register-Guard*. 29 August 2008.

Moseley, Rob. "In Todd's Memory." *Register-Guard*. 15 December 2008.

83. Notre Dame Comes to Town

Conrad, John. "Irish fear the Ducks' Irish will be up."

Conrad, John. "The Irish Tie One on for Zize, 13–13." *Register-Guard*. 24 October 1982.

Mosley, Joe. "Big day—and Almost a Big Upset." *Register-Guard*. 24 October 1982.

Mosley, Joe. "Oh Danny Boy, the Irish Are Playing." *Register-Guard*. 23 October 1982.

84. Mighty Oregon

Daily Emerald Online. "Might Oregon Sings of the Past." http://dailyemerald. com/2006/11/12/mighty-oregon-sings-of-the-past/

University of Oregon. "Oregon Athletic Bands. About Us: History." http://pages. uoregon.edu/bandadm/OregonAthleticBands/History.html

85. Tom Graham
Moseley, Rob. *What It Means to Be a Duck.* Triumph Books, Chicago, 2009.

86. Playing at Hayward Field
Tims, Marvin. "Semi-Retired Hayward Field Still to Play Important Role for University." *Register-Guard.* 17 September 1967.
Uhrhammer, Jerry. "Hayward Good-Bye." *Register-Guard.* 4 November 1966.
GoDucks.com. "Hayward Field." http://www.goducks.com/ViewArticle. dbml?DB_OEM_ID=500&ATCLID=205174795

87. Bill Moos
Bellamy, Ron. "A Chance for UO to Redefine Again." *Register-Guard.* 28 November 2006.
Bellamy, Ron. "Moos Intrigued by Washington AD Opening." *Register-Guard.* 14 January 2004.
Bellamy, Ron. "Moos' Legacy: Reach for Stars." *Register-Guard.* 26 November 2006.
Clark, Bob. "It's Official: Moos Will Resign." *Register-Guard.* 27 November 2006.
Clark, Bob. "What's Next for Oregon Athletics?" *Register-Guard.* 28 November 2006.
GoDucks.com. "Bill Moos." http://www.goducks.com/ViewArticle. dbml?DB_OEM_ID=500&ATCLID=22178
Moseley, Rob. "What's Next for Oregon Athletics?" *Register-Guard.* 28 November 2006.
Withers, Bud. "Nike Co-founder Is Spiritual Godfather to the Ducks." *Seattle Times.* 31 October 2006.

88. D-Boyz
Bellamy, Ron. "Secondary Hits Primary Goal." *Register-Guard.* 28 September 2008.
Moseley, Rob. "Call 'em the Pac-10's Best Secondary? The D-Boyz Will Drop and Give You 20." *Register-Guard.* 16 August 2008.

89. The Collapse at Cal
Conrad, John. "Schuler Not Bragging About Win." *Register-Guard.* 3 October 1993.
Conrad, John. "Cal's Record Comeback Kills Ducks." *Register-Guard.* 3 Oct 1993.

90. Stars of the '80s
Conrad, John. "Ducks Rush Right Past Sun Devils, 27–7." *Register-Guard.* 22 October 1989.
Conrad, John. "Oregon, Miller Find Their Redemption." *Register-Guard.* 27 October 1985.
Conrad, John. "This One Bounces Oregon's Way, 15–14." *Register-Guard.* 25 September 1983.
Moseley, Rob. *What It Means to Be a Duck.* Triumph Books, Chicago, 2009.

91. "Shout"
Baker, Mark. "Footoprints of Eugene's Past." *Register-Guard.* 30 September 2012.
Baker, Mark. "Rose Bowl Fans Will Be Jumping and Shouting." *Register-Guard.* 1 January, 2012.
Markstrom, Serena. "Knight's and Daze." *Register-Guard.* 14 December 2012.

92. Playing for the Platypus

Baker, Mark. "Trophy Fits the Bill." *Register-Guard*. 28 November 2007.

93. Conquering Saban's Spartans

Clark, Bob. "Duck Season Opens With a Bang." *Register-Guard*. 6 September 1998.

Clark, Bob. "Old and New Key Ducks' Romp." *Register-Guard*. 6 September 1998.

"Oregon Football Report." *Register-Guard*. 6 September 1998.

95. Billboard Blitz

Bellamy, Ron. "Bauman Gets Last Word." *Register-Guard*. 18 October 2001.

Bellamy, Ron. "Ducks' L.A. Ad Priceless." *Register-Guard*. 23 August 2002.

Clark, Bob. "Linemen the Subjects of Marketing Blitz." *Register-Guard*. 16 August 2002.

Hansen, Chris. "USC Wideouts Pose Problem." *Register-Guard*. 27 October 2002.

Moseley, Rob. "Billboard Puts Ducks Back in Big Apple." *Register-Guard*. 16 July 2002.

Fernas, Rob. "UO Billboard Draws Trojans' Ire." *Los Angeles Times*. 20 August 2002.

96. Pat Johnson's Catch

Conrad, John. "Ducks Turn Huskies to Mush." *Register-Guard*. 9 November 1997.

Conrad, John. "Smith Shows Ducks He's the Man." *Register-Guard*. 9 November 1997.

99. UO and UW Deliver Double Zeroes

Cawood, Neil. "It Was a 'Beautiful Site,' Says Beleaguered Owens." *Register-Guard*. 27 October 1974.

Cawood, Neil. "Washington Lineman Tips Off UO Defense." *Register-Guard*. 28 October 1973.

Newnham, Blaine. "As a Game, It Stunk." *Register-Guard*. 28 October 1973.

Newnham, Blaine. "You Hope a Game Like…" *Register-Guard*. 28 October 1973.

Withers, Bud. "Huskies Give Ducks Fitz." *Register-Guard*. 27 October 1974.

100. Don Essig: The Voice

Baker, Mark. "Still Quackin'." *Register-Guard*. 6 March 2010.

Wenstrom, Chuck. *It Never Rains in Autzen Stadium: The Don Essig Story*. Don Essig. 2012.